DAWN OF THE DUMB

Charlie Brooker is a writer and broadcaster. He created the satirical website *TV Go Home* in 1999, which in turn spawned Channel 4's *Nathan Barley* (co-written with Chris Morris). Prior to joining the *Guardian* in the year 2000, Brooker worked as a cartoonist and videogames 'journalist'. He currently writes and presents *Charlie Brooker's Screen Wipe* on BBC4.

Some qualified praise for Charlie Brooker:

'Anger drives Charlie Brooker – and makes him very, very funny.' *Observer*

'Charlie Brooker is a star . . . Funny, scathing and consistently brilliant.' *Independent on Sunday*

'He's lost none of his fury . . . which is what makes his rantings so good.' *Morning Star*

'The cleverest person I've ever sat next to.' Ian Hislop

'I hope you get jail time – I am complaining to your embassies, businesses that advertise with anyone who consorts with you, and our law enforcement over this matter.' Concerned American Citizen

'Childish? Yes. Hilarious? Well, I think so. If it was all fantasy dis-embowelling of nob-ends in colourful language Brooker could be dismissed as a one-trick pony, even if that trick is astonishingly amusing. But there's a real vision at work here . . . For all the apparent misanthropy there's a cornered and bruised altruism at work here too.' SpikeMagazine.com

'The funniest newspaper columnist in the world.' *Racing Post*

by the same author

Screen Burn

Charlie Brooker

Dawn of the Dumb

ff

faber and faber

*The*Guardian

First published in 2007
by Faber and Faber Limited
3 Queen Square London WC1N 3AU
on behalf of Guardian Books
Guardian Books is an imprint of Guardian Newspapers Ltd

Typeset by Faber and Faber Limited
Printed in the UK by CPI Bookmarque, Croydon, CRO 4TD

A CIP record for this book
is available from the British Library

ISBN 978-0-571-23841-5

20 19 18 17 16 15 14 13

CONTENTS

INTRODUCTION

Hello.

Thanks for buying this book. I hope you enjoy reading it more than I enjoyed writing it, because I hated every minute. Well, almost. It's fair to say I don't write for pleasure. To me, writing is like methodically chewing through a handful of corks. Thanks to the voices.

One voice tells me to stop typing because I'm rubbish and about to be rumbled; the other tells me to stop typing because it's too much like hard work. And recently they've been joined by a third voice – one that continually whines about a worrying, worsening form of RSI in my right arm which feels like a constant headache in my elbow. As a result, I'm often in a pretty sour temper during the writing process, and this occasionally comes across in print. Sorry about that. Hope it doesn't sully your enjoyment of an otherwise jubilant sunbeam of a book.

All the pieces collected here originally appeared in the *Guardian*, which is incredible, considering how puerile and witless they are. They fall into two categories: (1) *Screen Burn* columns on television, written for the *Guardian* Guide, and (2) other columns, on all manner of topics, written for the G2 section. Rather than split the book into two halves (with all the TV stuff at one end and everything else at the other), I decided to alternate them in shorter sections. I don't know why. I just know it's my book and I'll do what I like with it.

Anyway, like I said at the start, I hope you enjoy the damn thing, although to be frank that's unlikely. In all probability I've wasted your time and you've wasted your money. Which means you've somehow managed to lose out twice, simply by walking into a bookshop. This could be the start of a beautiful friendship.

Charlie Brooker
London, 2007

PROLOGUE

Towards the end of 2004, during the US election, I wrote a review of the televised Presidential debates which got me into a bit of trouble.

The dumb show   [23 October 2004]

Heady times. The US election draws ever nearer, and while the rest of the world bangs its head against the floorboards screaming 'Please God, not Bush!', the candidates clash head to head in a series of live televised debates. It's a bit like *American Idol*, but with terrifying global ramifications. You've got to laugh.

Or have you? Have you seen the debates? I urge you to do so. The exemplary BBC News website hosts unexpurgated streaming footage of all the recent debates, plus clips from previous encounters, through Reagan and Carter, all the way back to Nixon versus JFK.

Watching Bush v. Kerry, two things immediately strike you. First, the opening explanation of the rules makes the whole thing feel like a Radio 4 parlour game. And second, George W. Bush is . . . well, he's . . . Jesus, where do you start?

The internet's abuzz with speculation that Bush has been wearing a wire, receiving help from some off-stage lackey. Screen grabs appearing to show a mysterious bulge in the centre of his back are being traded like Top Trumps. Prior to seeing the debate footage, I regarded this with healthy scepticism: the whole 'wire' scandal was just wishful thinking on behalf of some amateur Michael Moores, I figured. And then I watched the footage.

Quite frankly, the man's either wired or mad. If it's the former, he should be flung out of office: tarred, feathered and kicked in the nuts. And if it's the latter, his behaviour goes beyond strange, and heads toward terrifying. He looks like he's listening to something we can't hear. He blinks, he mumbles, he lets a sentence trail off, starts a new one, then reverts back to whatever he was saying in the first place. Each time he recalls a statistic (either from memory or the voice in his head), he flashes us a dumb little smile, like a toddler proudly showing off its first bowel movement. Forgive me for employing the language of the playground, but the man's a tool.

So I sit there and I watch this and I start scratching my head, because I'm trying to work out why Bush is afforded any kind of credence or respect whatsoever in his native country. His performance is so transparently bizarre, so feeble and stumbling, it's a miracle he wasn't laughed off the stage. And then I start hunting around the internet, looking to see what the US media made of the whole 'wire' debate. And they just let it die. They mentioned it in passing, called it a wacko conspiracy theory and moved on.

Yet whether it turns out to be true or not, right now it's certainly plausible – even if you discount the bulge photos and simply watch the president's ridiculous smirking face. Perhaps he isn't wired. Perhaps he's just gone gaga. If you don't ask the questions, you'll never know the truth.

The silence is all the more troubling since in the past the US news media has had no problem at all covering other wacko conspiracy theories, ones with far less evidence to support them. (For infuriating confirmation of this, watch the second part of the must-see documentary series *The Power of Nightmares* (BBC2) and witness the absurd hounding of Bill Clinton over the Whitewater and Vince Foster non-scandals.)

Throughout the debate, John Kerry, for his part, looks and sounds a bit like a haunted tree. But at least he's not a lying, sniggering, drink-driving, selfish, reckless, ignorant, dangerous, backward, drooling, twitching, blinking, mouse-faced little cheat. And besides, in a fight between a tree and a bush, I know who I'd favour.

On 2 November, the entire civilised world will be praying, praying Bush loses. And sod's law dictates he'll probably win, thereby disproving the existence of God once and for all. The world will endure four more years of idiocy, arrogance and unwarranted bloodshed, with no benevolent deity to watch over and save us . . .

That's not where the column originally ended. No. It ended with a variant on the old 'Guy Fawkes, where are you now that we need you?' graffiti gag. It's an old, albeit tasteless joke that's appeared many times before – on soldiers' helmets during the Vietnam war, and on bumper stickers during the Clinton years, to name but two examples.

Unfortunately, in this case, it also appeared on the globally accessible Guardian website, where the usual context of the Screen Burn column – i.e. a TV preview page in an A5 entertainment supplement – wasn't clear, especially to overseas readers, who could be forgiven for mistaking it for a 'serious' op-ed article. End result: an old joke was interpreted by some as an earnest call for assassination, including the Drudge Report, which ran it as a headline.

This didn't do the Guardian's reputation any favours — nor mine, come to that (although in retrospect I'm mainly embarrassed I was giving the daft 'Bush was wired' conspiracy some serious consideration). The article was removed and replaced with a (sincere) apology for any offence caused. But, encouraged by a series of right-wing websites, outraged emails flooded in, hundreds of them: some abusive, some baffling, and some downright hair-raising. Here's a random sampling:

'We have sent your name to the FBI and Secret Service along with a copy of your wonderful article. Death threats are punishable and I am sure we can extradite you if need be since you are an American.'

'Bush will go down in history as one of the greatest presidents ever . . . while your name will be like a drop of water lost in the ocean . . . NOTHING.'

'I hope you get jail time . . . I am complaining to your embassies, businesses that advertise with anyone who consorts with you, and our law enforcement over this matter. Concerned American Citizen.'

'You have been reported to the Secret Service and I have urged that you be placed under arrest upon any entry to our country.'

'We don't give a flying fuck what you stupid Brits think. There was a reason we kicked your ass in the Revolution . . . you're all just a bunch of fucking sissy asses. I can't wait to watch as you and the rest of the European faggots turn into Third World countries that you all aspire to.'

'May those in your life survive under the curse you wish for others. Let them live long miserable lives. I look forward to reading your obituary on the back page of a paper sooner than later . . . You deserve the severest punishment that can be meted out. May the queen be soon rid of scum like you.'

'Come on over for a nice visit to the US. Let me know where you'll be, and I'll come and beat you to death.'

'Just to let you know I have forwarded your article to the US secret service who take these threats seriously. I can assure you that you will now be on the Homeland Security watch list. You can look forward to being hassled at every airport in the world from now on . . . Enjoy your life.'

'Die of AIDS, scumbag.'

'Look, shitface, I suggest you never try to come to the US . . . You will be under constant surveillance by the Secret Service should our incompetent immigration agents even let you slip in. Stay home and fuck your mother – and the horse she rode in on. Don't show your cretinous face here, scumbag. Many of us pack, you know. And the Tony Martin case would not happen here since we are not the decadent country England has become under the Guardianship of crypto-Communists. I can't picture twelve good men and true convicting any American for blowing you away.'

'Do you remember Jill Dando? And she was innocent! Have a care, cretin.'

'Your 9/11 is coming soon. We both know it. I'll be sure to telephone you when it happens and see if you've been personally affected. I can only hope.'

'Watch your back.'

And so on. And so on. Laughable now, but seriously disturbing at the time, especially given the sheer weight of complaints and death threats.

Later, I realised this is how modern campaigning works: partisan websites whip up a storm of controversy (wilfully misinterpreting the facts if necessary), then encourage people to email in their thousands. It's intimidation. And it works: initially, at least. But in the long run, it's an impotent howl: an angry, protracted bovine hoot. The Secret Service never contacted me. They have better things to do. Nor did the authorities place me on any sinister 'list': I've visited the USA several times since, had no trouble obtaining a visa or entering the country, and had a wonderful time while I was there. In fact, every American I've ever met in the flesh, at home or abroad, has been delightful.

But the neo-cons with email accounts? Bleh.

CHAPTER ONE

In which Nicky Campbell is mistaken for the Antichrist, John McCririck is likened to a womble, and Sir Alan Sugar makes his debut

Dripping with menace

Nicky Campbell: what's that all about then? If Judge Dredd burst in and ordered you to write down a list of all the household names in Britain, chances are you'd forget to include him. Campbell hovers somewhere just outside the mind's field of vision, yet in reality he's never far from eye or ear shot. So why doesn't he stick in your head?

Because he's the Antichrist, that's why. Now this is just a theory, coupled to an opinion, trundled into battle on the back of a vague feeling . . . but I reckon Nicky Campbell might be the most evil man in the universe. There's no evidence to support this, but come on – there's just something about him, isn't there?

Stare into his eyes and you'll be chilled to the core by the cavernous hollow within. They say true evil is fundamentally banal: that the wickedest serial killers operate unnoticed thanks to their blank, unremarkable nature. Campbell's fronted everything from *Wheel of Fortune* to *Panorama*, from Radio 1 to Radio 5, and yet you'd forgotten all about him, hadn't you? Doesn't that say something?

If you don't believe me, check out his regular performances on *Watchdog* (BBC1), which he hosts in the style of a man linking stories in a 1970s portmanteau horror movie. It's screamingly over-the-top, yet passes without comment. Dripping with menace, he stares straight down the lens, delivering lines about fly-by-night timeshare companies as though discussing the Third Reich. He's got to be taking the piss. Perhaps the whole thing's an arch joke, devised for his own amusement. Well, I'm not laughing. No. I'm hearing the theme from *The Omen* looping endlessly in my head.

Do you think Campbell really gives a toss about any of the issues raised during the average edition of *Watchdog*? I certainly don't, and I'm a Quaker, for pity's sake. It's virtually impossible to care about the kind of whingeing shitsacks on display here. They're idiots: idiots who express genuine surprise when the diamond ring they bought for tuppence from a satellite shopping channel turns out not to be worth £1,300 after all: idiots who jerk with indignant rage when the knock-off *Finding Nemo* cuddly toy they purchased in dumb faith from a ramshackle pound shop falls apart at the

3

seams, revealing a collection of rusty metal shards that scrape their children's eyes out.

And they're ugly. Unbelievably ugly. Hideous, puffy-eyed, bloated, blotchy-faced organisms with dry hair and lips as thick as forearms, droning away in their dull, grotty voices – droning and whining and grousing about the petty injustice of it all, in the vain belief anyone else gives a toss. If they really want to complain about something worthwhile, they should stand on top of a mountain waving an angry fist heavenward, loudly demanding to be told why God saw fit to curse them with a face like John Merrick's ballbag.

Still, as far as these clueless, dribbling sea cows are concerned, Campbell's a knight in shining armour, galloping into combat on their behalf in the show's most uncomfortable section – the bit where a shifting, blushing, dry-mouthed company spokesman gets an over-the-top grilling. Campbell seems to secretly relish these encounters – as well he might, being the Prince of Darkness. (Sometimes co-presenter Julia Bradbury does the honours – although since she possesses an indefinable quality that makes you suspect she's probably quite mucky in the bedroom, her interviews are less sinister and more like a sexually charged pre-shag tiff between two tipsy adulterers.)

I could go on about *Watchdog* till the cows start texting to say they're on their way home – I could discuss the confused researchers milling about in the background trying to look busy, or the tortuously contrived links in Paul Heiney's VT reports – but really, the most important thing is to draw your attention to Nicky Campbell's hilarious weekly performance, which I urge you to tune in and savour for yourselves. No, really, it's funny.

Just don't stare into his eyes for too long, or God knows what might happen.

Cannibal Holocaust [27 November 2004]

'Oh, good Lord! It's unbelievable. It's horrible. I can't understand the reason for such cruelty!'

4

That's a quote from *Cannibal Holocaust* (1980), the most sickening and notorious video nasty ever made. I haven't checked the yuletide schedule yet, but the chances ITV are showing it at four o'clock on Christmas Day are pretty slim, to be honest.

I'm a Celebrity . . . Get Me Out of Here! (ITV1), on the other hand – that's hearty primetime fare. Yet the similarities between this and *Cannibal Holocaust* are striking. In each, a group of naive media types ventures into the jungle in an attempt to raise their profiles, then rapidly descend into lunacy and infighting. Both groups must eat disgusting things to survive, both get tortured for entertainment, and both are ultimately gobbled up and flushed away. *Cannibal Holocaust* doesn't cut away to a rubbish First Choice holidays blipvert every 19 seconds, but apart from that, they're basically identical.

Anyway, who's in the cast? Of *I'm a Celebrity*, that is. Well?

First up, former All Saint Natalie Appleton, who spent the first 48 hours snivelling and squealing. This is Natalie's fourth stab at fame. First there was All Saints, then a role in a Dave Stewart movie (I've looked it up on the internet: apparently she played a pair of naked tits) and then, in 2003, a musical comeback successful enough to put her where she is today – in the outback, wiping her arse with leaves. Have you seen the size of this woman's ears? Each time she ties her hair back, bingo – it's Topo Gigio, the Italian puppet mouse (Google the name. See?).

Then there's Joe Pasquale, better known across the land as Oh God Turn Over I Can't Stand Him. Actually that's unfair: he's coming across as a genuinely likeable man, and is my favourite to win. Bear in mind I'm writing this on the morning of Tuesday 23 November – so if he's started whistling Nazi anthems and kicking wombats in the face by the time you read this, ignore everything I just said.

The decision to recruit badger-haired nobody Fran Cosgrave was initially baffling, because it's the first time they've included someone who's less famous than, say, your local GP. But on reflection, I think it's a bit of cunning philanthropy on ITV's part. Anyone with more than three friends is better known than he is, which means,

thanks to Fran Cosgrove, we're all celebrities now – and we'll
remain celebrities long after he's slunk back to obscurity (hey Fran,
Obscurity would be a great name for a club).

For some reason, Antonio Fargas has to walk around with 'Huggy
Bear' printed on his T-shirt, instead of his actual name. Presumably
this is to help thick viewers remember who he is, but it's a touch
demeaning because the others don't get the same treatment. It'd be
far easier to identify Nancy Sorrell if she simply walked around
with 'Vic Reeves's Wife' on her back; Sophie Anderton could be
labelled 'Cokey Model', Brian Harvey 'E17 Chav', and Sheila Fergu-
son 'Forget It'. Then there's Janet Street-Porter ('Shagged Normski'),
a cheery media tyrant famous for sounding like the cat from the
old *Charley Says* public information cartoon.

Finally, national whipping-boy and former royal butler Paul
Burrell ('My Rock') – facially, a cross between Jamie Oliver and a
simpering broad bean.

Apparently the nation is on tenterhooks, eager for whatever regal
gossip he'll spill. The only question I'm interested in hearing him
answer is: 'Did you ever get to see Diana's bum – perhaps just
accidentally, and only for a second – but did you?' Bet he did.

Anyway, them's the inmates – at the time of writing they're yet
to undergo any real torture, just a bit of foreplay in which Fran
was staked to the ground while bugs crawled round his privates.
Doubtless the real horror's to come. I'll leave you with a quote from
Cannibal Ferox, another video nasty with disturbing *I'm a Celebrity*
overtones: 'They castrated him with a machete and then they . . .
they ate his genitals!' And to think, he only won three bushtucker
stars for the trouble.

I love Frann he is wel fit   [4 December 2004]

So another *I'm a Celebrity . . . Get Me Out of Here!* (ITV) scuttles
to a conclusion, and what have we learned, fourth time around?
Absolutely nothing, except that Natalie Appleton should've been
forced to complete her trials with a cattle prod. Is this the frailest
woman in Britain? She's like a heroine in a Victorian novel: a pale

delicate flower, weakened by years of indulgence and pampering, who faints and dies of consumption if she so much as stubs a toe, or shakes hands with a beggar, or one of the footmen accidentally blows off in another wing of the mansion.

'I just can't physically do it . . . I'm gonna pass out . . . oh God I'm gonna be sick,' she whined, over and over again, until it became a theme tune. Her husband should sample it, loop it and use it on the next Prodigy album. Possibly as a recurring motif in a brand new mix of 'Smack My Bitch Up'.

What else? Well, Vic Reeves's big entry was a mistake: it's never a good idea to arrive fashionably late and to great fanfare on a reality show, unless you subsequently do something – anything – to justify the hype. Ages ago, in *The Smell of Reeves and Mortimer*, he did a terrifying and hilarious impersonation of Lloyd Grossman, hovering around with an outsized papier-mâché forehead and bits of cutlery for fingers. He should've gone in like that and stayed in character till the bitter end.

ITV2's live feed once again ran a coin-operated text-message window along the bottom of the screen, in a shameless bid to rake in money from illiterate cretins nationwide prepared to pay for the privilege of making the words 'I LOVE FRANN HE IS WEL FIT' appear on their tellies. How long until they start superimposing that over everything, even the news? Six months from now, you'll switch on the ITN news and there it'll be, running along the bottom: 'CONDOLEEZA U R SOOOO SEXY!!!'; 'FALLUJER IS A MESS PS MARTIN WIL U MARRY ME LUV KIRSTY'.

Oddly enough, that sort of caper might actually outclass Channel 4's new political offering, *Morgan and Platell* (C4). It's not that the show itself doesn't include at least some level of political debate, it's just that it's impossible to concentrate on the issues at hand when your brain's busy trying to work out which of the hosts you'd like to smack in the cakehole first.

Who's the more repugnant? In the red corner, Piers 'Fake Photos' Morgan, a man who recently sparked panic amongst *This Morning* viewers by inadvertently blabbering about an impending al-Qaeda attack 'in the next few days', then spent last week's *Morgan and*

Platell haranguing Commons leader Peter Hain for 'encouraging fear'.

In the blue corner, Amanda 'Antigay Malignity' Platell, former spin doctor for William Hague, famous for penning an *Evening Standard* column so nakedly homophobic and misleading that the paper's own theatre critic wrote to the letters page complaining it was 'a piece of gutter-press journalism . . . I have never been so upset or angered by an article as Amanda Platell's attempt to incite contempt.'

Morgan spends the entire programme looking twice as smug as a man who's just learnt to fellate himself – yet miraculously it's moon-faced, putty-nosed Platell who ultimately snatches first position in the punchability stakes, because there's something about her that suggests she thinks she's gorgeous and pouting. It's a bit like watching a drunken old spinster pinching the waiter's arse at a wedding reception.

Still, there's one remarkable side effect to all this: it's the only political show in living memory where the politicians are the most likeable people in the studio by far. Under these conditions, even Dick Cheney would come across as warm and approachable – if I were him, I'd book an appearance at the first opportunity.

To quote Miss Appleton, I think I'm gonna throw up.

Mr Logic on holiday [1 January 2005]

Why are we here? What is the sound of one hand clapping? If a tree falls in a forest, and there's no one around to witness it, will Alain de Botton write an entire book about it anyway?

Probably. In case you don't know who de Botton is, let me explain: he's an absolute pair-of-aching-balls of a man – a slap-headed, ruby-lipped pop philosopher who's forged a lucrative career stating the bleeding obvious in a series of poncey, lighter-than-air books aimed at smug Sunday supplement pseuds looking for something clever-looking to read on the plane – yet if you pick up one of his books and read it cover to cover, you'll come away with less insight into the human condition than if you'd worked your way through a copy of *Mr Tickle* instead.

For some mad reason, his books keep getting made into TV shows. Last year, he rocked the world to its very foundations by revealing that human beings sometimes experience an emotion called 'envy', in his book and TV series *Status Anxiety*. Now he's popped up again, to instruct us on *The Art of Travel* (C4), just in case we didn't buy his book of the same name, which was the toast of the aspirational tosspot community back in 2003.

And boy, has he struck the jackpot with the telly version, because rather than sitting at a desk typing about travel, he gets to roam the world stroking his chin in front of a camera crew.

It opens with Alain drearily watching a holiday ad on TV, but don't panic: within seconds he's hit on a way to put the budget to good use. 'I thought of going on a Mediterranean cruise,' he says, bold as brass. 'It seemed to offer everything I was looking for. Sunshine; the excitement of being on a glamorous ship; some destinations I'd always wanted to see.'

Cut to Alain boarding the *QE2*, which is 'even more beautiful than I imagined. There were chocolates on the pillow at night. There were artfully moulded toiletries in the bathroom. The ship was repainted every morning, and was resplendent in the Mediterranean sun.'

As is Alain's bald, shining head. Yet, despite his opulent surroundings, something's eating away at him, so he has a little think, and before long, 'a troubling realisation began to dawn on me . . . that I'd inadvertently brought myself along with me on my holiday . . . Wherever we choose to go, perhaps the underlying wish is for me to get away from "me".'

I'd only known him a few minutes, and I wanted to get away from him too. Later, he reveals that guide books are no substitute for exploring a place yourself, and that a hotel is an 'anonymous' place. Unless it's an East German swingers' hotel filled with naked people, that is – like the one Alain visits halfway through the show, ostensibly to illustrate a point about something or other, but probably because he was curious.

With their orange, wrinkled skin, the swingers look pretty grim, but they're not a patch on Alain, with his shiny dome, slit-like eyes and dark red lips. (They really are dark, like he's been suckling cranberry juice from a teat for the last six months, and set against his paper-pale skin they make him look like Ronald McDonald's serious older brother – or an inverted black-and-white minstrel, whichever is most insulting.)

Alain's entire travel philosophy boils down to 'wherever you go, there you are'. It's the sort of thing that might be explained in a single page of *The Little Book of Comforting Dribble*, in other words – the only difference is that Alain has to circumnavigate the globe to make the same cock-obvious point.

Still, never mind. At least you can point at him and laugh, and say, 'Ha ha ha, it's like *Viz*'s Mr Logic on Holiday' for the entire duration of the show. And if you feel bad about slagging him off, don't worry. He'd be philosophical about it.

Enter the Dragons' Den [8 January 2005]

Fool! You probably won't bother tuning into *Dragons' Den* (BBC2), just because of its stupid title. And who could blame you? A TV show called *Dragons' Den*? Sounds like a cheapo *Lord of The Rings* knock-off, aimed at children who can't tell how rubbish the special effects are.

Fortunately, it's not like that at all: instead it's an entrepreneurial take on *Pop Idol*. The 'dragons' of the title are a panel of super-rich businessmen and women, every single one of whom you'll want to smack in the face on sight, simply for making you feel like a medieval pauper by comparison. They're all quite psychotically odious, although the prize swine has to be YO! Sushi founder Simon Woodroffe: an obscene combination of unimaginable personal wealth and pretentious facial hair.

The premise: members of the public queue up to pitch their business ideas to the dragons. The prize: real money and real investment, from the dragons' real pockets. Not piddling little amounts of money either: we're talking hundreds of thousands, life-changing helpings of cold hard cash.

The result makes for merciless viewing. The wannabes are already nervous as they enter the room, via a staircase apparently designed to leave them puffing for breath. That they're immediately confronted by a row of scowling dragons, with huge stacks of banknotes literally piled either side of them, scarcely helps matters. But the poor sods need that cash, so they mop their brows, swallow hard, and start pitching – which is where things really go to pieces. Because almost without exception, their schemes and plans and hopes and dreams are absolutely bloody ridiculous.

This week's episode, for example, finds a man requiring thousands of pounds to fund the launch of a world-changing invention: the 'StableTable', an adjustable plastic widget that stops tables wobbling (you know, just like a makeshift cardboard wedge does, but for more money). Then there's a woman hawking a 'flower quiver' – quite literally a quiver you wear on your back to keep flowers in (this, she claims, eradicates the 'difficulty' of holding them with your hands). Most heartbreaking of all are two petrified young scamps attempting to drum up support for an online music service: one of them is so intimidated by the mere sight of the dragons he immediately forgets his lines and starts sweating so profusely he might as well be pumping 15 gallons of lactic acid through a blowhole on the top of his head.

Faced with this absurd parade, the dragons feel personally insulted. After all, it's *their* cash these bozos are after. And once angered, they speedily pick apart each proposal with ruthless efficiency. Business plans are derided, personalities are shredded, dreams are openly laughed at. The hapless pitchers stagger away, reeling and blinking as though they've just had a bagful of shit thrown over them. Like I say, it's fun.

Still a bad title though. Anyway, dragons don't have dens, they have lairs, dammit.

Even if you hate kids so much you just threw up because you saw the word 'kids' at the start of this sentence, it's worth catching this week's *Child of Our Time* (BBC1), because it includes a startling investigation into how much of *EastEnders* the average toddler can comprehend.

As part of an 'experiment' to see whether kids actually understand what they see on TV, a group of five-year-olds are shown the episode where Janine throws Barry off a cliff. They're then asked to explain, in their own words, what happened. Using puppets to represent the cast.

Naturally, their versions are a hundred times better than the original: according to one of the kids, Janine was upset with Barry because he wouldn't give her any sweets.

I hereby demand the BBC starts broadcasting live kid-puppet 're-imaginings' of their entire output, 24 hours a day, accessible via the red button. Come on, BBC. I for one can't wait to see their version of *Crimewatch*.

The amazing John McCririck [15 January 2005]

So, the BBC went ahead and broadcast *Jerry Springer: The Opera* in its entirety last week, enraging a hardcore band of extremist humourless oafs who decided before they'd even seen it that it was blasphemous and despicable and hideous and ghastly and wrong, and therefore Must Not Be Shown because They Didn't Like It.

Let he who is without brains cast the first stone. And cast they did. Prior to broadcast, they jostled, they shouted, they published contact details and made threatening phone calls – all in the name of Our Lord Jesus Christ, who, unless I'm grossly mistaken, was actually rather keen on tolerance and forgiveness and turning the other cheek.

Before *Jerry Springer* was shown, the BBC received 47,000 complaints. Afterwards, it received just 900 – plus around 500 calls of support. Which suggests that once people had seen it, it finally dawned on them that perhaps it wasn't worth getting quite so steamed up over a comedy musical. Nevertheless, a crusading fringe group calling itself Christian Voice, who published private phone numbers of BBC staff on their website, and who probably speak for, oooh, 0.0005 per cent of all practising Christians, plan to prosecute the BBC for blasphemy. And if that doesn't work, they could always throw Mark Thompson in a lake to prove he's a witch.

You'd have thought human beings had evolved beyond this kind of idiocy – but since Christian Voice probably don't believe in evolution, I guess they're exempt. And as for the many thousands who objected to the broadcast on the grounds that it represented a 'misuse of their licence fee', I suspect that if you counted all the people who've ever turned on their TV of a Sunday evening and said, 'Oh shit, *Songs of Praise* is on', you'd be looking at a majority of millions.

What would Jesus make of it? He'd probably watch the opera, laugh his halo off, and then appear before the protesting hotheads and say something wise and charming, like 'do not let your hearts be troubled' or 'love one another'. He certainly wouldn't be standing there indignantly stamping his feet. Well, not with his stigmata.

Anyway, onto more important matters, namely *Celebrity Big Brother* (C4), home of the Amazing John McCririck, who really ought to be imprisoned within a digital satellite channel for the rest of his days, where we can tune in and watch him skulking round a bear pit, rubbing his head against the walls and grumpily swinging on tyres – all of it backed up with some kind of interactive technology that goads him with a stick each time you press the red button.

Is it just me, or does McCririck look a bit like a Womble? An angry, recently waxed Womble, but a Womble nevertheless. He even dresses like one: witness the Great Uncle Bulgaria costume he sometimes throws on, or his Bungo hat. If any movie execs out there are planning a twenty-first-century 're-imagining' of *Wombling Free*, they could save themselves a lot of expensive CGI by simply covering McCririck in glue and rolling him in cotton wool. And asking him to provide his own clothing.

Here's hoping he's still incarcerated by the time you read this. As I type, Germaine Greer's just walked, which is a pity, because without her or Great Uncle Bulgaria there's little reason to tune in. Bez just bobs around staring at everything, like a man trying to make out individual atoms in the air; Kenzie is basically Mike Skinner's thick younger brother; forcing Brigitte and Jackie to square off on TV despite the child-custody issues involved strikes me as a sickening misjudgement; Caprice, Jeremy and Lisa are so bland they may as well be replaced with furniture.

Still, if McCririck goes prematurely, at least you know you can look forward to six months of hilarious, life-affirming Diet Coke commercials in which the corner shop runs out of his favourite fizzy drink and he throws a strop and slaps someone. Christ, that would be something worth protesting about.

Fear of vomiting [22 January 2005]

Don't you never say this column ain't educational. Your new word of the week is 'emetophobia', which means 'fear of vomiting'. There. You've learned something. Give yourself a big fat pat on the back, four-eyes.

I'm familiar with the word because I'm an emetophobe myself. It's an incredibly stupid phobia – for instance, the thing that scares me most about nuclear war isn't the death and destruction, but the vomiting caused by radiation sickness – but it's a phobia none-theless, and I've got it. Sometimes it's so annoying, I could puke. Except of course I can't. It's all very confusing.

Anyway, fellow emetophobes beware, because this week's edition of *Tribe* (BBC2) opens with the most spectacular on-screen vomit since *The Exorcist*. But worse, because it's real.

The spewing commences when masochist extraordinaire Bruce Parry decides to spend a month with the Babongos, an obscure African tribe whose initiation ceremony involves taking a powerful, sometimes lethal hallucinogen whose first side effect is to make you hurl the entire contents of your stomach up. And by Christ does Parry hurl with gusto. It all comes up: he practically coughs up his own kidneys.

The drug then sends you on an unstoppable three-day trip dur-ing which you experience visions, float free of your own body, drift inside the minds of other people, and relive every bad moment in your life in blistering Technicolor close-up. And just in case that isn't mind-mangling enough, the Babongos do their level best to exacerbate things by dressing up in vibrant costumes, dancing around with flaming sticks, dunking you in the river and making you pass through a symbolic gigantic vulva built out of sticks. At the end of which, you're reborn. As Bez.

Ah, Bez. The usual 'at the time of writing' caveats apply, but now Great Uncle Bulgaria's left, it's Bez and Bez alone who's making *Celebrity Big Brother* (C4) watchable. Adrift in a world of spliffless clarity, it's clear he finds sobriety as disorientating as most people would find the Babongo drug ritual. The housemates' reaction? They nominated him. 'I reckon yous lot are a bunch of tossers,' he replied – the wisest, most coherent thing he's said since he entered the house.

If his brain ever adjusts to normality, perhaps he'll muster yet more accurate insults, and hopefully aim them directly at Lisa I'Anson, who, at the time of writing, is still in there, apparently intent on single-handedly redefining the word 'smug'. And the word 'insincere'. And the phrase 'high-handed, self-satisfied, nauseating she-bore'.

Could Lisa I'Anson be the most patronising person on Earth? She swans around treating everyone as though they're six years old – pretty close in Kenzie's case, and Bez's mental age can't be far off, but even so, it's hard for me to stomach. She talked down to Jackie (who's funnier than Lisa). She talked down to John McCririck (who's more honest than Lisa). She talked down to Germaine Greer (who's . . . well, where do you start?).

I don't know if she's a religious woman, and I haven't seen her saying any bedtime prayers, but if she did, chances are she'd even talk down to God.

Under any circumstances, it's pretty bleedin' rich for an ex-Radio 1 DJ, who's currently reduced to picking her bum on CCTV, to believe she's in a position to offer any sort of advice to anyone (unless it includes a few handy pointers on the most efficient way to sob all the fluid out of your body), but when the advice on offer consists of nothing but cod psychology, artificial sympathy and dreary, witless murmurings of 'it's all good, babe, it's all good . . .', it veers straight past 'rich' and hurtles toward 'nauseating' with alarming speed.

All good babe? All good? No it isn't: shut your cakehole. Our stomachs are rising, and speaking as an emetophobe, that horrifies me to the core.

Celebrity bollockers [12 February 2005]

In today's cut-throat consumer marketplace, some names are synonymous with quality: Rolls-Royce. Bang & Olufsen. Alessi. Gucci. Smeg. And then there are other names. Names like Amstrad. Yes, Amstrad. My second-ever home computer was an Amstrad CPC6128, which came with its own built-in disk drive – as luridly futuristic back then as a computer with its own fully-functioning bladder would be now.

Trouble is, after a few weeks, the sound chip went all wonky and started guffing out bum notes at random. Then the disk drive, which I'd been so dazzled by, developed its own personality – which might have been fun if it hadn't proved to be a destructive personality that didn't like disks very much. Little things like that can wear you down, and before long, playing games on the thing was less fun than glaring at it and wondering which window to hurl it through.

The culprit responsible for my conked-out Amstrad CPC6128 was Alan Sugar, who today heads a £700m business empire, owns 13 per cent of Tottenham Hotspur, gets called 'Sir' by everybody including the Queen and is the star of BBC2's surprisingly enjoyable back-stabbing reality show *The Apprentice* (BBC2). In the US, *The Apprentice* starred Donald Trump, a man so obscenely rich he could afford to buy all the oxygen in the world, then rent it back to us at a profit if he so chose. The show was a hit, and Trump's hairstyle (which looks like a golf cap hurriedly assembled from rusting steel wool) became a major star. Sugar doubles for Trump in the UK version, which works like this: fourteen odious, over-confident wannabe entrepreneurs, every single one of whom you will learn to hate twice as much as Hitler, have given up their day jobs in order to dance to Sir Alan's tune. He divides them into two teams (one team of boys, one of girls), and sets them a weekly task

– at the end of which, one candidate from the losing team gets personally fired by Alan, in the grumpiest manner possible.

While unsweetened Sugar can't trump Trump in the preposterous haircut stakes, on the evidence of this first episode his name will soon be mentioned in the same breath as other famous celebrity bollockers like Simon Cowell and Gordon Ramsay. Looking eerily similar to Jon Culshaw impersonating Russell Crowe, he enters wearing the face of a man who's just stubbed his toe on the gravestone of a close relative, and continues to grumble and bark his way through the rest of the show. Even his introductory greeting is downbeat. There's not so much as a handshake. Instead, he glares at the line of hopefuls like they're a group of work experience kids who've just trodden dogshit into his boardroom carpet.

'I don't like liars, I don't like cheats, I don't like bullshitters, I don't like schmoozers, I don't like arse-lickers,' he announces, unwittingly dismissing every single one of them in the process.

Once Alan's set the weekly task – flower-selling for the opener – the focus shifts to the candidates themselves, as we watch them bicker, argue, scheme, moan, boast, brag, grandstand, plot and spout marketing bollocks until you want to squat on their chests and punch their jaws through the floor. By the end of the show, you'll want Alan to fire the lot of them. Preferably into the ocean.

Speaking of the candidates, whatever the collective term for a bunch of turds is (I think it's a 'fistful' of turds), it applies to both *The Apprentice*'s fourteen entrepreneurs and a scene in *Michael Howard: No More Mr Nasty* (BBC2) in which we're treated to the sight of John Major, William Hague, Kenneth Clarke and Iain Duncan Smith sitting round a table offering advice to Michael Howard.

Warning: the programme also contains repeated, severe close-ups of Howard, who has more than a touch of 10 Rillington Place about him, plus a talking-head interview with Anne Robinson, whose face now appears so tight and Botoxed she seems to be pushing it through the taut skin of a tambourine toward the viewer. Beware. Beware. Beware.

Mrs Spoon from Button Moon [26 February 2005]

Sorry to ruin your morning, but you're going to wither and die. There. I've said it. Forget all the aspirational stuff you'll read in the magazine supplements – your destiny consists of yellow hair and liver spots. In fifteen years' time you'll have a face like an elephant's kneecap and an arse like a chamois leather drying on a radiator. Your mirror's going to vomit each time you walk past. And there's nothing you can do about it.

Unless, of course, you bump into Nicky Hambleton-Jones, presenter of *Ten Years Younger* (C4). Essentially an hour-long commercial for Botox, *Ten Years Younger* is one of the cruellest shows around. Each week a dowdy, wrinkled member of the public is subjected to a series of ritual humiliations. First, they're paraded around the streets while members of the public guess how old they are (the answer is consistently upsetting). Then they're set upon by a team of experts who pick them apart in finer detail – pointing out their jowls, their shabby hair, their rubbish taste in clothes and their ham-fisted excuses for make-up.

Thus psychologically broken, they're offered a lifeline: Nicky and Co. offer to shave a decade off their fizzogs courtesy of a haircut, a makeover and a faceload of plastic surgery. This week, it's not a member of the public, but a celebrity – well, Sherrie Hewson from *Emmerdale* at any rate. Sherrie's fifty-four years old but the average street-plodding schmuck reckons she looks fifty-seven. Hardly a disaster, but that doesn't stop Nicky, who charges on regardless.

I say 'charges on', but there's nothing particularly charged about Nicky. She's slightly synthetic and ethereal: the ghost of a listless graphic designer. Weirder still, for someone fronting a show about facelifts, her own face is almost entirely featureless. She looks like Mrs Spoon from Button Moon. She looks like a baby new potato in glasses. She looks like Michael Jackson's mugshot snap. But most of all she looks like a Crayola sketch drawn by a very very stupid child. There's a *Ten Years Younger* spin-off book in the shops right now: the front cover features a simple cartoon drawing of Nicky Hambleton-Jones, and curiously, it looks more like her than her actual photo does. She's a freak. How *dare* she tell other people what to do with their faces when she hasn't grown one of her own?

By the end of this week's edition, Sherrie looks and feels like a million dollars – but the surgical bill can't have been far off. And you can't help suspecting that any surgical procedure carried out on behalf of a TV show is going to be performed with far more care than the average snip-'n'-slice facelift. If I had one done, knowing my luck I'd catch the surgeon on an off day and spend the rest of my life sneezing through my tear ducts and blinking through my arse.

In summary: *Ten Years Younger* is an irresponsible piece-of-shit show that plays on universal fears and snidely offers corrective surgery as the only solution – as opposed to, say, NOT JUDGING PEOPLE BY THEIR LOOKS IN THE FIRST PLACE.

And please, please don't carp on about how great the participants feel at the end of the show, as though that's some justification. There's got to be something seriously wrong with a society that can't let people age naturally without pointing at their saggy bits and laughing. If this programme had its way, we'd be walking around with identikit baubles for heads. What in God's name happened to character?

Jacko   [5 March 2005]

Someone's probably told you already. They've emailed, texted, phoned, or simply run up to you in the street, flapping their arms around and shrieking 'Jesus CHRIST – have you seen the *Michael Jackson Trial Reconstructions* on Sky News yet?'

I urge you to tune in today at 7 p.m. for the weekly catch-up. Because holy mackerel: this is either brilliant, or the most ominous paradigm shift for humankind since the creation of the downloadable ringtone chart.

No idea what I'm gabbling about? It's simple: in the absence of dedicated camera coverage of the Jackson child molestation trial, Sky have decided to ditch the traditional charcoal court sketches of old (which have a tendency to turn judicial proceedings into a

19

stark graphic novel), in favour of a full-colour day-by-day reconstruction of events using actors.

The end result is a truly spine-chilling cross between a daytime soap, an episode of *Judge Judy*, and a *Dead Ringers* Christmas special. If there weren't so many references to child molestation, they could run it with a laughter track and have an underground comedy hit on their hands.

The cast, who are uniformly rubbish, are made up as lookalikes, with Jacko himself being particularly impressive. Where did they find the actor responsible? More to the point, is that his real nose? Did he undergo surgery to land the role? Was he born that way? Or maybe he lost his original nose in an accident, so the make-up artist seized the opportunity to plop a Jackson-like triangular conk in the middle of his face?

His wig's not bad either – a bit *Planet of the Apes*, maybe, but a good effort. His defence attorney's hair is even better: a brilliant snow-white helmet that makes him look like Geppetto from Disney's version of *Pinocchio*. I can't wait for Liz Taylor to show up. Who's going to play her? Matt Lucas?

Sky are showing the reconstructions as stand-alone 'specials', but since they're also interweaving them with their actual news coverage of the trial, you're treated to the baffling spectacle of the real-life participants walking toward the courtroom (shot by the news crew), interspersed with the hammy lookalikes delivering lines inside the building. It's a bit like watching *Plan 9 from Outer Space*, the Ed Wood movie in which Bela Lugosi died halfway through filming and was hastily replaced by a stand-in for half his scenes. At the time of writing, Sky are running a phone-in poll asking viewers whether Jackson can ever truly receive a fair trial. So far, the viewers reckon the answer is 'no', but I'm confused. Are they talking about the real Jackson, or the pretend one? What if one gets off and the other doesn't? Can that happen? I reckon it might. And then he'll probably moonwalk home.

Still, having taken an exciting leap into the unknown, here's hoping Sky go the whole hog. For week two, why don't they resurrect the *Spitting Image* puppets and re-enact the trial with them? Or illustrate some of the grittier incidents with animated manga-style flashbacks, like in *Kill Bill*? How about cutting away at random intervals to show Beavis and Butthead watching the trial at home, calling the prosecutor a 'dork' and sniggering?

And why stop at recreating the Jackson trial? Perhaps next time Sky are doing a report on something Tony Blair's said, the screen could go all wobbly and slowly fade into a claymation *Numskulls*-style sequence set inside his head, in which polarised elements of his conscience (played by boggle-eyed plasticine sheep) debate the consequences of his actions?

They could liven up their Iraq coverage by dubbing *Eye of the Tiger* over the top and dropping in random sequences from *Saving Private Ryan*. Or use complex CGI technology to show the Pope having an out-of-body chinwag with God while laid up in hospital, with the words 'IMPROBABLE RECONSTRUCTION' flashing across the bottom in bright red letters.

Fuck it, they might as well. Let's face it, they've pissed their integrity up the wall already.

 – *In retrospect, that's a bit harsh. Sky News is gaudy and hysterical on occasion, but it's a damn sight better than ITV News has become.*

Colours and shapes [12 March 2005]

Brilliant. In case we haven't all got enough to worry about what with bird flu, terrorism, global warming, food scares, neo-conservatives, corporate megalomania, MRSA, phone tumours, asteroids, nuclear stockpiles, crime, plane, train and car crashes, depression, madness, ageing, anguish, Aids and G4's debut album going straight to number one . . . the BBC considerately toss another chunk of doom on the pile in the form of *Supervolcano* (BBC1), designed to strike terror into the hearts of everyone who watches it.

We're all going to die, apparently, because a huge glob of magma beneath Yellowstone Park could erupt at any moment. Sorry, 'supererupt' – causing widespread death and destruction as the gases and ash turn the world into a freezing, desolate, scarcely inhabitable hellball. Imagine a worldwide version of Doncaster. Yes, the situation's that bleak.

If you watch the 'drama' version of the show, that is. There's an accompanying documentary: *Supervolcano: The Truth About Yellowstone* (BBC2), which also does its best to scare you, but has to begrudgingly stick to the facts by pointing out, reluctantly, that although a supereruption will certainly happen 'some time in the future', it could occur 'at any point in the next 100,000 years'. In other words, it's just as likely to happen in the year 102005 as it is tomorrow. Phew.

Not that this stops the 'drama' version of the show making merry with the concept, presenting it as a cross between an episode of *24* and *The Day after Tomorrow*.

Why are they doing this? It's not like we can campaign to have volcanoes outlawed. If the BBC just wants to scare everyone, they could simply broadcast a nightly show called 'Boo!', consisting of two hours of blank, silent blackness, punctuated at random, infrequent intervals by a scary ghost face shrieking at the top of its voice. It'd have a similar effect, and at least we wouldn't think our lives were in danger.

Anyway, breakfast TV now: and Five's *Milkshake!*, a collection of shows aimed at toddlers, which I've just decided is the best option for anyone unlucky enough to be conscious at that time of day.

First thing in the morning most people have a mental age of three, which is why pre-school programming makes so much sense. Colours and shapes accompanied by basic descriptions of the alphabet is pretty much all the human mind can take at that time of day.

But that's not the only reason to tune in: the shows on offer are the most imaginative, lovingly crafted pieces of television you'll find at that time of day. Either that, or I'm easily impressed at 7 a.m.

This morning, for instance, I hugely enjoyed *Hi-5*, an Australian import which starts off looking like the single worst idea ever – essentially *Play School* hosted by a fresh-faced pop group in the Steps mould – but wins you over well before the end with a mixture of spirited performances and genuinely catchy tunes.

And I might be going mad, but I reckon there's a faint whiff of sex about Hi-5 themselves. Bet they all share a group shower at the end of each recording.

Then there's *Elmo's World*, a *Sesame Street* spin-off in which a scarlet squawking abomination with googly eyes scampers round a house made entirely of crayon drawings which spring into life at random intervals. It's what the world probably looks like when you get hit on the head with a croquet mallet and it's fantastic.

All in all, *Milkshake!* offers such a refreshing start to the day, it's hard to see why anyone would choose to spend time in the company of Eamonn Holmes instead (he's quitting GMTV of course – probably before he bloats to the point of actually exploding on-screen).

Milkshake! could cheer practically anyone up. If *Supervolcano* plunges you into a trough of despair, tune in the next morning and learn to smile again before the world ends.

Holding seances and going 'Woooh' [19 March 2005]

Hooray for me! Having lived for years in a house where the landlord forbade satellite dishes (although rat infestations were OK), I've moved to a place where no such ban exists. Which is why I spent last Saturday pacing the floor, staring at my watch and chanting 'When will the Sky Man come?' like an awestruck Amazonian native awaiting the return of his rainforest messiah. 'Soon the Sky Man shall arrive with his box of visions. It is written he will come from the south, from the Croydon installation centre, before the sun is at its peak, traffic permitting.'

In accordance with the prophecy, he arrived, did his job, and bingo: the magic box lives. Plus I've got that fancy Sky Plus impossible-o-vision thing that lets you pause, rewind, record, weigh, violate, polish and season whatever it spews out, for no good reason whatsoever. Finally, I can enjoy LivingTV's full range of psychic-centric programming to the full – something I'd been looking forward to, not because I'm interested in the afterlife, but because I simply can't believe the sheer audacity of the people who claim to be in touch with it.

Take *Crossing Over with John Edward*, a US import in which the host purports to receive messages from the dead relatives of vulnerable audience members. The show seems heavily edited, and Edward's messages are either hopelessly vague or clearly whittled down through methodical 'cold-reading' (the guessing-game process of elimination via which so-called mediums often appear to arrive at accurate revelations).

Nevertheless, his victims fall for it, possibly because they can't quite believe a fellow human being would exploit the pain of their bereavement for financial gain. Anyway, forget channelling spirits – Edwards seems rather better at channelling the facial mannerisms of Sylvester Stallone. Either that or he's recently been smacked in the jaw with a boat hook. Like he deserves.

Then there's *6ixth Sense* in which Colin Fry, who looks like a failed prototype Chuckle brother, pulls much the same shtick for a UK audience. Both shows feature heavy disclaimers in the credits – a wodge of text that shoots down any notion of plausibility, claiming the shows are not purporting to be taken as factual, and are simply 'entertainment'.

In other words, by their own admission, they're making grief-stricken relatives cry for entertainment. On a scale of moral reprehensibility, this isn't too far away from child porn. It's psychological rape: disgusting, dishonest and exploitative. Here's how to solve the psychic problem: make it a jailable offence for any 'medium' to charge for their services without a licence. How do they get a licence? Simply by demonstrating their abilities under laboratory conditions (something not one has ever been able to do). That'd sort 'em out.

Less sickening, though equally preposterous, is *Most Haunted* – an allegedly 'factual' cross between *Scooby-Doo* and the *Blair Witch Project*, hosted by Yvette Fielding and 'Britain's leading psychic' Derek Acorah. It's outrageous nonsense – nothing but a bunch of people lamely making stuff up, holding séances and going 'woooh', shot with night-vision cameras to make it look creepy. The only thing genuinely returning from the grave here is Yvette's career.

Still, Derek's hilarious, particularly when he gets 'possessed' by spirits and screams the word 'bitch' right into Yvette's face. If he believes in what he's doing, he's insane. If he doesn't, he's a laughable prat. Either way, Derek loses and we win. As a 'paranormal investigation', *Most Haunted* is about as scientifically rigorous as an episode of *Bod*, but the audience laps it up. I watched last weekend's 'live special' and was dismayed by the avalanche of texts the show received.

Mind you, many claimed to have experienced a strange sensation of 'nausea' and reported their sets 'switching off' during the show. Paranormal phenomena, or flickerings of sanity? You needn't be psychic to work that one out.

If a penis could choose its own wardrobe

[26 March 2005]

If a penis could choose its own wardrobe and hair stylist, chances are it'd end up looking like Duane 'Dog' Chapman, star of *Dog the Bounty Hunter* (Bravo). Essentially The Osbournes with pepper spray, it's a light-hearted docusoap chronicling the life of a family of bounty hunters – Dog, his wife Beth, son Leland, brother Tim and nephew Justin.

The Chapmans all dress like bombastic 1980s action movie heroes – particularly Dog himself, who stomps about wearing biker boots, leather trousers, open shirts and a haircut that makes him resemble the entire cast of *The Lost Boys* crossed with a gay lion.

It's worth tuning in for about five minutes simply for that haircut, but sadly Dog soon turns out to be about 10 per cent as interesting as he and the producers think he is.

In fact, I only mention it because Dog spends most of his time hauling poverty-stricken heroin addicts out of shit-encrusted trailer homes, thus providing a perfect contrast to *The Queen's Castle* (BBC1), also a docusoap, but set in one of the most expensive homes in the world: Windsor Castle. Unlike *Dog the Bounty Hunter*, no one gets kicked in the nuts or zapped with a Taser gun in this show and, for reasons which will now become clear, that's a crying shame.

As the programme begins, a great hoo-hah is made of the fact that the crew has been granted 'unprecedented access' to Windsor Castle, as though we should be somehow grateful for being granted a peep at the glittering opulence within – opulence we've paid for and which the royals take for granted. But before you come to terms with that, the programme hits you with something else: polishing.

Lots of polishing. Hours of it. Too much in fact. I now understand how the Windsor Castle fire broke out: a member of staff had been ordered to polish the Queen's teaspoons till they glowed white-hot.

There's also dusting, wiping, mopping, folding, ironing, arranging . . . you name it: priceless trinkets and pieces of furniture painstakingly manipulated by subservient staff on behalf of Her Grumpiness the Crone, who turns up hours later and doesn't even say thank you.

Naturally, the inmates of this slave-labour camp are filled with pride, mesmerised by the prestige of a lifetime spent in pointless backbreaking servitude. One woman almost blubs for joy, recounting how as a girl she dreamed of spending each day on her hands and knees, needlessly wiping any object the Queen might waft within 500 metres of. Now her wildest childhood fantasies have come true.

It doesn't stop with housework. Every imaginable convenience is taken care of by a crack squad of fawning serfs. Guests staying overnight don't unpack their own cases: a team of maids does it for them. Diners tucking in to a helping of swan-and-unicorn terrine have it practically spoon-fed to them by grovelling footmen. Nip off for a crap and chances are there's a cap-doffing peasant stationed by the bowl, punching himself in the face with pride as he wipes your bum, pulls the chain and holds a sprig of lavender under your nose till the stink fades away.

Just when you think things can't get any worse, you're treated to the sight of Queen and Co. sitting down to enjoy some modest after-dinner entertainment – the musical *Les Misérables*, transplanted in its entirety from the West End to one of Windsor Castle's

8,000 drawing rooms. And what's that the cast are singing? Why, it's a song about the miserable lot of the underclass: 'At the end of the day you're another day older/ And that's all you can say for the life of the poor . . . Keep on grafting as long as you're able/ Keep on grafting till you drop' – all of which plays out over footage of the staff frenziedly washing dishes and licking the bog floor clean with their tongues.

Here's hoping the series ends with the castle burning down a second time. While the staff get pissed and polish off the wine cellar.

Show us your bum for ten pence   [2 April 2005]

Travelling at 7,000 m.p.h., 22,000 miles above our heads, a satellite orbits the Earth, beaming a signal to the dish on your roof. This signal then travels down a fibre-optic cable to a receiver which unscrambles the image and sends it to your TV set, which in turn paints it on the screen, line by line, 15,000 times a second, fast enough for your brain to register as a moving image.

All this, just so you can watch girls waving their bums around on shows like *Babestation* (about a million different satellite stations, nightly).

Have you seen *Babestation*? If you've got a satellite dish, that's a stupid question – you can't miss it. Go randomly channel-surfing any time after 10 p.m. and you'll bump into more *Babestation* variants than you can shake a stick at. If you catch my drift.

In case you don't, here's what I'm talking about: *Babestation* is a bit of night-time 'adult fun' (i.e. pornography) consisting of several inset windows. One houses live footage of thick girls in various states of undress. Below that lies another window full of texts from even thicker viewers, begging them to blow kisses and jiggle about a bit. Sending the texts cost a fortune, and that's why *Babestation* is there. It's a coin-operated wanking machine, in other words, and it's just as glamorous as that sounds.

Other stations house countless spin-off variants on this theme: generally dingy webcam footage of girls in rooms as small as coffin interiors, chatting to viewers on premium-rate phone lines.

Grimmest of these is the alarming *Babestation Contacts*, which displays phone-camera snaps of sagging viewers accompanied by voicemail messages encouraging you to get in touch, come round and muck about with them.

This is almost enough to signal the end of civilisation as we know it, which is currently scheduled to occur the day a major network broadcasts a show I've recently invented called *Show Us Your Bum for Ten Pence* – a four-hour live broadcast in which viewers nationwide are encouraged to send in phone snaps of their backsides in exchange for a 10p discount on their next mobile bill. Scoff all you like, but I guarantee it'll be on air within a decade.

Anyway: *Babestation* – it's seedy and gooey and yucky and bluurgh, but even so, it's nowhere near as puke-inducing as one of its daytime equivalents, the truly hideous *Psychic Interactive*. The name gives it away – yes, it's another bit of coin-slot bummery, this time aimed at the desperate and gullible (as opposed to the desperate and masturbating).

Psychic Interactive offers a range of services, from premium-rate one-to-one 'sessions' with on-air mystics to text-window Tarot readings courtesy of dowdy bags in the studio. People text in to discover whether their relationships will survive, or their job prospects will improve . . . even to find out whether they're pregnant. It's one of the most nauseating things you'll ever see. Well, until *Babestation Contacts* turns up later on.

And there's an incongruously surreal twist: since *Psychic Interactive* is currently only broadcast during 'dead time' on a channel normally aimed at video-game fans, it's interrupted every few minutes by an 'ad break' largely consisting of stills of Pac Man accompanied by captions in Italian, or Mortal Kombat characters backed with heavy metal music. This must irritate *Psychic Interactive*'s natural audience immensely, which is why I laugh out loud each time it comes on.

Regular readers will know I don't have much time for 'psychics' of any description, and a few weeks ago I fantasised aloud (well, in print) about a law aimed at shutting them down.

I didn't realise one already exists: the 1951 Fraudulent Mediums Act, aimed at people who purport to 'act as spiritualistic mediums or to exercise powers of telepathy, clairvoyance or other similar powers' in order to deceive people for financial gain. Clearly this law doesn't apply to anyone appearing on *Psychic Interactive*, or they'd have all been booted off screen ages ago.

Be not afraid   [9 April 2005]

Chunky, golden CGI lettering farts its way across your screen, accompanied by ominous music: 'One man . . . One calling . . . One world . . .' What is this, a trailer for the next Vin Diesel beat-'em-up? Nope. The slogans vanish and are instantly replaced by a cut-out photo of the late Pope, accompanied by his name, spelled out in a medieval font presumably selected for its religious overtones, and a quote along the bottom: 'BE NOT AFRAID.'

It looks like a computer-generated version of a knowingly tacky Terry Gilliam animation, but it's not supposed to be funny. It's supposed to be solemn. It's a break bumper on Fox News, which is bringing you up-to-the-minute coverage of the death of the Pope.

Of course, Fox can confidently claim to run more coverage of this sad event than anyone else. After all, they got a head start by announcing his death a day early, on April Fool's day.

Again, this wasn't supposed to be funny. It was a mistake. The only joke is Fox itself, and running the 'BE NOT AFRAID' bumper while simultaneously doing its utmost to keep viewers in a state of perpetual ill-informed terror is presumably the punchline. I may not know much about the Pope, but I'd put money on him feeling thoroughly sickened by everything Fox stands for – particularly their star turn Bill O'Reilly, notorious host of *The O'Reilly Factor*, who spent much of last Monday's show lambasting the dead Pontiff for (a) criticising the Iraq war, and (b) not doing enough to halt the rise of 'anti-Christian' activity in the US.

Bill himself, of course, does his best to promote Christian values. Why, he regularly preaches tolerance and forgiveness – virtues he drew on last year when he settled out of court with a woman who'd accused him of sexually harassing her over the phone. He accused her in return of extortion. In the Christian spirit of tolerance and forgiveness, they've agreed to end the battle – although if you fancy a laugh, you can still find the statements lurking on the internet.

From one belligerent monster to another – namely Saira Khan, the most irritating woman in the world, still hanging on against all the odds in *The Apprentice* (BBC2). Saira is a self-professed business supremo who endlessly babbles about her brilliant vision, drive and interpersonal intuition. By her reckoning, these are three great business skills, although she may be doing herself a disservice, because judging by her progress she possesses four key business skills: 'missing the point', 'bullshitting', 'hectoring' and 'backstabbing'. Above all, though, she's patronising. If Saira spoke to an unborn foetus through a stethoscope for five minutes, it'd come away feeling somehow demeaned by the encounter.

The Apprentice being what it is, the stage is set for an ultimate showdown between Saira and Sir Alan Sugar, who, as he reminds us in the opening titles each week, 'can't stand bullshitters'. It's got to happen soon – Saira's managed to cock things up more than anyone else, yet has miraculously escaped dismissal week after week. At this rate, she'll win – thereby turning the show into one long hideous parable about the inexorable rise of obstinate morons everywhere.

Horrifying it may be, but *The Apprentice* is also brilliant fun. And Sir Alan's so good, he deserves a second knighthood. Sir Alan Sugar Squared has quite a ring to it, don't you think?

Before I go, a quick mention of *Doctor Who* (BBC1), despite the blanket coverage the series has received elsewhere. Thing is, I simply can't stand by and let this week's episode, *The Unquiet Dead*, pass by without comment, for the following reason: I think it may be the single best piece of family-oriented entertainment BBC has broadcast in its entire history. It's clever, it's funny, it's exciting, it's moving, it's got shades of Nigel 'Quatermass' Kneale about it, it looks fantastic, and in places it's genuinely frightening. TV really doesn't get better than this, ever. Resistance is futile, as Davros or Saira or even Bill O'Reilly might say.

Cargo of pebbleheads   [16 April 2005]

Europe! It's got everything! Golden beaches! Snow-dappled mountains! Dingly dells! Cities! Cutting-edge modern buildings shaped
like kitchen utensils! Culture! Moaning! Welcome to the horrid
world of *Coach Trip* (C4), the bargain-bucket daily reality show,
which thunders to a climax this week. I say 'thunders', I mean
'trundles'. And I say 'climax', but I mean 'sorry conclusion'.

It works like this: get a coachload of idiots in pairs and drive
them round Europe, stopping at tourist spots where they can potter around and disapprove of everything, including each other. At
the end of each show, the couples vote to eject one pair from the
group, thus souring an already fractious mood even further, before
the coach shuttles its now diminished cargo of pebbleheads on to
the next location.

Unfortunately, each time a pair leaves, they're replaced by an
equally unpleasant couple. Recently we've suffered a pair of substantial hosepipes called Gavin and Nathan, self-regarding oily
siblings who work on a 'freelance basis' in 'the music industry'.
Gavin doesn't so much demonstrate an eye for the ladies as openly
waggle a penis at them, thereby rendering himself the least agreeable member of the party. But only marginally. Most of the others
are standard tutting, parochial Brits, apparently incapable of
enjoying or appreciating anything.

Overseeing the whingeing, whining lot of them is glamorous tour
guide Brendan, whose faintly camp air of detachment ensures fun
is never more than a six-hour air-conditioned coach journey away.
As you'd expect, Brendan is also a seasoned diplomat. Last week he
playfully chastised a 73-year-old passenger for wearing a miniskirt
(to be fair, her exposed legs did have the textural appearance of
Peperami sticks), before stoking the holiday-makers' enthusiasm
for the Spanish bullring they were about to visit by describing, in
unflinching step-by-step detail, just how grisly the public slaughter
of a large angry mammal can be.

I hope they make a second series of *Coach Trip*. Set exclusively in
the winding, perilous mountain roads of the French Alps. During a

blizzard. With a bomb in the boot. And with each losing contestant being nailed to a cross and hurled into the crevasse below. Directed by Michael Winner.

From one winner to another – yes, it's *The* (BBC2), and Saira Khan's still on the playing field, despite her stroppy, oblivious rudeness angering Tottenham Hotspur's corporate division so badly they virtually withdrew cooperation from last week's task. Another irritating trait I've noticed – She. Talks. In. Broken. Sentences. Very. Very. Slowly. Whenever. She's. Trying. To. Negotiate. With. Someone. I think she mistakes this for 'clear communication', as opposed to patronising baby talk.

If Saira doesn't win, the BBC should snap her up and give her a role in *Mind Your Own Business* (BBC1), a daily corner-shop makeover show starring Duncan *Dragons' Den* Bannatyne and a mysterious Cruella De Vil type calling herself 'Mrs S'. The show seems to work like this: Duncan and Mrs S visit a struggling small business, systematically knock all the joy out of it, and leave a ruthlessly efficient but character-free shark pit in their wake. In the case of a neglected village store, their prescribed changes included placing 'impulse purchases' by the counter, charging more for chocolate bars, and developing a 'brand identity' for the shop itself.

As a team, Duncan and Mrs S work pretty well – he's stiff and ungainly, she's downright terrifying – but they could do with a little added pizzazz, and Saira's the woman to provide it. While the others faff about installing laminate flooring and hypnotising customers into voting New Labour, Saira could lock herself in the back room with the owner and Talk. Very. Slowly. To. Them. Until. They. Agree. To. The. Programme's. Every. Demand.

Don't have nightmares   [14 May 2005]

What do we want? Bleedin' justice! When do we want it? Right bloody now! Pity, then, that the wheels of justice turn so slowly. I mean, the Michael Jackson trial reconstructions have been running on Sky News for ages now, and we're only just getting to the bit where they bring in the celebrity witnesses (with any luck, we should get a Stevie Wonder impersonator this week – I'm not making this up).

In our espresso-paced era, to spend months soberly weighing up the facts feels outrageously self-indulgent. Even *Crimewatch UK* (BBC1), once considered the last word in instant justice, takes too long to produce results. Oh, it's all very well to end the show with a nod and a wink and a 'we've had lots of interesting leads', but in this day and age we need speedier results. Or we'll have nightmares. Old-fashioned tip-offs from the criminal underworld take far too long to process, and besides, most of the viewers aren't members of the criminal underworld anyway – they're paranoid curtain-twitchers, and the programme should inject a little mobile-phone interactivity into its format in order to empower them.

How about encouraging viewers to stand by their living-room windows throughout the programme, taking phone-camera snaps of suspicious passers-by and texting them into the studio where we can all have a good look at them? Better yet, they could introduce a 20-minute break in the middle, so anyone who lives near a canal or secluded area of woodland can nip out, take the dog for a walk, and send in pictures of any bodies they find lying about.

And then the police can parade the suspects in front of us, and we can vote to identify the guilty one, press the red button to slam him in jail and the yellow one to throw away the key, or hold down both at once to bring back the rope and snap his neck like a breadstick.

Think I'm being flippant? Well I'm not. I've got ITV on my side: they're showing us the way forward in the form of *People's Court UK* (ITV1). Unfortunately, at the time of writing, it's being used to settle petty disputes, not murders. But give it time, and that'll change. This is progress.

The televised small-claims format has been around for years, but *People's Court UK* is unique because it lets the audience decide who wins, live, by texting in. They also send in comments, which scroll across the bottom of the screen throughout the 'case', affording a glimpse into the jury's mindset: 'Steves telling the truth and whats more hes cute!!! – Sally, Bracknell'; 'I hate Dave he thinks hes so clever well Dave u arnt all that!!! – Amy, Lowestoft'.

At a stroke, outmoded notions of 'impartiality' have been replaced by a system in which disputes are settled on the basis of who looks most honest, or shouts loudest, or has the prettiest nose – in the opinion of several thousand irredeemably stupid button-pushers. Watching *People's Court*, it's easy to see why ITV's audience has collapsed. Having spent years relentlessly pursuing the lowest common denominator, it's inadvertently become a specialist channel for the very, very thick, while its traditional audience (the slightly thick) is now openly courted by Channel 4.

Anyone who isn't thick is probably feeling slightly lost and unloved, so I'd encourage them to turn to BBC4 and be spoiled rotten by (ironically) *The Thick of It*, a fantastic new comedy series. 'A semi-improvised sitcom set in the back rooms of Westminster' might sound like the driest, most clever-clever, Bremner-ish bit of business imaginable, but that's precisely what this isn't: it's laugh-out-loud funny – so good, in fact, I watched the second episode on video immediately after finishing the first, then phoned up the BBC to badger them for the third. Don't let it be wasted on the cognoscenti alone: this sort of thing should be on all the channels, all the time. Tune in and get hooked.

A horse that isn't there [21 May 2005]

Bleak but true: last winter, I was strolling down the local high street when I passed a casino. Now, this is south London I'm talking about, not Monte Carlo, so when I say 'casino', stop imagining dinner-jacketed high-rollers playing roulette to a Henry Mancini soundtrack, and start imagining Frank from *Shameless* shambling round a cramped, smoky fleapit filled with fruit machines and despair. You know the sort of thing: windows full of 'prizes' (carriage clocks and decanter sets), and a name like 'Las Vegas' that only serves to highlight the glamour-gulf between it and its namesake. A losers' shithole, basically.

Anyway, something about this particular 'casino' made me stop dead in my tracks: there, in the window, was a cardboard sign promising 'FREE SOUP AND BREAD ROLL' to its patrons. Yes! You can gamble your last pennies into oblivion, but at least you won't go hungry! It's a soup kitchen and casino in one! What next – free second-hand shoes?

By ensuring its wrecked, reel-gawping clientele received at least one hot meal a day, was the casino being wildly irresponsible or just savvy? Was it being generous, or simply trying to keep them alive long enough to bleed a few more coins out of them? I don't know. And I'm similarly conflicted when it comes to the rise of interactive gambling on satellite TV.

For starters, there's poker. What's going on there? Suddenly, everyone's talking about it. Thousands of people are haemorrhaging money in online games, and poker-dedicated digital channels with names like *Instant Poker Whirlpool 24* are sprouting like weeds. Some of the stations offer interactive play: jab the red button and you can experience the thrill of automated losing from your very own armchair. (Downside: you have to provide your own soup.)

Then there's the openly moronic puzzle channels, with names like *Grab a Grand* or *Play 2 Win* or *Coins U Waste* or similar. These consist of a simple puzzle (a faintly blurred photo of Sean Connery, say, accompanied by the question 'Who is this famous actor? (CLUE: SCOTTISH BOND)' attached to a premium-rate phone-or-text service. And it's all hosted by a presenter (usually a woman, occasionally in a bikini) cheerily encouraging you to roll your sleeves up and have a go, as though she's running a coconut shy. It's a cash-pisser's paradise.

Most heartbreaking of all, though, are the games that rob the player of whatever scraps of dignity they've got left. Take *Virtual Horse Racing*, for example. This crops up on the Avago channel during the day, and on Sky Vegas through the night, and it's exactly what you think it is: a seemingly endless sequence of nonexistent race events, recreated with PlayStation-quality visuals – which you can gamble on. Somewhere, right now, there's a tearful addict

35

blowing their last remaining pennies on a horse that isn't there. It's almost poetic.

There's *Virtual Greyhound Racing* as well – that's a recent development. Personally, I'm holding out for *Virtual Cock Fighting*. Well, why not? It's not like any real birds get hurt, and it's surely more exciting than watching pixelated horses. What about a game in which a man runs round a small market town punching nine-year-old girls in the face, and the viewer has to bet on which ones will fall over? It's OK! It's not really happening!

Back to reality, and as far as interactive TV gambling goes, the absolute biscuit-taking winner has to be *Gerbil Roulette* on the Avago channel. 'When the wheel stops turning, it's up to you to decide which house our talented little rodent will enter,' claims the publicity. 'It couldn't be easier!' Or any more demoralising. All we need now is a coin-slot that bolts onto the side of your television and a hose that pumps soup into your mouth while you play. Bet you a tenner it happens by Christmas.

Shed a tear for Abi Titmuss   [28 May 2005]

Like a burned-out paramedic gazing tearfully at a blazing pile-up, it's time for me to sigh, roll my sleeves up and lurch towards *Celebrity Love Island* – the show that makes the score from *Requiem for a Dream* start playing in your head.

I was going to write something damning but I changed my mind because there's little point getting angry. It's just a rehash of *I'm a Celebrity*, minus the elements that made that show successful (i.e. the older participants, the bushtucker trials, and Ant and Dec). That's all. It's just depressing. So don't get angry. Get sorrowful.

Start by shedding a tear for Abi Titmuss. Although described on the show as a 'tabloid babe' (which is as low as a human being can sink short of gargling sewage for a living), she's actually rather homely – a bit like a neighbourly dairymaid. This, apparently, is a crime: because she's plumper than earlier *Nuts* photo-shoots had suggested, the programme openly sneers at her for being 'fat'. Let's hope she sees sense and develops a serious eating disorder at the earliest opportunity. Until then, weep for her.

Weep too for Rebecca Loos, the woodpecker-faced Posh-botherer who was presumably hired on the understanding that anyone who's previously masturbated a pig on television might be prepared to stoop slightly lower and perform the same act on ex-Hollyoaks actor Paul Danan.

Sob for Danan, who is a bell-end of considerable magnitude, and the ugliest person on the island – ugly in a unique fashion, like a man whose face was heading toward 'handsome' but took a wrong turn at the last minute. He looks like Jude Law crossed with the Crazy Frog, and he's an absolute aching backside. The only way the producers could possibly justify his presence would be to spike his cocktails till he goes mad and has sex with a melon or something. But that's not going to happen, because that would be fun, and *Love Island* isn't about fun. If it was about fun, they'd go the whole hog: call it *Celebrity Fuck Hut* and send paratroopers in to force them to form a grunting, humping human daisy-chain. It's not about fun, it's about despair, remember?

Bawl for Fran Cosgrave, whose 'celebrity' status is so low he doesn't actually exist outside shows like this. This is his reality: when the last edition finishes, he ceases to be, like a character in a video game when it's switched off.

Blub for the remaining islanders – blub as they loll about like dying sea-lions in a failing zoo, accompanied by the sound of gentle lapping as waves of public indifference break upon the shore.

Sniffle for Patrick Kielty and Kelly Brook – a man you wish would shut up before he even starts speaking, and a woman who can scarcely talk in the first place, marooned before an unimpressed nation. Curiously, Brook is listed in the credits as 'Presenter & Consultant Producer', which is a pretty impressive job title for someone apparently unable to read from an autocue. Cry for Kelly. Cry for her.

But mainly, cry for us all. If *Love Island* has left you entertaining dark notions, I understand. And I have a plan.

Here's what we do. We charter a boat. We sail to Fiji. We drop anchor offshore and we light candles and sing songs. And as dawn breaks, we stand on the deck and slit our own throats and splash wordlessly into the ocean. For the next 48 hours our bodies wash up on the beach, one by one. Our lifeless cadavers knock gently against Michael Greco's ankles as he goes for his morning paddle. Bloated, fish-pecked carcasses slap against the sand throughout the evening barbecue, souring the mood. Our non-violent suicidal protest turns the show into an unfolding Jonestown massacre for the twenty-first century, and ITV's ongoing ratings crisis is averted.

Alternatively: switch off the box, walk into the garden and stare at the stars while tears shine in your eyes. *Celebrity Love Island*: wish hard enough, and God might make it stop.

Twenty-first-century stocks   [4 June 2005]

When I first read about olde-worlde scoundrels being 'put in the stocks', it struck me as a quaint and toothless sort of punishment. Further reading proved me wrong. The locals didn't just lob the odd rotten tomato at you – they hurled rocks. They urinated in your face. They pulled your trousers down and performed vile-but-darkly-hilarious experiments with your rear end. Spend 48 hours in the stocks, and there was a pretty good chance you'd die, with a face like a popped blister and a rolling pin blocking your exit.

Which brings me to *Big Brother* (C4). Anyone volunteering to take part is surely the present-day equivalent of a medieval lunatic willingly locking himself in the stocks and inviting the world to do its worst. The viewers represent ale-sodden sadists only too pleased to oblige, while the producers are canny tradesmen standing at the side, selling shit-encrusted rocks for them to throw. And since I'm about to pile more abuse on top, what does that make me? Worse than the village idiot. No one's coming out of this well.

Anyway, if you sketched a diagram denoting the exponential growth of contestant idiocy levels throughout *Big Brother* history, you'd start low, run out of space at the top during series five, and scrawl demented swirls all over the page by the start of series six. Because this lot scarcely qualify as fully sentient humans – they're people-shaped amoebas existing on raw narcissism.

Take Anthony, the present-day equivalent of the utilitarian android gigolo played by Jude Law in Spielberg's *AI*, right down to the fibreglass eyebrows. Anthony achieved a *BB* first by turning the crowd against him before he'd even entered the house: he spent so long jigging, twirling, posing and preening during the brief car-to-door stroll, the crowd's initial cheering rapidly evolved into a chant of 'wanker, wanker' held aloft on a carpet of boos. It was like watching Tony Blair's eight-year fall from public favour distilled into 90 seconds.

Then there's Lesley, who donned a PVC nurse's outfit that afforded us a gruesome peek up her arse on her way into the house (another great *BB* first) shortly before baring her gargantuan breasts in the plunge pool. This delighted the witless Maxwell, a Norf Lahnden bozo best described as the human equivalent of a clipping from *Nuts* magazine bobbing in a fetid urinal.

At the time of writing, Maxwell has designs on Sam, a slightly less skeletal version of Calista Flockhart, who spent most of her audition tape outlining what a strong, independent, hot-pants-wearing sexbomb she is. In practice, however, she's little more than a slightly pretty, self-regarding plastic peg.

Worse still, she fancies Anthony: by the time you read this, they'll probably be going at it hammer and tongs in the diary room, while viewers text in whoops of encouragement.

Other notable inmates include Makosi, a woman with the head and worldview of a plastic doll, and Roberto, an Italian with a face like a cartoon sketch of a foolish horse.

The most foolish horse of all, though, is Science. That's not his real name. His real name's Kieran. Science is his 'street name'. His 'screen name' is Prick.

Science seems to spend 70 per cent of his time shouting at Kemal (cross-dressing Leo Sayer lookalike), and the remaining 30 per cent shouting at everyone else – shouting about how no one but him understands what it's like 'in the hood' (which is rather unfair on Nookie Bear-eyed white witch Mary, who entered the house wearing a hood so huge she literally couldn't see which way she was going).

Still, you can't fault Science's intentions. He's not there to get his mug on the box – no. He's there to 'represent the ghetto', which, if he's genuinely representative, is full of pretentious hotheads throwing juvenile tantrums when they don't get salad cream with their fish fingers.

Big Brother 6, then: simultaneously more *and* less sophisticated than the brutal stocks of yore. Pass the mouldy turnips.

A ham-eyed poltroon   [11 June 2005]

Is it just me, or is there something about young, over-confident male idiots that makes you want to smack the entire world in the mouth? I'm asking this because I've just discovered bookies are offering odds of 5–1 for Maxwell to win this year's *Big Brother* (C4).

This depresses and baffles me in equal measure. The man's a goon, a berk, a gurgling bore, a ham-eyed poltroon and a great big swaggering chump. There are only two things in life he passionately cares about: whether Arsenal win and whether Saskia (who could pass for Giant Haystacks's sister on a dark night) wants to blow him. If I ran the country, people like that would be chemically neutered the moment they learned to rut.

Worse still, I've heard people describe him as 'really funny'. That's what they said about Joe Pasquale on *I'm a Celebrity*, and he's hardly had the world shattering its ribcage with giggles since emerging from the jungle, has he? He may well seem 'funny', but only if you compare him to, say, Roberto, who just lopes around gruffly moaning about coffee. Maxwell's the sort of person who openly breaks wind and then makes a trumpet noise with his mouth to underline how hilarious it was, for God's sake.

Science – now he's funny. I had a pop at Science last week; since then my attitude toward him has mellowed immeasurably. For one thing, he perpetually argues with Maxwell (who, as we've already established, deserves harsh treatment at the hands of the state). Better still, he intimidates Anthony, and anything that makes that tweeting Geordie ferret uncomfortable immediately rises in my estimations. For the record, if Anthony ever contracts pubic lice,

I'd like to shake every single one of them individually by the hand (provided they'd washed them first, obviously).

Actually, the more I think about this year's housemates, the more I start praying for an extinction-level meteorite to strike the Earth. I'll tell you what just dropped into my head: Craig's voice. His ceaseless, dull-month-in-Dorking of a voice. It's surely the worst noise in the universe. Listening to him is like lying in your own coffin, hearing rainwater seep through the cracks.

Still, at least no one in there seems happy to be taking part. The housemates are all either under twenty-five or over thirty. With no angst-ridden late-twentysomethings to smooth things over, what you're left with is a couple of set-in-their-ways curmudgeons being forced to cohabit with a bunch of squawking know-nothings. I'll be astonished if it ends without open bloodshed.

All hands on deck [18 June 2005]

Years ago, a girlfriend of mine booked us on a make-or-break holiday cruise. It sounded great – we'd be sailing to Spain aboard a luxury liner complete with its own casino, a cinema, a cocktail bar and a selection of high-class restaurants. Best of all, she'd got it on the cheap by collecting tokens from a newspaper.

We were young, OK? Young and naive.

The 'cruise liner' was a car ferry. The 'restaurants ' would've shamed a motorway service station. The 'cinema' consisted of a video projector beaming *Mortal Kombat: The Movie* onto a suspended rectangle which swung left and right along with the ship. The 'casino' was an enclave of fruit machines servicing a handful of wheezing alcoholics.

Our cabin was deep in the bowels of the ship. It didn't even have a porthole. It had a painting of a porthole. Quite a shit painting at that. You couldn't go on deck because the freezing gales would strip your carcass bare in seconds.

You couldn't stay in the room because the violent rocking combined with the lack of visual reference points made you spew. All you could do was sit in the cocktail bar, downing whisky and watching the live cabaret – by far the cheesiest thing I'd ever seen, yet strangely uplifting under the circumstances.

All of which brings me to the point: the ship's cabaret wasn't a million miles from *The New Variety Show* on SoundTV – and it's had a similar effect on me: uplifting for no discernible reason.

The New Variety Show is a family-oriented extravaganza presented by Tucker, a 'new comedy sensation' and former Pontins Blue-coat. I sat transfixed through last Saturday's edition: a two-hour cavalcade of ventriloquists, geezerish stand-ups in spangly jackets, a Sinatra impersonator with the face of a farmhand, and a star turn from Duncan Norvelle. It's like stumbling across an old edition of *Summertime Special* on VHS. Which isn't always a bad thing.

The high point came when chunky crooner Tony King sang an anti-war anthem so impossibly, hilariously crass it demanded three immediate repeat viewings. Funniest thing I've seen in weeks.

SoundTV itself is 'the brainchild of established television entertainers Jethro, Richard Digance and Mike Osman . . . its team of executives includes Chris Tarrant [and] handyman Tommy Walsh'. Which explains why, alongside *The New Variety Show*, the channel broadcasts *Golden Moments*, in which a galaxy of stars including Jethro, Chris Tarrant, Brian Conley and Tommy Walsh discuss their fondest memories, and *In Conversation*, in which a galaxy of stars including Jethro, Chris Tarrant, Brian Conley and Tommy Walsh talk to Richard Digance. There's also *Richard Digance and Friends*, *A Day in the Life of Status Quo*, *Status Quo in Concert*, *Chris Tarrant's Golden Moments* and *A Day in the Life of Jethro*.

Who says variety's dead?

Just when you think SoundTV can't get any more Alan Partridge, along comes something to take your breath away: according to the website, we'll soon be enjoying *Tommy's Ark*, 'an enchanting series of specials in which Tommy Walsh recreates the famous biblical vessel as a travelling playground for sick and underprivileged children . . . animals for the ark will be supplied by top celebrities, who'll beg, steal or borrow the furry passengers to present to deserving children as the ark travels the country.'

Read that back again and picture it in your head. Go on.

Anyway, I suspect SoundTV might just succeed. It's gaudy and cheap, but there's something curiously endearing about the all-hands-on-deck nature of its schedule. Among the chintz you can also get genuine belly laughs from the likes of Mick Miller, and in satellite terms, it beats watching UK Lifestyle *Hollyoaks Plus*. More power to them.

Oh, and that 'make or break' cruise I mentioned? We only got 90 minutes in Spain at the end of it. Then back on the ferry for the return trip, during which we finally 'broke'.

Now that's a holiday.

Pure bling in action   [25 June 2005]

This heatwave's sending me crackers. Night-time's the worst. Since I live in London, I can't sleep with the window open in case someone crawls in and kills me with a bit of railing or something. So it's humid. The air tastes like it's been strained through a hot leotard. I lie sleepless, thrashing like a fallen horse, tortured by stuttering flashbacks from this week's television, convinced the apocalypse is nigh.

Yes, I'm a hair's breadth from becoming the sort of person who stands shirtless at the side of the road shouting into traffic about the forthcoming end of the world – and it's somehow due to television, to shows like *Pimp My Ride UK* (MTV) which leave me seriously questioning the human race's grip on existence.

The original *Pimp My Ride* is an American import in which a team of butch mechanics (under the aegis of rapper Xzibit) perform extreme makeovers on clapped-out automobiles. This British incarnation is exactly the same. Well, almost. Instead of Xzibit we're lumbered with the preposterous Tim Westwood, a white forty-something son of a bishop whose interminable 'wigga' stance inspired Ali G. Watching him in action is like watching a sequence in a crap Hollywood comedy in which Leslie Nielsen has to black up and infiltrate a record label.

The British mechanics aren't as convincing as their American counterparts either. In the US version, they look like a gang of death row inmates crossed with a group of surfers – all tattoos and cool attitude. The British mechanics look like . . . well, like British mechanics – apart from their hairstyles, which are suspiciously modern. I suspect they've been 'pimped' themselves by a team of stylists, although the end result leaves them resembling the cast of *EastEnders* circa 2019.

Anyway, above all else, *Pimp My Ride* is phenomenally and frighteningly shallow. Each edition tracks a single car as it's resprayed, rebuilt, reformed and kitted out with a universe of unnecessary extras – spoilers, bumpers, giant stereos, in-car games consoles, singing windscreen wipers, passenger-seat bidets and so on. All of which happens for no discernible reason at all. It's pure 'bling' in action – the celebration of gaudy, self-aggrandising, shallow, meaningless shit for its own barefaced sake.

At a time when extreme global poverty and environmental sustainability loom high on the international agenda, driving around in a car encrusted with golden baubles is just taking the piss, isn't it? It's like squatting in front of a beggar and wiping your bum on a banknote. If I see a *Pimp My Ride* motor humming past I'll be tempted to leap in front of it. I might die, but on the bright side, the dent and the bloodstains might temporarily wipe the vapid grin off the face of the idiot driving.

Speaking of vapid grins, at the time of writing the *Big Brother* (C4) house is still hopelessly infected with Maxwell – a witless droopy-eyed thug and the most despicable housemate in the programme's history. Despite single-handedly making the show impossible to sit through, in his own mind he's guaranteed a career in broadcasting the moment he leaves. Lolling around in the loft the other day, he spent several minutes confidently discussing his future media-career options with Anthony the Formica Android.

As the words 'I wouldn't turn down a radio job' farted through his pukesome little blowhole, I was suddenly confronted by a terrifyingly plausible vision of the future in which Chris Moyles is suddenly only the second most gormless and insufferable prick on Radio 1. Here's a better idea: give Maxwell a job on *Pimp My Ride*

UK. He won't take much convincing – it's a show about selfish boasting. And he can perform a valuable service by testing the cars' safety features. With Maxwell in the driving seat, I'd happily watch hour upon hour of blinged-out motors thundering headlong into ditches, walls, oncoming trains, the ocean . . . whatever. Provided it's fatal, I'm there. Might even help me sleep nights.

Nigella. Nigella. Nigella. Nigella [9 July 2005]

Nigella. Nigella, Nigella, Nigella. It sounds like a playground nickname for an effeminate boy. They might as well have called her 'Malcolmina'. Or 'Keithette'.

Nigella. Nigella. Nigella. Nigella.

Tell you what else it sounds like: a brand of antiseptic cream. Or an island off the Italian coastline. Or an incredibly pretentious kind of tiny ethnic hat. Or a cheap and horrible car ('Police are on the lookout for a light blue Fiat Nigella').

Here's what it doesn't sound like: an ITV daytime show. But that's precisely what *Nigella* (ITV1) has become. She's become a celebrity chat show, and a cookery show, and a human-interest debate show – all at once.

Confused? Try watching it. It opens with a kitsch credit sequence in which Nigella flutters her eyelashes and smiles a lot. Then she appears in person, looking far more ill at ease – like a minor royal who's somehow been coerced into presenting a Christmas edition of *Blue Peter*. A minor royal who started regretting it the moment the lights went up.

After a spirited, doomed attempt to read naturally from the autocue, Princess Nigella meets her celebrity guest-of-the-day, then cooks a meal for them while simultaneously conducting an interview. Naturally, since she has to concentrate on making sure she doesn't overcook the salmon or inadvertently hack her thumb off, she can't absorb anything they're saying, and the conversation flows like granite. It's hardly fair: even a veteran presenter would struggle. Nigella's clearly inexperienced, yet she's literally expected to spin plates. What next? Make her do it on stilts?

It's bewildering just watching it. In fact, it makes your brain hurt. Are you supposed to follow the recipe, or the discussion? Or both? Is it some kind of test? If so, perhaps next week they'd like to super-impose an animated pie chart over the screen at the same time.

Anyway, once the baffling cookery-interview is out of the way, it's time for a REALLY horrible bit in which a dowdy, downtrodden member of the public is wheeled on to discuss a personal problem while HRH Ovenglove does her best to sympathise and give coun-sel, like Princess Diana getting dewy-eyed at a peasant's hospital bedside. It's toe-curlingly awkward, but at least Nigella's not being asked to toss pancakes at the same time. Yet.

Just as you've got to grips with that, there's another awkward gear-shift and the show suddenly turns into *Loose Women*, as Her Sacred Cookliness and a couple of guests loll around and discuss an 'issue', apparently just for the hell of it. On Tuesday's edition, the 'issue' was 'old folks' homes' – not because they're in the news, but because Nigella had just read a book about one. Come week three she'll be reading the nutritional information panel off the side of a soup carton and asking her guests to guess the carbohydrate content. While deboning a herring. On stilts.

Then there's an unbelievably condescending phone-in section (members of the public whine about their problems: Nigella and Co. offer sympathetic platitudes), a competition, and another bloody recipe. Then it's all over and you're out the other end, with an icky taste in your mouth. Never a good sign for a cookery show.

Hysterical blindness [16 July 2005]

Oh, my eyes have seen the glory of the coming of the Lord! I'm talk-ing about Paul McKenna, obviously. Yes, Paul McKenna, formerly ITV's favourite celebrity hypnotist, now repackaged in *Paul McKenna: I Can Change Your Life* (Sky One) as a kind of self-help cross between Derren Brown and Jesus.

From the off, the show is hell-bent on depicting the Archangel Paul as a bona-fide miracle worker. The opening credits even seem to show him floating in heaven, swooshing beams of celestial light around with his hands, knitting them into patterns and plugging them together as though they were Scart leads. He looks like a god. An impish little god who, facially speaking, is vaguely reminiscent of Brian the snail from *The Magic Roundabout* – but a god nonetheless. And the rest of the programme does little to dissuade you.

Using a curious blend of hypnotherapy and general psychological tomfoolery, McKenna sets about curing the ills of members of the general public. How does it work? 'The human mind is like a computer,' he claims. 'When someone has a problem, I can help them reprogram themselves.' Great. That's cleared that up.

Paul's 'reprogramming' generally seems to consist of getting, say, an obsessive chocoholic to imagine eating a chocolate cake smothered in dogshit, over and over again, until they start looking like they'll never eat anything again. It all looks pretty straightforward, and (unless his subjects are lying, which I doubt) it seems to work. The problem is Paul sometimes bites off a little more than he can chew. Such as when he attempts to cure the blind.

Yes, last week, Paul McKenna set about healing a blind man. Initially, this didn't seem quite as absurd as it sounds, since Ray, the man in question, had been diagnosed with 'hysterical blindness', a condition in which the cause of sightlessness is entirely psychological. Following intensive hypnosis, Paul encouraged Ray some way down the road to full vision, to the point where, incredibly, he could make out light, shapes and perspective.

So far, so miraculous, but Paul was aiming higher still. To speed the treatment, he sent Ray to 'a healer', who, we were told, could help 'clear the energy blocks' around Ray's eyes (simply by waggling her fingers around, by the looks of it). It was around this point I began to have my doubts about Paul.

And then the bad news arrived: a doctor (a real one) re-examined Ray's case and decided the cause of blindness was physical after all. No amount of finger-waggling was going to let him see again. The relentlessly positive Paul took this in his stride.

'I don't think I would've taken this case on if I'd known it was a physiological problem, because I'd have thought that was out of the realm of what I could treat,' he said, modestly. 'It just goes to show: when you don't know something's impossible – look what you can do!'

Er, yeah. So what exactly did he do? There seemed little doubt the subject himself felt his vision had improved – not returned, but improved. Had Paul helped him make more sense of the impaired images he'd always been seeing? Or had he literally worked a miracle and returned some of the man's sight? The show was frustratingly ambiguous.

This is entertainment, not science, of course, but I can't help finding it a little unsettling that a large part of the Sky One audience is walking around right now convinced that Paul McKenna can heal the blind (although I suppose we should just be grateful he's using his hypnotic powers for good – ever seen *Omen III*? We don't want him pulling that kind of stunt, thanks very much).

Speaking of science, before I go, can I just say: *Big Brother 6* (C4) – Science to win. I know I said he was a prick in week one but he's also the most deserving winner by a long chalk. Even a blind man can see that. With or without the assistance of Our Lord McKenna Almighty.

The no-pity-for-toffs rule   [23 July 2005]

Hard scientific fact: unless you're a member of the gentry yourself, it's neurologically impossible to feel in the slightest bit sorry for posh people under any circumstances whatsoever. It's true. A team of researchers proved it in a laboratory. They took a random bunch of proles, wired them to some electro-magnificent brain-scanner widgets, and showed them footage of top-hatted aristocrats falling from buildings, tumbling into threshing machines and inadvertently poisoning their own children. No one exhibited the faintest glimmer of pity for any of them. I think it's something to do with the accents.

Actually there is one exception to the no-pity-for-toffs rule, and that's journalist James Delingpole, who pities them so much he's made a documentary called *The British Upper Class* (C4) – a passionate defence of roaring snobs and everything they bally well stand for. Delingpole himself is middle class and sincerely wishes he wasn't. 'I'm no toff, and I never will be,' he confesses. 'But I've always been curious about the upper class – it all started when I was at Oxford back in the 80s.'

Having established his credentials, James (who went to Oxford) sets out on 'a journey' to discover just what it is about the gentry that gives him such a broom-handle. First port of call is a posh party thrown by historian Andrew Roberts, who reckons the upper classes are 'impossibly romantic and splendid'. Rubbing shoulders with earls, viscounts, dames and princes, James (formerly of Oxford University) seems happy as a pig in shit. But alas! Not one of the toffs he approaches wants to take part in his documentary. Not even Earl Spencer. Not even when James walks right up to him and bellows, 'I'm James Delingpole, I reviewed your book about Blenheim,' by way of introduction.

The poshos, James reckons, are 'terrified of being stitched up', although I suspect their reticence has more to do with James himself, who looks like a cross between Mick Jones and Mr Logic, and is cursed with a floppy bottom lip which dangles so perilously low it's a wonder he doesn't trip over it. They're probably just freaked out.

Never mind. James leaves the party and sets about persuading us the upper classes are inherently admirable because they're jolly keen on rough-and-ready games. To prove it he visits St Moritz and has a crack at the Cresta Run (an extreme tobogganing event favoured by blue bloods). It's dangerous and thrilling, sure – but a taste for perilous activities is hardly limited to the aristocracy. You don't need a coat of arms to go skateboarding, just a benevolent attitude toward shattering your hip on a concrete step. Idiotic thrill-seekers exist in all classes. As do tossers called James.

Next, James mourns the passing of two other favourite posho sports – fox-hunting ('a magnificent sight!') and hare-coursing. The latter, he reckons, is under attack because it's 'a ritual that flies in the face of sanitised bourgeois morality . . . it's too messy, too visceral – too real.'

49

'Nowadays it's the middle classes who are running the show. For many of them, traditions are all very well, so long as they're cleaned up, packaged, and sold back to us as products in the National Trust gift shop. But [hare-coursing] isn't "chocolate box" heritage, it's the real thing – and the chattering classes simply can't hack it.'

Yeah, James – you tell 'em! Screw the nanny state! Let's see that rabbit blood fly! Let's get naked and dance around in a big fat spray of it! And since you're keen to preserve noble English customs that celebrate 'the cycle of life and death', let's reintroduce some others – such as the tradition of sticking criminals' heads on poles above the entrance to London Bridge, where they can be pecked at by crows until they go a bit mushy and topple off and burst on the cobblestones below! Like to see what those Islington pussies make of that! Ah well. At least Delingpole succeeds in improving the image of the upper classes. Whenever he opens his mouth to defend them, they magically become fifty times less irritating. Than him.

Drunk on the news   [30 July 2005]

I appeared drunk on the news once – as a pundit. Beat that. This happened way back in the mists of time. Well, six or seven years ago – although at the rate the world's accelerating (right now we're eating our way through a decade's worth of history every week) that's equivalent to six or seven millennia. Way back yonder, back when I was a video-games 'journalist', and I used to turn up around midnight on BBC News 24 to be quizzed about (a) the PlayStation games chart and (b) whichever vaguely technological stories were in the news (all of which I knew nothing about).

Anyway, one week I was supposed to arrive at TV Centre around 9 p.m., until they called to say the slot was being pushed back because of a big developing story. God knows what that was – the news was always nice back then – probably a teddy bear falling over, something like that.

Anyway, since I was delayed, I decided to sit down and read a paper. In a pub. First mistake. Then I bumped into some people I knew, and had a pint with them. Second mistake. I soon forgot all about the news and concentrated firmly on making mistakes until closing time, when the news people rang to say the big story was over and could I be there in 30 minutes.

I couldn't think straight. I couldn't even walk straight. But disappointingly enough, the anecdote fizzles out right here, because I got away with it. I didn't wee on the desk, punch the presenter or have sex with the weatherman's leg. I just yabbered away like a dullard. Which is why I don't appear in *Rowland Rivron's TV Drinking Club* (C4), a cheery scamper through television's most degrading alcohol-induced disintegrations.

Obviously, the late Oliver Reed features heavily. We see him drunk on *The Word*, drunk on *After Dark*, drunk on *Saturday Night at the Mill*, drunk on *Aspel*... wherever you look, Ollie's there – wrestling invisible bears, barking, growling, boggling his eyes, ripping his shirt open and almost certainly soiling himself: an out-of-control cross between the Hulk and an entire chimps' tea party. Rivron calls him a 'hero', but the wisest words come, impossibly, from the mouth of Michael Winner, who calmly explains that while drunken Ollie was an appalling bully, sober Ollie was a genteel and thoughtful man who'd have been horrified to see his antics on tape.

Undeterred by this strong whiff of tragedy, the programme steams on, coughing up clips of George Best, Lynne Perrie, Tracey Emin and Shane MacGowan (whose face, following years of hard-core glugging, now resembles a puff-pastry model of the moon, speckled with broken teeth).

So far, so predictable, although along the way we're also offered more unusual and well-researched clips than you might expect. There's some great footage of monkeys getting drunk and falling from trees, and an astonishing snippet from a 1960s booze experiment in which a clean-cut middle-ager explains that he drinks very little – 'just a couple of beers in the morning, maybe an aperitif, wine with every meal, and cognac in the evening...'

We even get to see Sir Robert Winston smashed out of his mind during an episode of *The Human Body* (although sadly he's simply illustrating a point about the effect alcohol has on the brain – he doesn't get pissed and fight a conjoined twin in a bid to prove fists work better when you're drunk, more's the pity).

The overall effect is pretty weird. On the one hand, the show is offering a snickering ironic 'hurrah' to acts of public self-destruction, and on the other . . . well, the clips ARE funny.

But that's alcoholic abandon through and through. It's funny watching someone twirl round with a traffic cone on their head. It's less funny when they shit themselves and punch you. And it's miserably unfunny when they continue to do it until their liver conks out and they turn yellow and die. Unless they do it on a chat show. Then it's hilarious.

London's village idiot   [6 August 2005]

Foul and unsettling? Yes siree! As per tradition, let's put all human decency to one side, hold a pistol to our collective temple and celebrate the approaching finale of *Big Brother 6* (C4) with a pointless little awards ceremony, coming to you live from an A5 piece of newspaper held in front of your eyes right now.

First up, the prestigious Most Sickening Housemate award, which this year goes to a couple: Maxwell (London's village idiot) and Saskia (burly, wrathful harridan with a face that could advertise war). Their daily routine consisted of bullying, bellowing, cackling at their own dismal non-jokes, glaring, sniping and discussing their imminent ascent to the topmost peaks of stardom – until the last week, when, faced with eviction, they settled for sulkily rutting like doomed livestock. The latter surely ranks as the least sexy thing ever broadcast on television. I'd get more aroused watching a dog drown in petrol.

Next, it's the Stupidest Single Statement award. This year's show contained dumber utterings than ever before. There was an early classic from Anthony, who, while frolicking semi-naked in the pool, carped 'What's the matter with youse, you're sitting there like you're watching a television show' to a disapproving Science. Sadly, that's ineligible because it was immediately followed by the year's wisest rejoinder (Science: 'I am.')

Which means it's a race between Craig's frank admission that 'I aren't too familiar with the rules of the English language' and Anthony's claim that he's 'more developed than a plant' – both of which are beaten by Saskia's jaw-dropping assertion that the Second World War started in 1966.

The award for Most Alarming Behaviour goes, inevitably, to Craig – a high-risk FBI profile made flesh. When he wasn't proclaiming his own brilliance, weeping, masturbating, or shrieking uninformed opinions at a uninterested world, he was mindfucking his beloved Anthony – a man so profoundly thick you could sell him a pair of his own socks for £500, even if he was already wearing them.

Their relationship reached its nadir the night Anthony got paralytic and Craig sensed an opportunity. A bleak farce ensued – Anthony vomiting and crying for his gran, Craig frantically cuddling him while shouting, 'I'm your only friend in here.' It felt more like an extended out-take from *Deliverance* than a reality show. How Craig passed the psychological vetting process, and why he wasn't quietly removed from the house and given some gentle guidance, is a deeply worrying mystery.

The Cheated Winner award is a close call between two acquired-taste housemates. Only a heartless warlord couldn't warm to Eugene, a well-meaning human pylon whose ineptitude and timidity meant he was out of his depth from the off. But he's narrowly pipped by Science, a bull-headed, one-man belligerence engine who delighted in provoking Maxwell and Derek to breaking point. For services to torture alone, Science should've won.

Just time for a few parting gongs. The award for Snidest Conniving Prick goes to Derek, a man so devious he probably pisses cobra venom; the Ugliest Body award is split between Sam and Orlaith, for poking their fake, motionless tits in the viewer's face (presumably to attract the sort of person who'd like to screw their way through the plastinated corpses at Professor von Hagens' *Bodyworlds* exhibition).

Finally, the award for Unprecedented Dignitycide goes to Kinga, who, just when you genuinely believed TV couldn't possibly shock you from your jaded, end-of-the-world ironic detachment bubble, celebrated her second night in the house by masturbating with a wine bottle in the middle of the lawn – an act of such gruesome self-abasement, even the other housemates were appalled. Considering they're the most undignified people in Britain, that's an astounding achievement. Mark my words, we'll be celebrating it on commemorative stamps before the decade's out. Preferably self-adhesive ones.

CHAPTER TWO

In which children are despised, King Kong's toilet habits are discussed, and colourful lies about Robbie Williams are gleefully spread across the page

New, improved reality   [23 September 2005]

They say beauty is in the eye of the beholder. They're wrong. It's in the hands of the retoucher. These days, almost every photograph you see has been Photoshopped to perfection, just for you, because you're so bloody special.

Celebrities aren't beautiful until someone rearranges their pixels. You should see the original snapshots. Johnny Depp looks about ninety years old. Angelina Jolie's eyelids are spattered with warts. Keira Knightley? Face like a Rotherham coroner.

But a few swipes here and there with an electronic pencil, and bingo: they're gorgeous. It's not fair, because real life can't compete. Retouching techniques are constantly improving. Real life isn't. The aesthetic gulf between the two widens by the day. Drag your face away from the magazine covers for a moment, walk down the street, and what do you see? Muck. Greyness. Bored pedestrians. A dog being sick. You live on the shit side of the chasm, and Keira Knightley lives way over there.

But what if you could Photoshop real life? The technology can't be far off. Ten years from now, you'll be able to stick a chip in your brain that retouches all the images flowing into your eyes, improving them on the fly.

Imagine. You wake up and look in the mirror. The bags under your eyes are invisible. And you appear to have lost weight. The postman knocks on the door – as you open it, the chip removes his stubble, sucks his paunch in, and replaces his uniform with a butler's outfit. Your partner joins you in the kitchen. They're the most beautiful person on Earth. And they're naked.

You go outside. Blue skies. Blazing sunshine. There's a solitary cloud up above, and it's shaped like a cuddly sausage dog. The tramp begging by the cashpoint machine isn't a tramp – he's Joey from *Friends*! And thanks to another chip in another part of your brain, instead of hearing him whine about change, you're hearing him belt out your favourite show tunes. In Dolby Surround. You wave and walk past; instead of seeing him scowl, you watch him give a cheeky thumbs-up. Your world's a nicer place, and it costs less than usual to boot! Everybody wins! Except the tramp.

Additional chips would go to work on the other senses. You could eat a polystyrene roof tile and your brain would claim it was made of chocolate. And when you spewed it up, the bile wouldn't sting – it'd be so delicious you'd spend an hour gargling with it for fun. If a burglar broke into your house and started thrashing you with a broom, you could replace the sensation of terror with the sensation of ironic amusement, and the sensation of pain with one of having a nice sit-down. And then another chip would kick in, and your memory would wipe the entire incident and replace it with a delightful pastel sketch of a butterfly instead.

These chips are set to revolutionise our lives. Once they arrive, you need never undergo a negative experience again. You'll be lolling blissfully on the sofa 24 hours a day, transfixed by an endless string of shimmering delusions while your carcass gently bloats to the size of a waterbed. A bit like you do already. Assuming you've got Sky Plus.

I hate kids   [30 September 2005]

I hate kids. Hate them all without exception. Even yours. Especially yours. Especially if it's a boy and you named it Jake. And if you've ever written a chummy diary article about Jake for a Sunday supplement, I wish nothing short of death upon you. Death by wasps and bombs and razor wire. In a thunderstorm. While Jake looks on in horror. Because I hate parents too.

As luck wouldn't have it, I live slap-bang in the centre of Nappy Valley, a wedge of South London with one of the heaviest kiddy-wink-and-parent populations in the universe. It's a sickeningly self-satisfied place where the high street heaves with aromatherapy centres, organic-honey shops and cosy little cafés with cutesy lower-case names like 'munch', 'toast', 'smug', 'twee' and 'bum'. And the pavement heaves with buggy prams.

Naturally, I'm so riven with confused rage, I don't really belong in Pretty Pretty Niceland – but oh, how I'd love to. I dream of being able to relax awhile in the café; to ruffle my *Berliner*, sup a tea, chew a wholewheat tofu crumpet or whatever. I wish I could do that.

But I can't. Because wherever I go, there's a repugnant Jake nearby, shrieking, kicking the table, bellowing its hot little face off. And sitting beside Jake is Jake's moron parent, doting on his every noise, dribble and splurt, as though he's somehow special or charming.

Well, he isn't. Jake is a selfish, dot-eyed shouting machine hellbent on sabotaging whatever scraps of tranquillity remain in this pitiful world, and every right-thinking person within earshot despises him with a coal-black intensity that would make your head spin like a centrifuge if you ever got wind of it.

But as a horrified onlooker – one who genuinely believes children should be seen and not heard, and preferably neither – what can you do? I've tried glaring at the parents, but their minds are so hopelessly warped by 24-hour brood-worship they mistake my consternation for admiration. I've tried glaring at Jake, which isn't entirely bad, since it usually causes him to shut up and start gazing back with a sort of affronted blankness for a few moments, but also makes the waitresses regard me with open suspicion.

I've contemplated having an 'I HATE CHILDREN' T-shirt made up, in the hope that it might shock attendant parents into scurrying away with Jake in tow, but in today's kiddie-reverent times I'd be sectioned in minutes. As for the most obvious solution – leaning forward and politely asking the parent to curb Jake's noisier excesses – that'd end in a fistfight.

I've come to realise that what's required is a distress flare – a smaller, indoor version of a trawlerman's distress flare, one you can fire over your head at the point when Jake's incessant babbling is starting to turn you homicidal. A distress flare solves two problems at once: it warns Jake's parents you're about to lob a plate at his head, while simultaneously rendering Jake himself dumb, as he stares at the glittering firework like a particularly stupid jackdaw with half-eaten beans round its gob. Oh, and if it sets the café roof on fire, killing everyone inside, that's another bonus.

Hey, don't blame me. Blame Jake and his mummy.

Dying of boredom   [7 October 2005]

So the other day someone's talking to me about something important to them, and I feel their grip on my attention start to loosen and my mind drifts away from the conscious reality of sitting there listening to them, gently rises like a hot-air balloon ascending the heavens and glides across a landscape of idle thoughts, while back on Earth my face sits beside them saying 'mmm' and 'ooh' and 'really?' and occasionally arching its eyebrows like an actor in a commercial who's been asked to wordlessly indicate that hey, these cough sweets really work.

As I gazed down at the idle thoughts, wondering which to toy with, I became aware of the fuzzy, trance-like state I was in, and realised that although I'd entered this reverie out of boredom, the experience of boredom itself was proving pretty interesting.

In fact, I don't think 'boredom' itself actually exists. There's no such thing as boredom, just varying degrees of fascination.

For example, when I was thirteen I was off school for weeks, literally bedridden. I couldn't walk or run. A recipe for boredom, especially since back then there was no internet or satellite TV. Furthermore, I couldn't move my right arm without experiencing blinding pain, which meant most existing forms of entertainment, from reading to self-appreciation, were off the menu. All I could do was watch terrestrial TV. Unfortunately, it seemed my illness was taking place in the middle of a non-stop televised bowls tournament.

So there I was, forced by God to lie still and watch bowls for hours. Did I lose my mind with boredom? No. I got into it, without even trying. Easy when there's nothing else to do. First, you choose a favourite player – not consciously, it just happens. Perhaps one of them's a bit slick, or you don't like his glasses. Instantly, you root for the other guy. Then there's the game itself, which largely consists of tantalising footage of bowls gently swerving to a halt as close to the jack as possible. This struck me as twice as exciting as the climax of *Die Hard* (which was prescient of me, since *Die Hard* didn't come out for another four years).

What I'm saying is the mind entertains itself no matter what.

Which makes me wonder what we mean by the phrase 'bored to death'. It can't happen: even if it were possible to be literally bored to death, the actual process of dying is intriguing enough to wipe any traces of boredom out.

Imagine it. You've been locked in a cupboard for six years, with nothing but some string and an old cork to amuse you. Eventually, you get so utterly fed up your subconscious decides to shut you down. You start dying without noticing, when out of the blue, a startling thought strikes you – something like 'Jesus, my heart's not beating' – and suddenly life's exciting again.

You're doomed to enjoy life, in other words. You can't win.

Anyway, back to my little balloon ride. I cruised internal skies for the best part of an hour before being rudely awoken by a loud sob: in my absence, my face had erroneously smirked at a tragic anecdote. And now apparently I'm a bastard.

Well, come on. That's not fair. I wasn't even bloody listening.

Sir Yes Sir   [14 October 2005]

What's the most offensive thing you could possibly do in public? Squat down and crap on the pavement, or eat a bag of Wotsits? Pretty soon, it'll be the latter, because eating healthily is now the law, and anyone who disobeys is a demented suicidal pig.

Just last night, for instance, a TV commercial from the Food Standards Agency commanded me to eat no more than 6g of salt a day. It wasn't a suggestion, or a bit of friendly advice. It was an order, plain and simple. EAT NO MORE THAN 6g OF SALT A DAY, it said.

At first I stood and saluted. And then I thought, hang on, it's *my* bloody throat – I can stuff as much salt down it as I like. At which point the Thought Police kicked the door down and arrested me for impudent reasoning.

Don't get me wrong. I'm not disputing whether these Anti-Pie, Pro-Skipping campaigns have the potential to save lives. I'm sure they do. But come on – are human lives really worth saving in the first place? I mean really?

Take a look around: there's far too many of us, and we're not much to write home about. We spend more time picking our noses and wondering what famous peoples' kitchens look like than we spend doing anything worthwhile or interesting.

The average citizen is a cretin in sore need of a good hard culling. If we can slowly reduce our numbers by gently guzzling snacks till our hearts burst – thereby saving the government the hassle of herding us into a stadium and blowing our heads off, one by one – then that's a good thing, isn't it? Well?

Besides, all these health promotions really do is make you neurotic and miserable, thereby ruining what's left of your lifespan anyway. What would you rather do – spend every waking moment joylessly assessing your diet, and live to be a wizened 500-year-old mantis? Or die fat, young and merry, with caramel smeared round your mouth?

It's time they launched a campaign actively encouraging the population to gorge its way to an early grave. We need gigantic billboards with big colour photos of chocolate éclairs and beer, accompanied by slogans like 'Tuck in and Get It Over With!', or, 'Hey, Bollocks to Everything, Right? Enjoy!'

Actually, sod the billboards. Let's just erect shelves all over the place. Shelves heaving with pork pies and marshmallows and chocolate biscuits and piping-hot ready meals. Cut out the middleman and pass them round for free. The streets'll be full of cheery, wobbly, blobby people, munching their way to oblivion. It'll be one big life-affirming, population-reducing party!

Come to think of it, let's hand out wine, cocaine and heroin as well! And handguns! Free loaded handguns, on a shelf, on every street corner! Life would become markedly more dangerous, sure – but imagine the buzz you'd get each time you simply made it home alive (and besides, your chances of survival would be higher than you think: there'd always be loads of fatsos puffing about between you and the bullets).

They should do that. Our quality of life would improve.

Till it does, I'm going to eat precisely 6.1g of salt a day. In protest.

Rage with the machine [21 October 2005]

Planet Earth is an angry place, a searing bauble of rage. Wherever you swivel your eye, someone's losing their rag like a rag-losing machine. There's a worldful of furious people. Look. In the street – a man thrashing a traffic warden. On the telly – two guests on a daytime talkshow trying to bellow each other to death. And in the newspaper – some tooth-gnashing maniac demanding the public execution of anyone who breaks wind.

(Actually that last one was me, and I stand by every word – hey, it's particles of *their* excrement going directly up *your* nose. It's an ASSAULT, for God's sake.)

All this fury, roaring round the ether – and where does it go? The answer is it simply dissipates; flitters up toward the clouds, where it hangs around making pigeons sick and causing thunderstorms.

Not good enough. The planet sorely needs clean, sustainable energy sources; this waste can't be allowed to continue. We've got to work out a way of harnessing all this spare rage and using it to power our kettles and our mopeds and our iPod Bassetts (or whatever the bumming heck Apple have decided to call the latest incarnation).

For example, imagine a car powered by raw anger. If you pulled into a lay-by for a mean-spirited argument with your partner over their inability to read a bloody map and announce the bloody turning in time, you wouldn't be dismantling what meagre love still existed between you, you'd be gathering fuel for the rest of the journey. Brilliant.

Trouble is, you'd have to find ways to maintain your irritation. If you're driving between the hours of 7 and 10 a.m., that's simple – just tune into Chris Moyles on Radio 1 and the car will hurtle along (but be sure to restrict your listening to 20-minute bursts or both the engine and your heart will explode).

But for those barren moments when the nation's airwaves are less cluttered with mindless, foghorning warthogs, you need to plan ahead. You might, for example, scatter a few uncomfortable objects across the seat before you sit down. A couple of three-pronged plugs and a live cat should do it.

Or you could simply replace the windscreen with a sheet of frosted glass, thereby forcing you to squint at the road ahead, sustaining a constant level of mild irritation. And to make it slightly more annoying, scratch the phrase 'THIS IS PROGRESS' into the glass before setting out, leaving you gazing directly into some deadpan sarcasm for the duration of your trip.

Or the government could rebuild all the roads in infuriating squiggles, with huge sections that loop back on themselves so it takes an extra five hours to go anywhere, leaving everybody perpetually angry and late. Well, more than they are already.

And rage wouldn't just power cars! You could generate enough wattage to light up a skyscraper simply by introducing random bumps on the carpets so the residents continually stub their toes. The possibilities are endless. The world of science should investigate immediately.

Immediately, I said. Come on, science. Hurry up. You wouldn't like us when we're angry.

Dead famous [28 October 2005]

The police have charged a man with committing murder in an Oxfordshire village occasionally used as a location for the TV series *Midsomer Murders*. I know this because I read it in the paper, in a single-paragraph story with the heading '"Midsomer" Murder: Suspect Charged'.

Surely it's bad enough being murdered, without the news of your death being reported solely in relation to a TV phenomenon that's nothing to do with you. Imagine the coverage if you were run over and killed by the bloke who played the Honey Monster. I'd rather not make the papers at all.

I live in fear of this sort of thing. Earlier this year, I was in Edinburgh at festival time, and at one point found myself standing in a hot, cramped bar with a group of people that included Ricky Gervais. This bar was a couple of floors up; it had low ceilings, was heaving with smokers, and felt like a tinderbox.

All the while, I was acutely aware that should a fire break out, my death – and the death of virtually everyone around me – would go unmentioned in the resulting news story, which would be headed: 'TV RICKY IN BLAZE HORROR – Joy as *Office* star battles past scum to reach exit'. Of course, Ricky Gervais is so famous that even your closest relatives would forgive him for kicking you down a blazing stairwell as he fought his way to freedom. But how insignificant does a celeb have to be before you'd receive equal coverage in the event of you both dying in the same incident?

I suspect there's no bottom limit. Even if you were involved in a fatal coach crash with, say, ex-Children's BBC presenter Andy Crane, the headlines would likely read, 'FORMER BEEB MAN KILLED – Someone else dies also' rather than 'TWO DEAD IN BUS MESS'. It's a sobering thought, but in terms of raw news, you are worth less than a dead Andy Crane.

It's less clear how this grim hierarchy might work among celebrities themselves. If the Iranians launched a rocket at the Baftas, killing everyone, how would the tabloids respond? Would they print '100 CELEBS DEAD'? Or would they lead with the most famous victims first – 'ANT & DEC: THE DAY THE GRINNING STOPPED' – and work all the way through to the guy who plays Martin Fowler somewhere around page 247?

Actually, given the seismic impact a mass celeb wipe-out of this kind would have on the mindset and sales prospects of the tabloids, it's likely they'd simply go nuts and print no headlines whatsoever – just a load of violent, abstract scribbles, accompanied by a library snapshot of a monkey on a trike.

It'd take them a good six weeks to stop hyperventilating and actually explain what happened. And even then, you can bet all the dead waiters, doormen and catering staff wouldn't get a mention, unless one of them had been hit in the eye by a chunk of Cat Deeley's shinbone or something.

The only way to guarantee yourself fair coverage is to travel somewhere European and get killed at an awards ceremony there. Since British readers wouldn't have a clue who all those foreign TV stars were, your nationality would instantly elevate you to a starring role.

Yes! 'BRITISH WAITER DIES IN GERMAN OSCARS HORROR' – and at last the tables are turned!

The National Excuse Hotline [4 November 2005]

Q: When is a lie not a lie? A: When it's an excuse.

I love excuses. They represent the human imagination at its finest. A good excuse hovers somewhere between plausible and absurd – credible enough to be thoroughly believable, daft enough to sound like it couldn't possibly have been invented.

It's important to choose your excuse carefully. Once, a few months into a relationship, I told a girlfriend I was deaf in one ear, in an attempt to explain why I hadn't been listening to her. It worked in the short term. But we stayed together for another six years. During that time I kept forgetting which ear it was, or the level of deafness, or that I'd said it at all. I lived in constant danger of exposure. Got away with it, mind. And if you're reading this now, Roz – sorry about that.

A good excuse won't backfire like that. Here's one of the best I've heard:

Let's say you're meant to be at work by 9 a.m., but you've woken up at 10. By the time you get dressed and travel there, you're going to be two hours late. Well sod that – you might as well stroll in wearing a dunce's cap, clanging a bell, bellowing what a failure you are. The only sane course of action is to throw a sickie. So you phone the office. But rather than trying to pull off an 'ill' voice, use the following brilliant excuse. Your opening line, bold as brass, is: 'Sorry I'm late – I shat myself on the tube.' (Or on the bus. Or in your car – delete as applicable.)

You then go on to sheepishly explain just how embarrassing it was; how you think it might've been something you ate last night; how you had to waddle home to change your clothes – make it as vivid as possible. Don't forget to chuck in a bizarre, unrelated, detail for good measure – claim the actress Pauline Quirke was on the bus at the time, for instance. A mild surrealist dash will, para-doxically, make the entire story more credible.

Then you offer to travel in again. At which point they'll suggest you stay home and recuperate. And after you've hung up, they'll share a collective chortle at your expense. But you have the last laugh, because you get to spend the rest of the day lolling on the sofa, eating crisps in your (unsoiled) pants.

It's a great excuse, but sadly, you can only use it once. That's why I've decided to market a page-a-day calendar with a creative late-for-work excuse for every day of the year – everything from 'Cows were blocking the road' to 'Aunty put a spade through her foot'.

If you're a publisher, get in touch. Let's do this. We'll make mil-lions. And I'll use my profits to establish Britain's first National Excuse Hotline – a 24-hour call centre dedicated to providing the perfect excuse for any situation, round the clock. Want to explain those mysterious entries on your credit-card bill but can't think how? Give us a call. Police on your back about the disturbed soil in your garden? You know where to come.

And if our excuses backfire, and your marriage collapses, or you wind up in jail, don't even think about suing us. You won't win. We're the National Excuse Hotline, stupid. We know every excuse in the book.

The Instant Suicide Button   [11 November 2005]

How much does it take to break you? To break you to the point of wishing you were dead?

Quite a lot, for most people – a couple of bitter divorces, plus a total career collapse, followed by bankruptcy and a dash of exist-ential woe. Whereas my threshold's far lower. Simple everyday chores do it for me. During the average washing-up experience I'll wail about not wanting to live any more at least six times. And I genuinely mean it.

That the slightest personal drawback leaves me huffing like a toddler denied sweets is a good indication of just how cosseted my existence has become. It's a life of luxury taken for granted.

Not that I live like a king – the same applies to everyone in the West. We spend our lives flopping on the sofa, moaning about the telly – but the sofa's upholstered with pauper skin and the TV runs on baby blood. Our double-glazed windows block out the sound of lashes and screams from the workhouse next door, while an electrified fence surrounding our garden frazzles any potential intruders to a sizzling carbon turd – which we feed to our dog. Our tiny, pedigree dog. Our dog in a sodding tiara.

To make matters worse, every now and then, we'll come across something in the paper that reminds us just how much injustice it's taken to put us where we are, and we'll get a bit angry and sad, and we'll roll our eyes and turn to our partners and tut and say 'Have you seen this? The world's so unfair' and then we'll get distracted by a car advert on the telly that's got that bloke who was in that thing in it. What was it again? Was it *Holby City*? Pass us a Malteser.

We're pigs.

Perhaps if we'd all been born with a suicide button on the back of our heads – a 'death button' that would kill you instantly and painlessly on a single press – we'd all be a bit more grateful; more aware of our good fortune. Yes, a single press and tee hee hee – it's dead as a cardboard box you be!

Incidentally, it's a button with its own fingerprint detection system, so only the owner can use it – it's not like some prankster can hide behind a hedge and prod it with a long stick as you walk by, then laugh as your corpse lands face-first in doggy-doo. It's yours and yours alone.

Of course, few would make it past adolescence. What? I've got to go to school with this huge spot on my chin? Click. And that's only the first of a long line of push-button temptations. There's exam pressures – click – your first heartbreak – click – your mid-twenties breakdown – click – your shitty job – click – turning thirty – click – your first grey hair – click. And so on. But it's all for the best. It thins out the populace and spreads the comfort around for everyone.

Besides, anyone voluntarily pressing their button is a fool, and the world's got too many of them. Stroke it, by all means. Flirt with danger. Run your finger round the rim and contemplate choice. But don't press it. Who cares how big that pile of dishes gets? You're alive, stupid. And you're lucky to be here. Now get on with it.

Pray for Stumpy Ralf   [18 November 2005]

Who's the world's biggest celebrity? Let's say it's Ralf Little. Obviously it's not, but for the sake of argument, imagine a version of Ralf Little that had made some different career choices, and starred in a string of hit movies, and written fifteen best-selling albums, and was better-looking and taller and had a different head and face and voice and outlook and mind. Imagine that Ralf Little.

Right. So Ralf is the world's biggest celebrity. Wherever he goes, bedazzled plebeian scum congregate to take photos of him with their phone cameras and scream themselves to death. He's on the cover of *Heat* magazine so often they end up incorporating his face into the logo. In a survey, more people can tell you what Ralf Little got for Christmas than can tell you what 'milk' is. He's insanely bloody famous.

Then some ghastly accident occurs and Ralf loses a leg. But hey – he's still Ralf Little! And the way he hops is so cute, people love him all the more. Then a week later, during a garden party, he inadvertently hops into a gigantic whirring fan and loses all his other limbs. PRAY FOR STUMPY RALF scream the tabloids. It looks like he's finished.

But then they wheel him onstage at the Oscars – in a brightly coloured toy truck pulled by Hilary Swank – and everyone leaps up and applauds. The worldwide audience sheds a tear and Ralf's still completely famous.

But on the way home from the ceremony, Ralf's limo somersaults into a tanker full of concentrated acid. He's almost completely dissolved. All that's left is a single lip that, miraculously, is still alive. So now Ralf Little consists of nothing but a lip. Surely his career is finally over?

Not necessarily. A single lip could maintain a decent profile. He could do cameos. He could slither down a window in the next Ben

Stiller movie. Or play a small pink slug that befriends Dakota Fanning. He could even star in his own action blockbuster – a new *Die Hard*. Just dangle him from a bit of fishing wire at face height, shoot his scenes as normal and fill in the rest of his body later using CGI. Easy.

Failing that, his agent could glue him onto an orange, draw some eyes over the top, ram the orange onto a pencil, and hey presto – he's a puppet. Book him onto a hip, ironic, late-night American talkshow where all he has to do is sit there while the host smirks at him and he'd soon rekindle his following.

And then they could market him as a doll! Or even just as a lip – a single plastic lip that you stick onto an orange yourself (or an egg, or a tennis ball, or your own knee – whatever, it's your plastic lip). Suddenly he's the new Mr Potato Head! Phoenix from the flames!

It seems the only way his career can falter now is if someone were to deliberately and maliciously slice him in half with a Stanley knife. And unfortunately, that's exactly what happens, on his birthday, following a backstage row with his PA. So Ralf now comprises twin chunks of cold, chapped lip. At which point the public finally desert him. And why? Because they're fickle.

A two-minute howl of despair   [25 November 2005]

On the first anniversary of 9/11 I accidentally stood in a pub bellowing into a mobile phone throughout the two-minute silence. Now, I'm not in the habit of shouting into my phone like a cunt, but this was a heated argument – plus it was a huge metropolitan pub, full of noise and clatter as I entered: I was SPEAKING VERY LOUDLY to be heard above the din. Suddenly everyone else fell silent, while I continued my fevered yabbering at maximum volume, scattering swearwords like rice at a wedding.

It took a while to realise what was going on, and oh oh oh, the contempt on their faces. I couldn't have been less popular if I'd danced in dressed as Bin Laden, hopped on the bar and unveiled my scrotum (something I inadvertently did on the second anniversary, but that's another story). It felt like a huge spotlight had swung round to single me out as the Scummiest Bag in Existence.

Furthermore, my telephonic opponent took my sudden hush as a mark of defeat, so I had to endure him crowing 'See? Haven't got an answer for *that*, have you?' in my ear while I withered in the glare of a hundred sickened faces.

Still. Two minutes silence. Scarcely a week pops by without us being asked to bow our heads and remember; to mutely contemplate sacrifice, or tragedy, or the grisly misfortune of others. It makes us feel slightly better – hey, we've done our bit, yeah? – but it's otherwise useless. The tragedies continue and the world becomes a sicker joke by the day – and the best you can do is stare at your shoes and shut up for a while? No wonder you feel helpless.

I mean, you switch on the news and here's what you see: rhetoric, death and white phosphorus. You see a furious, ignoble arsehole claiming the divine right to blow himself and innocent civilians to pieces, and then you see a grinning presidential meerkat incapable of opening a door. You see bombing and lying and lying and bombing and it comes from both sides and there's no end to it. And you think 'What can I do?' but there's no answer. And the tension and nausea rises in your gut, because all you know is *something's coming* and *you are powerless*.

In Orwell's *1984*, the citizens vented frustration in the state-sponsored 'Two-Minute Hate'. I'm proposing something slightly different: a citizen-led two-minute howl of despair. We set a time and date, and we pass it on – we fire a simple email at everyone we know.

'Feeling trapped in the middle of a fight you didn't pick? Mad as hell? Not going to take it any more? Well hip hip hooray – it's venting time. At the allotted date/hour, stop what you're doing, put down your tools, step into the street and join us, the sane remainders of the human race, as we howl inarticulately at the skies.'

Futile noise beats futile silence, people, so howl till your throat burns – howl yourself dizzy. Millions of us, simultaneously, howling round the world. Who knows: maybe it'll prompt the man in the moon to float down and save us. It's worth a shot – for crying out loud.

Things Robbie Williams hasn't done

[9 December 2005]

Rubbish singer Robbie Williams has won 'substantial damages' in a libel action against the *People* newspaper, which had alleged he was 'pretending' to be heterosexual, that he 'engaged in casual and sordid homosexual encounters with strangers', and was 'about to deceive the public' over his sexuality in an autobiography. Pretty strong stuff, considering it turned out not to be true.

Now I'm no Robbie Williams fan – I'd rather shatter my jaw on a concrete bollard than sit through one of his videos – but I'm worried this legal action might lead to a reduction in the number of gossipy articles written about him, thereby creating a dangerous vacuum at the centre of modern tabloid culture.

In the absence of regular double-page spreads about Williams' latest notional high-jinks, the red-tops might start printing other things, such as step-by-step photo guides instructing their readers how to wield pitchforks, form mobs and overthrow democracy.

Civilised society? I give it three weeks.

Only two things can save us. First, David Walliams needs to plug the gap by cranking up his colourful social life yet further, to the point of having sex with hollowed-out potatoes in public. And second, rather than printing stories that claim to be true yet turn out to be false, the celebrity press should start printing stories that claim to be false and remain that way.

After all, ultimately no one cares whether any of them *actually* get up to this shit. That secretary flipping through *Heat* in her lunch break knows full well she's not reading vital information – just something dimly glitzy that'll take her mind off slashing her wrists and spraying blood in the faces of her co-workers for 10 seconds. That's all she wants. They can print what they want – even a row of numbers will do, so long as it's broken up now and then with the names of a few celebrities.

With this in mind, I'd like to dedicate the rest of this week's column to a list of things Robbie Williams would absolutely, positively *never* say or do. Read it in your lunch break. OK? Let's go:

Robbie Williams would never shoot a man just to watch him die. Robbie Williams would never wrap a mouse's head in blotting paper and crush it with his heel. Robbie Williams would never threaten to gore a sales assistant to death with his antlers.

Robbie Williams would never jump on to Philip Schofield's back and demand to be flown to the nearest star-gate. Robbie Williams would never suddenly turn into a two-dimensional diagram of himself printed on the inside of a ball bearing which continually rolls out of your field of vision the second you realise it's there.

Robbie Williams would never deliberately break a dairymaid's heart with a sarcastic puppet show. Robbie Williams would never attack a hill with his feet, hands and forehead. Robbie Williams would never change his name to Baron Plop-Plop and fly across Devon in an undersized Sopwith Camel with a hole in the bottom so he could stick his bum out and poo on people trying to enjoy picnics below. Robbie Williams would never seal himself inside an immense iron drum for fifteen years with only a bee and a puddle for company.

Robbie Williams would never drink chalk, steer clouds, bite France or breathe deckchairs. And nor would Tom Cruise.

God: massive bastard   [16 December 2005]

If you're looking for proof that God doesn't exist, don't bother investigating the big stuff, like earthquakes or famines or the tsunami. Start small. Right now I've got a sore throat and as far as I'm concerned that's evidence enough.

The constant awareness is the worst part. Usually I walk around blissfully ignorant of my throat. I never think 'Ooh, aren't I lucky to have a throat?' or anything like that. But right now I'm obsessed with it. It's like the early days of a love affair, when the other person is all you can think about, except here the 'other person' is played by my own throat, and there's no sex involved because that would be impossible and probably just make it even more sore.

I'm also extremely conscious of just how often I must noncha-lantly swallow saliva in an average day without even realising, because suddenly it hurts like hell each time it happens. Every few minutes it feels like I'm trying to squeeze a splintered cupboard door down my neck – yet I can't stop doing it. It's humiliating.

Even sleep brings no respite: I wake spluttering in the middle of the night, feeling like a cat's just clawed through my gullet, trailing furballs in its wake. I hate it, I hate it, I hate it.

In summary: a mere sore throat is proof enough that there is no God – or that if there is, he doesn't give a toss about human suffering. In which case why bother worshipping him? That's like fellating someone who intermittently stubs fags out on your head for no good reason. And we all know how unsatisfying that can be.

Still, perhaps I'm wrong and perhaps there is a God. Perhaps he's reading this right now, on the toilet in heaven. In which case, perhaps he'd like to do something to prove his existence. Once he's washed his hands.

Yes, perhaps Mister so-called 'God' could create a highly infectious disease that was both non-fatal and fun. And by 'fun', I mean something that generates symptoms that feel nice instead of nasty. How about an illness that induces the sensation of sliding into a warm bath? Or the satisfaction of having just finished a really good novel. Or one that spends an entire week gently but firmly bringing you to a thundering orgasmic finale.

Wouldn't it be great? You'd jump for joy at the first symptom. If a doctor gravely ushered you into his office and said you were infected, you'd end up kissing him. If the virus was transmitted via saliva, he'd kiss you back (and if it was sexually transmitted, he'd lock the door, take his phone off the hook, and bang you round the room like a dirty little doctor-loving bitch. Ain't that right? Say it, ho: say you love doctors. Mmmm. This be some prime medicinal lovin', right here. I be taking your temperature real good. Uh. Uhhh! Uhh-hhhhh!).

Yes, that's how great the world of sickness and disease could be. But it isn't, because God's being an arsehole about it. If you're the sort of person who prays every night, ask him to stop dicking around, yeah?

I'd do it myself, but my throat's too sore.

King Kong times two   [6 January 2006]

Last night I saw Peter Jackson's remake of *King Kong* for the second time. This makes me an idiot. Partly because it's three hours long, and partly because it's rubbish, but mainly because even though I'd already seen it, I'd been in such a state of denial about it being three hours long and rubbish that, on being invited to see it again, I cheerfully accepted.

Ten minutes in to my second viewing, I suddenly realised I'd made a terrible, baffling mistake. And now not only was I going to have to sit through the whole thing again, but I'd somehow have to explain to my two companions (who spent the duration yawning, writhing and fouling themselves with disgust) just why I'd been prepared to waste six hours of my life watching such a mammoth fountain of shit.

There simply isn't space to list everything wrong with it. Its most glaring flaw is being sixteen times more overblown and histrionic than necessary. For instance, Kong doesn't just fight one T-Rex, as per the original. No, he fights a whole bunch of them, while entangled in vines, dangling above a ravine, and tossing Naomi Watts from paw to paw like a Hacky Sack – for ages.

If there'd been a scene in which Kong went to the toilet, it would've run like this: (1) Kong unfurls his 10km penis and piddles into an erupting volcano for 45 minutes; (2) Kong turns around and passes a stool the size of a blue whale, in slow motion, to the strains of a 20,000-strong choir, while Naomi Watts stares at him, her eyes brimming with love; (3) his bowels emptied, Kong plucks the planet Jupiter out of the sky and swallows it for no reason, while fighting fifteen giant crocodiles. And a robot. And a pig.

What's more, the cast are just plain weird to look at. Jack Black looks like he's playing the lead in *Young Prescott*, Adrien Brody resembles a cross between Ross from *Friends* and a disappointed sundial, and Naomi Watts spends the entire film gawping, sobbing, screaming or turning into Nicole Kidman in your head. Until the final scene, when she does all three at once. In slow motion. Atop the Empire State Building. In 3D.

75

As a film, it's the fattest, most swaggering, numb-headed and pointless assault on the senses it's possible to imagine. What I can't understand is why I enjoyed it first time round.

I suspect it was something to do with my state of mind at the time. I'd been Christmas shopping in a particularly miserable shopping mall – one of those modern ones consisting entirely of shiny floors and echoes, JD Sports and Nando's Chickenland. I was thoroughly sick of it and, by extension, of life itself.

At which point I was faced with a choice. I could drop to my knees and headbutt the floor until my skull split open in front of thousands of horrified shoppers. Or I could go and see *King Kong*, which I figured would probably be far too long and not very good. My expectations thus lowered, I actively enjoyed it. I'd adjusted my filter beforehand.

It's all about adjusting your filter. Just don't try adjusting it twice.

The root of all stupid [13 January 2006]

So the other day I'm watching *The Root of All Evil*, Richard Dawkins' new Channel 4 series about religion, and it's alternating between terrifying and hilarious. Terrifying because it feels like a report detailing the final seconds before the world slides into an all-out holy fistfight, and hilarious because every time Dawkins meets a religious spokesman, which he does at regular intervals throughout the programme, he quickly becomes far too angry to conduct a civil conversation with them – visibly fumes, in fact, and adopts the expression of an outraged Victorian gentleman who's just been mooned by a cackling street urchin while escorting a lady across Bloomsbury Square. It doesn't exactly move the debate forward.

Still, his central point (that the irrational dismissal of logic encouraged by religion often leads to tragically irrational behaviour, such as blowing yourself up on the tube or listening to Christian rock) seems pretty valid from where I'm standing, i.e. cowering on the sidelines of a fight I didn't pick, and which seems to be escalating out of control. Life on Earth would be simpler and less blowy-uppy if religion didn't drive so many of its followers crazy – so why isn't anyone researching a drug that can cure it?

It can't be that far-fetched. After all, there's no shortage of boggle-eyed drug-guzzling bores out there willing to describe their spiritual experiences at punishing length. They can crack on for hours about the time they took a nuclear strain of hallucinogen they found on the internet. They ran outside in the moonlight, glanced down at a bit of old stick on the floor, and suddenly found themselves journeying inside its mind – suddenly the air tasted of wood, they felt bark growing on the outside of their brain and they slowly realised that when you really bloody think about it, we're all sticks, in a way, and let me tell you that revelation was bloody life-changing, it absolutely was. Do you want some? Do you? Do you want to take some now? Go on. I need someone to talk to, someone on my level. TAKE THE PILL!

If we're smart enough to create drugs that tickle the spiritual node in the brain, perhaps we can create a few new ones that'll shut it down completely. I'd make it mandatory for all schoolkids, worldwide. Actually sod that – I'd pump it into the water supply myself.

Imagine! Nothing to kill or die for! And no religion too! It's amazing literally no one's ever had that thought before.

OK, so there's always the possibility that the same part of the brain that handles fuzzy spiritual feelings is the same part that handles love and sorrow and pity and joy; the same part that makes us create songs and jokes and books and art and brightly coloured computer games in which an animated weasel collects starfish in a fountain; so once we wipe it out we might all be left scampering around the planet like thick, bipedal, cultureless mice – rutting, foraging, scratching behind our ears and doing very little else. But look on the bright side. No more religious conflict *and* no more novelty ringtones. Two almighty evils erased for the price of one. Bargain.

CHAPTER THREE

In which Jeremy Kyle interrogates the unfortunate, Neighbours *celebrates two decades of bland existence, and George Galloway impersonates a cat*

Beating them off with a stick   [20 August 2005]

Last weekend I went to the Natural History Museum and got
seriously impressed by spiders. It's the way they catch flies. There's
your standard web – which is incredible in itself – but there are
also exotic variants on the theme.

Take the purseweb spider, which constructs a tubular web that
protrudes from the ground, ready to swallow anything dumb
enough to land on the tip. Or the bolas spider, which creates a glob
of webby goo on the end of a silvery thread, then twirls it around
like a lasso until it catches a moth.

I'm not that fussed about eating flies myself, but I've got to hand
it to the spiders: their determination is astounding.

I was reminded of this while watching *Studs of Suburbia* (C4),
a documentary about men who know what they want (sex with
ladies) and know how to get it (charm).

Oops – did I say 'charm'? I meant the opposite. In fact, imagine
embroidering the word 'charm' on a piece of satin, wrapping it
round a rock, and blasting it skyward through a high-velocity
cannon, all the way over to the other side of the universe. Then
walk away from the cannon and accidentally step in some dogshit.
Now examine your shoe. That's what these men have instead of
charm. But they also have countless notches on their bedposts.
As a fellow man, this upsets me.

Take Alan. Alan is fifty-two and hails from a small town in Yorkshire. He looks like a cross between Rodney Bewes and John
Prescott. He lives with his mum. He speaks with a bloated jowly
gargle and has nothing of interest to say.

He's beating them off with a stick.

His secret? Suggestive chat and dogged persistence. Apparently
he gets turned down 'eight times out of ten', but despite closely
resembling the animated mascot from *Bullseye* he succeeds with
the remaining 20 per cent. He once got three women pregnant
simultaneously. OK, not literally simultaneously – he's not that
potent – but it's still quite an achievement, if you measure success
by the number of people you've slept with, which all men secretly

do. (Even Magnus Pyke. In fact he's probably even drawn up a pie chart detailing how many naked ladies he's seen. And then he's drawn a pair of boobs underneath it. Great big pink ones. And he's dead, for Christ's sake.)

We also meet Clive, a fifty-five-year-old Welshman who claims to enjoy similar success using a high-tech spin on the same basic technique. He spam-mails women on dating websites, firing off the same flirty messages again and again until he scores a hit. At one point in the documentary Clive tips a carrier bag full of knickers all over his bed, then sorts through them, chuckling to himself. It's his trophy collection.

I can criticise Clive until I'm blue in the neck. He's a selfish, dough-faced tail-chaser with the moral outlook of a skunk, and I'm not. But then I've never tipped a carrier bag full of knickers over my bed and sat about laughing. No. I spend my weekends gawping at spiders in a fucking museum.

Somehow, Clive has won.

Lost   [27 August 2005]

Like about 6 million other people, I tuned in for the two-part premiere of *Lost* (C4) a few weeks ago, and mightily enjoyed it.

Yeah, so they all look like supermodels, apart from token Blobbo Boy. And yeah, so despite the plane crash, they've only sustained cosmetic little injuries – a dainty scratch here, a neat graze there, and absolutely no one with a whopping great shard of metal jutting from their eye. And yeah, so a few of the characters could be replaced by simple glove puppets with 'Tormented Hero' and 'Selfish Macho Guy' stitched on them, and you wouldn't really notice. So what? I liked it.

Because oooh, I thought to myself, oooh, it's a bit like a cross between *The Twilight Zone* and *24*: schlock, but quality schlock. What's the mysterious force that keeps smashing down trees? How come there's a polar bear on the island? Will they get to the bottom of the looping sixteen-year-old distress signal? Pointless questions, but they intrigued me.

And just like everyone else, I started theorising about what might be going on. Perhaps they're in purgatory. Perhaps they've gone back in time, or been zapped into an alien theme park. Perhaps the last episode will end with the camera pulling back to reveal the whole thing's been happening inside the brass knee of a gigantic clockwork robot. Perhaps, perhaps, perhaps. Now, several weeks in, perhaps it's just a big con. I was halfway through this week's episode when I realised, with a bit of a jolt, that I was finding it profoundly irritating. I stopped wondering about the mysterious island, and started wondering whether *Lost* itself is worth bothering with – because it's starting to strongly resemble a load of navel-gazing soap claptrap that passes itself off as something more stimulating by going 'woo, woo, I'm mysterious' every five minutes. It reminds me of the sort of rubbish 'surreal' painting you do during art class aged fourteen (you know – a giant eye hovering over a desert landscape, surrounded by floating question marks, the kind of thing even a Marillion album cover would consider embarrassing).

Lost? They should've called it Metaphor Island.

The flashback format doesn't help. This week's episode keeps nipping back in time to examine Jack's past – which is hard to care about. And I suppose over the coming weeks we're going to go through all the other characters, one by one, discovering there's more to them than meets the eye, and they're all running away from something, and they've all got demons to face and so on. Instead of enjoying some good old-fashioned spooky fun, we've got to wade through a load of narcissistic 'look deep within' bumwash: whiny self-obsession masquerading as a spiritual quest. That's not a supernatural thriller, that's a psychologist's chore.

Well I don't care about their wounded inner children. I just want to watch them fighting ghosts on monster island. But they won't let me. They're too busy running around with their heads up their backsides. No wonder they're lost.

If I sound annoyed it's because I started out enjoying the show and I'd quite like to go back there, thank you very much. Maybe it'll improve. I wouldn't know: I've been dodging spoilers like nobody's business. One thing's for sure – if the series ends with a big wobbly question mark and a promise of further revelations next year (instead of a neat *Twilight Zone* ending that solves the mystery), I'm going to sue the entire American TV industry for wasting my time.

Actually, I won't. But only because they've also given us *Deadwood* (Sky One), which I genuinely think I could watch from now until the end of time. Sky seem to be nudging it further and further back in the schedules – hopefully not a sign they're losing faith in it (it's a 'hard watch', but worth it). When the series is over they should broadcast the whole thing again, back-to-back over a single weekend.

Not for their benefit – for mine. Saves me leaving the sofa for a good 48 hours.

Hooray for telly! [3 September 2005]

There's a general consensus among TV folk that one of the greatest crimes you can commit is making a show that's too 'in' – i.e. one that concerns itself with the process of programme-making. Shows that analyse, explain or satirise TV are of interest solely to people who work in the industry, whereas the actual audience couldn't care less.

Cobblers. The schedules are already full of programmes so 'in' they're in danger of physically imploding – those cheery list-show retrospectives that celebrate the past while promoting the idea that telly today is more sophisticated than it used to be. In other words, if all you're saying is 'hooray for telly!' you can be as 'in' as you like on the box.

If you want to be 'in' in real life, however, you have to go somewhere like the MediaGuardian Edinburgh TV Festival (last weekend, Scotland), where you'll find hundreds of like-minded folk talking, debating, whispering and occasionally bellowing about nothing but telly, for three whole days on the trot.

The telly business involves more guesswork than most professions (largely in the form of execs sitting around debating the mores of the aforementioned mythical, unknowable, thick, ugly, stinking, ignorant audience). Consequently, the Edinburgh TV sessions consist almost entirely of questions such as 'Is the audience sick of celebrity reality shows?'

That one was posed during a panel discussion featuring Jade Goody, James Hewitt and Jayne Middlemiss, all of whom took quite a while to conclude that the answer was 'maybe'. Still, perhaps the audience's opinion will finally get off the fence if *Celebrity Shark Bait* (ITV1) scores a kill, eh? Fingers crossed.

Not all the questions were so straightforward. One session simply asked 'Can working in TV make you happy?' I can answer that one, because on the first night of the festival I found myself in the temporary Edinburgh incarnation of Soho House at 2 a.m., swigging champagne, surrounded by stars, listening to a fellow media type making crass jokes about the London bombings while a woman in the background exhibited the kind of facial spasms I'd normally associate with strychnine poisoning, and I started wondering aloud whether it's possible to commit suicide using nothing but a small Yale key, which was the sharpest item I had to hand. (I eventually worked out the correct method would be to tear your throat open with the ragged edge, then firmly drive the key into your tearduct using a flattened palm – but by this time I was talking to myself.)

What I'm saying is no, it doesn't make you happy.

The rest of the festival was less depressing. There was a spirited row during a session on 'TV controversies' in which Stephen Green from Christian Voice boo-hooed about *Jerry Springer: The Opera*. 'If they know we may be offended by a programme, they have the chance to stop it, but they just keep going,' he said. I share his pain, having recently read a Christian Voice pamphlet against gay policemen (sample quote: 'Homosexual police are involved in the most disgusting perversions imaginable – how can they bring clean hands to any investigation?'). Astoundingly offensive, but Christian Voice just keep going.

Usually, the big event is the MacTaggart lecture, traditionally a horrified wise man ranting about plummeting standards. This year Lord Birt performed the honours and was widely acknowledged as a damp squib, being neither horrified nor ranty enough to draw blood. But as with any industry convention, most delegates' personal highlights take place either during the silly 'fun events' (this year, a live version of *Simply Come Dancing* featuring pirouetting TV execs) or back at the hotel bar. All of which probably explains why, despite the festival's annual questioning, navel-gazing and proclamations about 'commitment to quality', the inherent nature of TV itself rarely changes. It's a big dumb wash of tinsel and jabber, specked with intermittent flashes of quality. And it probably always will be.

Ha ha you're grieving [10 September 2005]

'Hey, Channel 4 – pay attention to me! Because I've just seen *Balls of Steel*, right, and it's given me a great idea for a new TV series, yeah? It's a comedy show called *Ha Ha You're Grieving*, and it stars me as a wizard, yeah, in a hat and everything, and what I do is I go up to people who've been bereaved, not actors, but real members of the public, and I tell them I've got, like, 'magic information' about how their dead relatives died! And they get upset, so we zoom in on that quite a bit, but the funny thing is I'd be, like, totally straight-faced and serious throughout? Cos I reckon I can do that. Cos I'm, like, heartless and reprehensible and that?'

Yuk. But Channel 4 wouldn't actually broadcast the above programme. Partly because it would be revolting. And partly because it's already available on Living TV, albeit in a slightly different form and going by the name of *The Psychic Detective*.

'Who do you turn to when the case is closed?' asks the blurb. 'Tony Stockwell is the Psychic Detective who uses his extraordinary psychic gift to help ordinary people investigate the unexplained and mysterious deaths of their loved ones.'

Now, I'm not calling Tony a liar. I can't do that unless I want to get sued, so I won't. I can, however, point out that if Tony really does possess a 'psychic gift', it follows that the rules of science will have to be rewritten.

This is usually the point where some bleating moron emails me to say that 'science doesn't know everything'. You're right. It doesn't. I mean, what is science anyway? Only a rigorously tested, peer-reviewed, continually evolving system of knowledge about the way our world works, built up over centuries – that's all. It's not a patch on mindless superstition, which has been around far longer, and is responsible for bringing us such exciting gems as ghosts, demons, witch trials, the tooth fairy and the Psychic pissing Detective.

Another thing the blurb doesn't mention is that Tony's a fat-faced Prince William lookalike, which is the first thing to strike you when you tune in. He's also got one of the weirdest accents I've ever heard – a cross between Cockney and Klingon. And he's incapable of pronouncing the letter G: rather off-putting in a psychic.

'I'm connectin' to the spirit world now – I'm pickin' somethin' up – your grandmother's tellin' me somethin' . . .'

If you're going to exploit my grief, you could at least make an effort to speak properly.

Mind you, maybe that's how dead people speak in the spirit world, and Tony's just picked up their mannerisms. That would also explain his corpse-like facial expressions: he continually flops about with his gob hanging open, like a dim cartoon yokel trying to work out an optical illusion. Perhaps they should've called it *The Psychic Farmhand* instead.

This isn't the first time I've had a pop at psychics, and regular readers could be forgiven for thinking I'm obsessed. But I'm attacking them because they're an easily identifiable symptom of a far deeper malaise – the widespread rejection of rational thought in favour of emotional response. That's what's messing the planet up for everybody at the moment, if you stop and think about it.

In other words: people like Tony may be microscopic fleas drawing blood from a big dumb backside, but having claimed the moral high ground, I can do what I like, stupid.

Ooh – just time to recommend the funniest show of the week: Chris 'SAS' Ryan's hilarious *How Not To Die* (Sky One), an unbelievably shouty worst-case scenario survival guide, little short of pornography for neurotics.

The high point of the series so far came during the 'Holiday' edition, which, in between coach crashes and hotel fires, carried a truly gruesome reconstruction of a man being mugged by bandits, then getting his kidney sliced out and sold.

At which point Chris popped up to say, 'Thankfully, this is just an urban myth.'

Phew! And thanks for drawing it to our attention.

Dickless [17 September 2005]

Although by and large I enjoy being a man, I've always had an awkward relationship with some of the niche aspects of maleness, such as the dull preoccupation with sport and pubs, or the deluded belief that breaking wind is funny. I like to think there's more to us than that.

Apparently I'm wrong. That's all we are. We're goons.

Well, according to the telly, anyway. We're not portrayed as sex objects. We're not portrayed as bastards. No. We're portrayed as bell-ends, and it's getting embarrassing.

He's Having a Baby (BBC1) is the final straw. The premise: each week, Davina McCall hosts a live studio show following a group of first-time dads (some whose partners have recently given birth, some who are still expecting). And each week, a couple of these dads are given hilarious tasks to undertake – such as organising a toddlers' party, or teaching a kiddywink to swim. These reach us in the form of side-splitting VT segments, generally accompanied by comedy parp-parp music. After which we cut back to the studio where Davina takes the piss out of them while the audience laughs. Because men are hilariously rubbish! They're big useless boys! Ha ha ha! But they're cute, too, bless 'em! A can of beer and some footie on the box and they're in heaven! Awww! Wook at his wickle face! He's dreaming about pubs! Tee hee! Men! Lovable, huggable, tumbling ninnies, the lot of 'em!

NO! NO! JESUS CHRIST, NO! If we men must be reduced to paper-thin cartoons, I'd rather see us depicted as warmongering rapists-in-waiting than dickless pudge-faced clowns. Every man involved in *He's Having a Baby* is a sex traitor who should hang his head in shame (except for Danny Wallace, who should hang his in a box of seriously irritated rats).

It isn't the only offender, of course. We've also got to contend with the downright jaw-dropping *Bring Your Husband to Heel* (BBC2), in which 'misbehaving' men have their behaviour 'modified' by a dog trainer, and *Kept* (VH1), a reality show about a wizened hag (played to perfection by Jerry Hall) choosing a pet boy from a bunch of dismal, preening bimbos.

You could be forgiven for thinking Michael Buerk's recent grumble about women ruling TV was correct. But you'd be wrong. There are loads of women in television, but few are network controllers; ultimately men are nodding these through. Why?

Well, since the anal study of demographics became a number-one priority in TV land, it's been noted that men are a tough audience to snare. So perhaps it's an act of revenge. Here's a quote in which Nick Elliot, ITV's controller of drama, explains why most of his output is aimed at women: 'You can bash your head against a brick wall trying to make dramas for sixteen- to thirty-four-year-old males, but if they only want to watch football or videos and PlayStation, there's no point . . . I'm not sure what a very male drama is. Maybe it's about business or something. We do guns and violence for boys occasionally . . . We actually thought *Footballers' Wives* would appeal to men, but it doesn't very much . . . they soon suss out it isn't about football.'

Jesus! He hates men! And no wonder: from the sounds of it, they're morons! Because that's what you see when you study any demographic: a hateful, ignorant, unthinking mass. And in this case, a mass which doesn't watch much telly.

Everyone in telly studies demographics. And I think that's why they hate us.

So – how about a Saturday night show called *Tumblebloke Twit Time*, in which men in nappies bounce around inside a large revolving drum, while Jerry Hall sits at the side laughing whenever one of their balls pops out? And in the second round they climb greased poles to reach a can of beer perched on top? And in the third round we let them off their leads in a park, and they scamper about and blow off and talk about football – and it's cute! Because that's where we're headed, chaps. Pass the noose.

A deep-fried sofa   [24 September 2005]

Somebody somewhere is having a Toffee Crisp. And the chances are that somebody is Barry Austin – Britain's most overweight man.

Let's not beat about the bush here: Barry's quite fat. He weighs 50 stone and looks like he's just eaten a sofa. A deep-fried sofa with cheese pillows. He's so hopelessly blobsome, his legs aren't recognisable as legs. They resemble a pair of doner kebabs that have stopped revolving and started melting. Thick, gutty rolls of skin hang in heavy folds across his body. He looks like a sweating, heaving heap of outsized blubbery tits, all stacked on top of each other, with a swollen spluttering face poking out the top, like an overweight tortoise that's exhausted itself trying to clamber out of an obscenely plump Yorkshire pudding.

Just to reiterate: Barry's quite fat.

Now, it's often the case that when you're physically repellent, celebrities don't want anything to do with you (that's the voice of experience talking – I've been phoning Jenny Powell non-stop for seven years now, and all she ever does is hang up or apply for injunctions). But TV's Richard Hammond is clearly made of more sympathetic stuff. He's perfectly happy to get intimately acquainted with fat Barry. In fact, he's prepared to physically enter him on television.

The result is *Inside Britain's Fattest Man* (Sky One), best described as a cross between *Fantastic Voyage* and an extended public information film. This is high-concept stuff for a documentary – the concept being that Hammond has magically shrunk to minute proportions and been injected into Barry's backside. Using his hi-tech nano-explorer craft, we're told, Hammond can travel around Barry's hulking carcass for 24 hours and see what sort of state the internal organs are in. Cue computer-generated footage of Hammond peering through the window of a bubble-shaped spaceship, pointing at bits of stomach and looking disgusted.

As well he might, because Barry's interior is a wreck. His lungs are so restricted by the surrounding blubber, he sometimes stops breathing in his sleep: his liver is 5lb heavier than average and is marbled with grey fat, like a slab of pâté. Well, it is in the CGI re-creation we're shown, anyway – although by that point the show had become so overwhelmingly disgusting they could've shown his liver vomiting into a bucket and I'd have taken it at face value.

These 'indoor' CGI shenanigans are accompanied by live action 'outdoor' segments following Barry's grotesque daily routine. Over an average 24-hour period, Barry wolfs down two or three full English breakfasts before moving onto fish and chips at lunchtime and a couple of curries for dinner – interspersing this ceaseless carnival of food with around twenty packets of crisps and count-less pints of lager (each of which he swallows in a single gulp). His mouth's like a plughole to another dimension: a vacuum hell-bent on magnetically inhaling all the edible matter in the universe.

The programme recounts much of this with a sort of amused respect, backed by comedy parp-parp music, even though you're keenly aware that you're watching a man eat his way to the grave, especially during the sections when you see him suffering with leg ulcers and almost wheezing to death.

For a show involving large quantities of food, it all leaves a funny taste in the mouth. We understand Barry's extremely unhealthy the moment he waddles onscreen – so to then spend a whole hour circling his gall bladder feels morbidly pornographic. To sit through the entire broadcast, you'd have to be a seriously committed vulture.

Still, as a dietary aid, it's unbeatable. Here's my advice: tape it, then watch it in eight-minute segments, every morning for a week, eating a pork pie as you do so. You'll be anorexic by Sunday. You might lose your hair, your skin and your sanity, but those jeans'll fit you like a condom. And who knows? Instead of playing parp-parp music behind your back, those nice TV people might invite you to form a girl band instead.

Half an hour of stab wounds   [1 October 2005]

If you live in a town, venturing outside at night is dangerous. Anything could happen to you. Here are just seven examples.

1: You could get stabbed in the chest. 2: You could get stabbed in the neck. 3: You could get stabbed in the knee, which would really hurt, because the blade would sort of glance off your kneecap without puncturing it, and – ugh, it doesn't bear thinking about, does it? 4: You could stab yourself to death in an argument over which half of your brain hates prostitutes the most. 5: You could get stabbed in the neck again. 6: You could witness a stabbing so hideous, the images continue to haunt you for the rest of your life, so that even if ten years later you sat down to watch *Finding Nemo* on DVD, all you'd actually see is that blade going in again and again and again, which isn't quite what Disney had in mind. 7: You could get stabbed in the neck some more.

Basically, what I'm saying is it's a world of knives out there: knives, and hands holding the knives, repeatedly jabbing them in your direction. You'd best stay indoors and watch *MacIntyre's Toughest Towns* (Five), the show that convinced me the outside world is one big knife-fight in the first place.

In case I haven't made it clear yet, what I'm saying is this pro-gramme is chock-full of knives. If you don't like sharp objects, don't go near it. It basically consists of half an hour of stab wounds being described aloud by Donal MacIntyre. During the first 30 seconds there's a hideous colour photograph of a man with a kitchen knife buried hilt-deep in his chest, and it just gets nastier from there.

OK, there's more to it than knives. A bit more. Five are actually showing a double-bill of MacIntyre episodes: the first one, dealing with Glasgow's criminal underclass, is the knifey one; the second episode, examining Liverpool's drug gangs, focuses more on guns, crowbars and nail bombs – which by this point simply makes a nice change.

Disappointingly, MacIntyre himself doesn't go 'undercover' at any point in either show – a crashing shame, as I wanted to hear him ask for heroin in a Scouse accent. Instead, he just pops by every now and then to shout at the camera, in a series of links shot against generic backdrops signifying 'urban hell' (i.e. graffiti, rubbish strewn about, cars with smashed windscreens, tattooed babies begging at cashpoints, etc). The show itself is cobbled together from interviews with local crime reporters, hospital staff and police, and footage of silhouetted youths bragging about the number of times they've seen people having their legs broken.

It's all rather depressing. What with this and *Ross Kemp on Gangs* (Sky One), it's a good week for hair-raising tales of urban violence and a bad week for songs about dandelions. The only question is why anyone would want to broadcast this kind of thing in the first place.

The answer? It's the 'Coast effect', innit? *Coast* was a huge hit for BBC2, partly because each week, cuddly middle-class people who lived on or near the coast tuned in to see if their locale was going to be on the telly. MacIntyre's *Toughest Towns* and Sky's grisly Ross Kemp travelogue are doing the same thing for townies.

The major difference is that while people tuning into *Coast* were rewarded with glorious scenery and classical music, MacIntyre and Co. offer nothing but incidents in grimy stairwells. And since the people who have to live in this squalor won't want to be reminded of it, its primary audience is middle-class urbanites seeking a vicarious thrill.

After all, if you've got no rolling scenery to speak of, you might as well brag about something else, such as how brave you are for living where you do – a stone's throw from the local sink estate, where people eat smack for breakfast and chop each other's arms off with sharpened bits of tin. You know: as seen on TV.

The Little Bo Peep Show [8 October 2005]

Kids rarely make me laugh, but a few months ago I saw a bunch of youngsters doing something hilarious. It was late afternoon – about 5 p.m. – and they were dancing in a West London street, belting out Eamon's number one hit 'F**k It (I Don't Want You Back)' at the top of their minuscule lungs. In case you're unfamiliar with the lyrics, they're as follows: 'Fuck what I said, it don't mean shit now/ Fuck the presents, might as well throw 'em out/ Fuck all those kisses, they didn't mean jack/ Fuck you, you ho – I don't want you back!'

Lovely. Anyway, the kids were word-perfect, and their spirited performance was accompanied by an equally spirited dance routine. This was happening in the centre of a relatively busy pavement a stone's throw from Olympia, so every few seconds the kids were passed by a disapproving adult – which just made them sing that little bit louder. The words were rude, but the innocent joy on their faces was a marvel to behold.

I was reminded of this while watching *Whatever Happened to the Mini Pops?* (C4), a documentary examining the storm that erupted in 1983 when Channel 4 broadcast a series in which kids impersonated pop stars.

On its original outing, *Mini Pops* actually did pretty well in the ratings. I'd imagine the core audience consisted of doting grandmothers who smell faintly of biscuits – you know: the sort of person who actually buys those hand-painted porcelain figurines of Little Bo Peep that get advertised in the *News of the World* magazine. The sort of harmless old love who thinks kiddywinks are charming no matter what they're doing – and who, if you showed them a gory reconstruction of the My Lai massacre re-enacted by toddlers, would simply point at the kids' outsized shoes and gently chuckle themselves to sleep.

Yes, grandmas enjoyed *Mini Pops*. But children didn't. Not normal ones, anyway. I was twelve, and can still recall recoiling in horror at the sight of it – but only because I thought they were a bunch of show-offs. The papers, however, were outraged – because unbeknown to the simpering grandmothers who loved it, it was a disgusting assault on the innocence of youth that bordered on child pornography.

Given the size and nature of the furore surrounding the show, you'd expect any archive copies to have been erased, impounded or picked up with tongs and tossed into a pot of molten steel by a man wearing a biohazard suit. But no. Consequently, this documentary features plenty of footage from the original *Mini Pops* series itself – which now doesn't seem pornographic at all, just ill-advised and rather creepy.

Don't get me wrong. It's undeniably distressing to watch a

heavily made-up pre-pubescent girl dancing in a nightdress while singing about 'making love'. But there's something funny about it too – funny because the poor bastards filming it had no idea anything was amiss in the first place. As far as they were concerned, she was just doing a cute Sheena Easton impersonation (which, in all fairness, she was).

The documentary contains interviews with the series creator, the choreographer and the commissioning editor, none of whom saw the criticism coming: a bit like a team of well-meaning bakers who've accidentally created a child's birthday cake in the shape of a penis, and served it up at a party without noticing. It's hard not to feel sorry for them.

And as for the Mini Pops themselves, now in their late twenties and early thirties? Well, judging by the interviews on offer here, they've got nothing but fond memories of the show itself, and some residual sourness about the arguments that surrounded it.

One thing's for sure: they're far less bitter than any past *Pop Idol* or *X Factor* contestant you care to mention. Especially Steve Brookstein – who, ironically enough, is probably impersonating Sheena Easton somewhere right now, just to make ends meet. But that's showbiz.

Thank God for Harold Bishop   [15 October 2005]

You know that feeling when you unexpectedly bump into somebody you were at school with years ago, and they look far older than they used to, and you find yourself staring at the silvery streaks in their hair, and the way their face has puffed out and gone saggy, and their stoop, and their middle-aged clothing, and their yellowing, desperate eyes, and you think 'I hope I don't look as bad as that', and then you realise it's not an old schoolfriend at all but your own reflection in a shop window, and you come to understand, fully and permanently, that youth has deserted you forever, and that basically you might as well be dead? You know that feeling?

Well, that's the feeling I got watching the twentieth anniversary episode of *Neighbours*, which is on this week.

I haven't seen *Neighbours* in years, so I wasn't sure what to expect. As it is, it starts like any other episode. The theme tune is as colon-twitchingly cheesy as ever. Less reassuring is the fact that most of the 'young' cast members look about nine years old.

OK, so *Neighbours* has traditionally had a lot of teenagers in its cast – but surely they never looked *this* young? During the title sequence, which, as per tradition, displays each Ramsay Street householder in turn like a lab specimen, the cast seemed to decrease in age before my very eyes, to the point where I actively expected it to end on a shot of a foetus in a crop top grinning down the lens.

Thank God, then, for Harold Bishop, who looks precisely the same as he always did – just slightly more so. His is probably the friendliest face on television – a cross between ten Toytown mayors and a baby. Furthermore, something about his mannerisms reminds me of a man pushing his cheeks between a tubby pair of breasts then spluttering side to side for comic effect. So thank God for him.

He's not the only old face hanging round the street, mind: Stefan Dennis is back as Paul Robinson. I've got no idea how long that's been going on, nor do I know how come he's lost a leg, or why all the other Neighbours seem to hate him *because* he's lost a leg. But to be honest I doubt it really matters.

So. You think you're getting a contemporary episode starring Harold and Paul and a bunch of nine-year-olds – when suddenly a load of characters from yesteryear show up, thanks to an improbable storyline in which glamorous former resident Annalise, now a famous film-maker, returns to screen her documentary about Ramsay Street.

Next thing you know, blast-from-the-past Joe Mangel's strolling around Erinsborough, rubbing shoulders with Phil, Lance, Doug and God knows who else, all of whom are greyer, fatter, or more knobbly and wizened than you recall – turning what's intended as a cheery retrospective salute to a much-loved soap into a heart-breaking visual meditation on the ageing process.

And just as you've come to terms with that, the show goes into freefall: Annalise screens her film, and the entire episode turns into a bizarre clipshow in which former cast members reprise their old roles for a few seconds apiece. And again, they all look a bit old and puffy – even Holly Vallance, who only left about five minutes ago.

Scott and Charlene are notable by their absence – although Annalise has thoughtfully included footage of their Ramsay Street wedding, apparently by going back in time and hiring a four-man camera crew. Having tested our suspension of disbelief with that, it's a shame they didn't go the whole hog and include updates from those characters who left Erinsborough in a coffin. I'd have loved to see, say, Jim Robinson bellowing a few lines from heaven (never spoke without shouting, that man).

Anyway, by the end you're left feeling monumentally blank: a bit like someone who's just had 20 minutes of their life stolen by an idiot. In other words, it's classic *Neighbours*. Here's to another two decades of televised Valium.

The Jeremy Kyle Show   [22 October 2005]

Breaking a leg. Watching a burglar shoot your cat. Eating a punnet of vomit and faeces. Unpleasant experiences all – but none, surely, is quite as unpleasant as grimly chewing your way through an entire edition of *The Jeremy Kyle Show* (ITV1).

Officially, it's described as a 'confrontational talkshow in which guests thrash out their conflicts, dilemmas and relationship issues in front of a studio audience', although that doesn't come close to capturing the flavour of it. That just makes it sound like Trisha, the show it's replaced. It isn't like Trisha. It's worse. It makes Trisha look like a dainty philanthropists' tea dance.

The key word in that official description is 'confrontational', because Jeremy's USP, you see, is that he's unafraid to hurl abuse at his hapless idiot guests. So when some greasy bi-toothed, boss-eyed scumball is guffawing about how many times he shoved it up his girlfriend's mother, Kyle shouts something like 'You amoeba of a man!' The audience applaud, the chav is humbled, and Jeremy seems secretly pleased.

In other words, everything about *The Jeremy Kyle Show* is completely and utterly horrid, starting with Jeremy Kyle himself. At first glance, he looks like a cross between Matthew Wright and a bored carpet salesman. Harmless, you think. But then something draws you back for a second look, and this time – ugh!

I mean, look at his eyes. There's a spine-chilling glint to them – it reminds me of the 'shimmering pupils' effect used in Russell T. Davies's *The Second Coming* to denote which characters were agents of Satan. Not that I'm saying Kyle himself is an agent of Satan, you understand. I'm just saying you could easily cast him as one. Especially if you wanted to save money on special effects.

You know that weird 'thing' about Nicky Campbell? That indefinable 'thing' that makes him ever so slightly creepy, like you wouldn't want to get stuck in a lift with him, because you half suspect he might suddenly pull a Stanley knife from his sleeve and start wildly slashing at you with a terrifyingly blank expression on his face? Well Jeremy Kyle's got that same 'thing' about him, but amplified by a factor of twelve.

Every time I see him, it's like someone's just walked over my grave. I'm starting to think it's some kind of premonition. The spirit world is reaching out, trying to warn me that Jeremy Kyle is somehow destined to kill me. I'm not sensing the word 'murder' – chances are it'll be an accident. Yeah. That's it: next week I'm crossing the road and bang – Kyle's vehicle inadvertently mows me down as it carries him en route to his shit and awful show.

Brrr. Just typing this makes me shudder. Look, if I'm found dead in the next few weeks, can someone tear this out and hand it to the police?

I'm veering off-topic. Back to the programme itself, which is infected by a curious linguistic virus: everyone in the studio uses the phrase 'on national television' at least five times per minute, meaning the show consists entirely of exchanges like this:

Seacow: 'Oh, so you're admitting, on national television, that you cheated?'

Baboon: 'Ha! I can't believe you can sit there on national television, and accuse me of that – on national television!'

Satan: 'Woah, you two – is this any way to behave on national television?'

Do they always talk like this? If an argument breaks out in their kitchen, do they say things like, 'I can't believe you're telling me this now – in the kitchen.' Well?

Actually, perhaps they're just trying to remind themselves where they are. After all, sitting there with Jeremy and his iridescent pupils glistening before them, confronted by a studio audience so ugly they'd make John Merrick spew down the inside of his face-bag, the poor sods could be forgiven for forgetting they were on national television and starting to believe they were somewhere in the bowels of hell instead.

As could the viewers at home.

Mariah Carey bullshit   [29 October 2005]

So winter's virtually upon us. The nights are cold and dark. The skies are bruised and drippy. Bird-flu victims litter the pavements. It's depressing. No wonder all you want to do is stay indoors swaddled in your duvet, drinking tea and watching *The X Factor* (ITV1). Who can blame you?

After all, some of this year's contestants can genuinely sing – by which I mean they invest their performances with genuine passion and soul, instead of just doling out the usual technical wibbly-wobbly note-bending you see in contests like this (you know – the sort of hark-at-me Mariah Carey bullshit that only the very thickest breed of moron could possibly enjoy).

Yes, some of this year's contestants are the best yet. And some very very much aren't.

Take Chico – or to give him his full name, Chico Time. Chico can't really sing at all – not even the wibbly-wobbly way. All he can do is yelp like a dog getting its prostate examined by a vet with sandpaper hands. That's a drawback in a competition like this, and Chico knows it. Fortunately, he's hit on a way to compensate for his lack of vocal expertise: leaping about like a ninny. He also grins, flashes his pecs and shrieks 'It's Chico time!' quite a lot.

Chico's performances are so rubbish, they quickly plunge beyond 'crap', 'rotten' or 'abysmal', drop off the bottom of the chart, and reappear at the top, next to 'brilliant', 'visionary' and 'epoch-making'. He inadvertently borders on greatness. As such, he thoroughly deserves his place in the contest.

Unlike Journey South, a pair of excruciatingly earnest male Gillette models who specialise in shouting and looking slightly pained. I say 'slightly' pained – I mean 'extremely'. Each time they hit a particularly sincere section of the lyric, they go all red-faced and funny-looking, like they've been stuck in a lift for three hours and need to go to the toilet, but can't because there are ladies present. They creep me out.

And as for their name – they're not fooling anyone with this 'we're two northern lads who got in a caravan and headed down to London to seek our fortune, hence Journey South' bullshit. It's a euphemism for cunnilingus. I know it, you know it . . . hell, even Kate Thornton knows it, and she probably doesn't even have a vagina – just a smooth Barbie-style bump. Journey South. For God's sake. I mean, come *on*.

Who else is in it? Well, there's Shayne (good voice, pleading eyes, looks like every male *Hollyoaks* cast member ever rolled into one), Phillip (so off-key last week he seemed to be showcasing a new avant-garde vocal style which takes utter disregard for melody as its starting point), Maria (top-heavy Mariah Carey type), the Conway Sisters (a Poundstretcher version of the Corrs), and Chenai (so blub-prone she's in danger of crying all the fluid out of her body).

Which leaves us with three genuinely excellent performers. There's Nicholas (who last week managed to cover Marvin Gaye's 'Let's Get It On' without desecrating it in the slightest), Brenda (sassy Aretha Franklin type with a voice the size of Jupiter) and finally, forty-one-year-old Andy, who according to the official *X Factor* website 'works as a Dustbin Man' – not a 'binman', you'll note, but a 'Dustbin Man' – which makes him sound like some kind of waste-disposing superhero. They keep banging on about him being a binman as though it makes him part of a different species, which is a touch patronising, and probably a little depressing for any binmen watching at home, hunched before the screen in their Dickensian hovel. Anyway, whatever he is, he can certainly bloody sing.

In my book, those final three make equally deserving winners. Simon, Louis and Sharon might as well call the contest off now and manage one each. But sod it, like I said, it's almost winter, and bird flu's on the way. They should stay on air. Cooped in our hatches, we're going to need all the telly we can get.

. . . And it smells good too [5 November 2005]

So we return, initially, to *The X Factor* (ITV1), since last week's edition can't pass without comment. Not because arse-voiced skittering marionette Chico Time's still in the running, although that's incredible in itself. No. What we're interested in here is Sharon Osbourne, and her ever more disturbing preoccupation with contestant Shayne Ward.

A fortnight ago she yelped that she wanted to grab hold of his 'private parts' while he sang a high note. Last Saturday she outdid even that. The twenty-one-year-old Justin Timber-like had just performed a yawnsome trudge through Bryan Adams's 'Summer Of '69' when he found himself impaled on an outrageously flirtatious spike in chatter, courtesy of La Osbourne. 'I've got something to give you,' she cooed, batting her eyelashes. 'It's warm and it feels good – and it smells good too.'

It sounded like the set-up for a *Carry On* gag – ah, I get it, it's a mug of cocoa! – but as it turned out, there wasn't a punchline. She really was talking about her Jemima Puddleduck, and didn't care who knew it. What's she going to do for an encore this week? Draw him a picture? Vault the desk and wipe it down his leg?

For all their faults, it's hard to imagine Simon Cowell – and impossible to imagine Louis Walsh – spouting similar stuff at the female contestants. 'Oh, Chenai! Chenai, Chenai, Chenai! I've got something to give you Chenai. It's long and it's straight and it's twitching with joy. And what's more – it stinks.'

It's all the more curious since the great British public recently decreed Sharon their 'Most Popular TV Expert' at the National Television Awards. An expert in what exactly? Behaving like a mad aunt at a wedding? Going into sexual meltdown? Gordon Ramsay was a runner-up – perhaps if he'd livened up *Kitchen Nightmares* by threatening to bugger the chefs, he'd have won (although he'd also have had to hand back all those hygiene awards).

Currently, all Sharon does is ooh and ahh over the contestants as though they're made of freshly-baked gingerbread. Still, perhaps it's part of the build-up to the moment in the final few weeks when she finally snaps – just like last year when she launched into a bizarre personal attack on luckless Steve Brookstein. Here's hoping.

Anyway, on to *Bleak House* (BBC1), whose place in the weekday schedules is enough to make you take leave of your senses and get all dewy-eyed about the BBC's contribution to our collective spiritual well-being. It's the primetime soap equivalent of *Deadwood*, and I don't mean that disparagingly.

Unlike every other TV previewer on Earth, I'm a scarcely educated ignoramus who's never read *Bleak House*, nor had it read aloud to me in sonorous tones by a mortar-boarded master. So I can't tell you how faithful Andrew Davies's adaptation is, or whether Johnny Vegas's repellent, slobbering Krook is so stunningly accurate it's like he's stepped off the page and blown off in your living room. I can't even tell you precisely what's going on, because just like *Deadwood*, my brain seems to be several steps behind the actual storyline at any given moment – but in an enjoyable, wallowing sort of a way.

In other words, I like it a lot. The one criticism I can muster is that it suffers slightly from cameo-overload syndrome. Occasionally the absurd number of well-known faces involved makes the process of watching it feel like lolling on a sofa, drunk, at Christmas, while a relative systematically fast-forwards their way through a comprehensive DVD box set containing every television drama serial ever made.

Come to think of it, just about the only famous person who hasn't shown up is Sharon Osbourne. Well, not yet. Perhaps the final episode revolves around a mad gothic aunt at a wedding, coming on to the best man, berating the groom and biting the head off a bat. Who knows? I haven't read it. And don't lie: neither have you.

Slough of despond   [12 November 2005]

Everybody hurts. Everybody bonks their head against the hull of despair now and then. Everybody finds themselves drifting along the pavement, fuelled only by the gentle throb of sadness – their eyes fixed on a distant thundering nowhere, while the rest of the world babbles idiotically in the background. Everybody's turned their smile upside down and felt it drip off their face. Yes, everybody hurts. Everybody's got a headful of boo-hoo.

Well, OK – not everybody. Just people who live in Slough. And can you blame them? It's a concrete-and-brickwork heckhole; a broken diagram of a town, famous solely for being (a) the setting for *The Office*, and (b) the subject of a Betjeman poem that wished a blitz upon it. Slough looks like it was never actually built, merely crapped into position by a misanthropic, mediocre God. It's not a town – it's a misery engine.

And that's why the positive-thinking gurus faced with *Making Slough Happy* (BBC2) have their work cut out for them. Yes, it's 'social experiment' time, folks – a new series in which a team of 'happiness experts' descend on Slough in a bid to stop the populace sobbing openly in the streets. Heading up the project is former journalist Richard Reeves, author of a book on happiness in the workplace and a man so eerily, robotically pleasant, you wouldn't be surprised if his face suddenly fell off, revealing a set of circuit boards and flashing LEDs.

But Reeves isn't quite as frightening – or as happy – as Dr Richard Stevens, a hippyish, silver-haired 'psychologist of well-being' who we first encounter literally prancing about in a dingly dell, grinning so violently he's in danger of splitting his face in two.

Together, they're unstoppable. Their first action is to draft a Happiness Manifesto for the Sloughsters – a ten-point personal improvement plan that includes simple advice like 'take some exercise', 'count your blessings' and 'have a good laugh'.

Reeves, bless him, walks around Slough handing this document to glum passers-by. The sequence in which he stands in a branch of Gregg's, attempting to pass the happiness bug on to a line of people miserably queuing for pastries, is heartbreaking.

Stevens, meanwhile, is leading a group of volunteers into a forest, where he encourages them to dance around and, yes, hug trees.

On the face of it, all the experts' advice sounds insipid and moronic – but you can bet your sweet bippy that if you stifled your cynical snorting and followed their suggestions, you'd end up feeling far better than when you started. That's the trouble with jovial hippies. They're often right – the happy bastards.

Happily fertilised [19 November 2005]

It's a day much like any other. Bob and Mike are dangling from a mucus rope, slowly revolving, with their bodies intertwined . . . when quite without warning, translucent penises begin to emerge from the back of their heads. Said penises writhe and intertwine also: undulating, throbbing, swapping sperm between the pair of them. Finally, when they're all pumped out, our loving couple let go of the rope, tumble to the ground and wriggle away – both happily fertilised.

It sounds like the sort of sexually confusing dream you might have after eating six pounds of cheese and falling asleep in a sleeper carriage, but amazingly, this whole psychedelic adult-fun encounter is(a) entirely real, and (b) broadcast in close-up, slap-bang in the middle of BBC1.

Of course, I've made it sound more shocking than it actually is. When I say 'Bob and Mike', what I actually mean is 'an anonymous pair of hermaphrodite slugs'. I don't know what their real names are. Although the one on the left definitely looks like a 'Bob'. But that bit about the penises growing out the back of their heads? I'm not making that up.

But perhaps Sir David Attenborough is. Because *Life in the Undergrowth* (BBC1), Sir Dave's latest natural history epic, contains so many jaw-dropping moments it's hard to shake the suspicion he might be having us on. He might've had a bonk on the head and gone a bit crazy, and convinced the BBC to let him spend two years making a series about things that only exist in the darkest corners of his mind.

The footage is the clincher – it's far too clear, far too spectacular and hypnotic. It must be CGI. They've plugged a USB lead into his brain and asked him to dream really hard down the pipe.

It's the only explanation. At one point he introduces us to a ruddy great foot-long centipede that hangs from the roof of caves in order to catch and eat bats. Come on, pull the other one, Dave – it's got a translucent penis sticking out of it.

Lord knows what Freud would make of the sexual connotations of the centipede dream – not to mention the same-sex snot-rope slug-shag incident I mentioned in the first paragraph. In fact, sex is clearly one of Dave's overriding obsessions, because he returns to it again and again.

Take the segment with the arachnid 'harvestman' thingamajig, which attracts females by building a showroom full of eggs, then walking around methodically polishing them all day, like an eight-legged jewellery-store owner. Initially, it's all rather charming, the sight of this chap impressing the ladies by setting out his stall and keeping it tidy. You almost expect him to pop on a bow tie and wax his moustache.

But no. Before long, Dave wanders down a hot velvet alley in his head, and it's bumpy-thrusty time. A shot of yet *another* translucent penis fills the screen – and it's *Lovers' Guide* time, Davey-style: 'He has a rod with which he injects his sperm. He withdraws, and she's been fertilised.'

Yeah, yeah. So far, so human. Come on, Sir D – get sick on our ass.

'Half an hour later, she lowers her white tubular ovipositor . . . she thrusts the egg into the floor of the nest and covers it with a thin blanket of mud.'

Hoo boy. I tell you, this is some of the hottest white tubular ovipositor action I've ever seen. That egg-thrust? And the thin blanket of mud? That's one heck of a money shot right there. I give it five stars. Bring a tissue.

I'm being both flippant and a moron: *Life in the Undergrowth* is a fantastic programme – captivating, stunning, and occasionally downright poetic. And I'm not fit to wriggle under Sir David Attenborough's boots.

Eye-brain mindwipe syndrome [26 November 2005]

Why, it seems like only yesterday we were discussing the last series of *I'm a Celebrity . . . Get Me Out of Here!* (ITV1) – when we thrilled to the antics of, um . . . Janet Street-Porter. And. Er. Oh yes: Vic and Nancy. And all the other people who were in it. Those were great days, weren't they? Vintage times. Ahhh. I'd get dewy-eyed just thinking about it, if I could just remember what happened.

Unlike good drama or comedy, which can resonate somewhere round the back of your soul for years after the event, your memories of *I'm a Celeb* wither on the vine the moment the credits roll. The same is true of every other reality show ever: they exist in the moment, nowhere else. Nothing wrong with that, in moderation: that's their job. They're like a fun, throwaway version of the news.

Trouble is, it's getting to the point where I'm forgetting what's happening while it occurs. It's a medical condition known as Concurrent Eye-Brain Mindwipe Syndrome, and it makes writing a column like this very tricky. I have to record each episode and watch it six times over, taking extensive notes as I go. And even then, I still thrash about with astonishment each time the camera cuts to Jenny Frost. Try as I might, I simply can't remember she's there.

Recalling the others is easier. David Dickinson's a doddle, because he's so audio-visually arresting. With his sagging 32A breasts, cow-length eyelashes and oaky complexion, he vaguely resembles a retired Thai ladyboy who's jacked in the nightclub act and applied for a DJ position at Magic FM. Unforgettable.

Then there's Sid Owen, who's easy to remember on account of his sole facial expression – a cross between a confused boy and a frightened pug. The moment he leaves the jungle someone should cast him as an adult Ron Weasley in a down-at-heel 're-imagining' of the J. K. Rowling books: *Harry Potter and the Fight Down Wetherspoons*, or something similar. No idea what happens in it, but with Sid in the cast, the job's half done. Innit.

Carol Thatcher's also hard to miss, chiefly because every time she opens her gob, gruesome memories of her mother pump through the veins in my head, and I have to clench my fists so hard my knuckles pop out and shatter against the wall.

Annalise from *Neighbours* is the first one I really have trouble with, because she looks identical to the Annalise from *Neighbours* I spent countless afternoons developing a pathetic stoner's crush on ten years ago. Either she hasn't aged, or *I'm a Celeb*'s become so ephemeral, it's ceasing to exist before it occurs, thereby causing a loop in the space-time continuum that's allowed her to step straight out of 1995, unscathed, into the present.

The others drift in and out of my head like repressed abuse memories. There's Antony Costa (who looks like a novelty inflatable condemned man), Jilly Goolden (plum-gobbed ghost-train skeleton), Jimmy Osmond (played by Teddy Ruxpin, the creepy 1980s bear), and Sheree Murphy (about whom – and this is a *fact* – it's impossible to say anything funny or interesting).

Of these, only Antony Costa has made me laugh so far – not because of anything he's done on the show, but because of his docile expression in his worm-eating publicity shot.

Still. Early days.

Finally, what is there to say about *OFI Sunday* (ITV1) except: how many weeks, d'you reckon, until Chris Evans slows to a halt in mid-sentence, stares down the lens for a full minute, then silently produces a handgun and starts walking round the studio, firing wildly at the crew, the cameras, and the audience? How many weeks till that occurs? Not sure if William Hill are taking bets on it yet, but I say three weeks. A friend of mine reckons one.

Who's right? Doesn't matter. Regardless of the timeframe, it's clearly destined to happen.

– *It didn't happen.*

Phil Mitchell fighting a reindeer [10 December 2005]

When, in your head, does December stop being December and start being Christmas instead? For me, it's nothing to do with the physical signs you see in the street – lamp posts swaddled in fairy lights, a drunk in a Santa hat throwing up in a doorway, shoppers kicking each other to death to get their hands on an Xbox 360 . . . that's part of the build-up, not the event itself. Because as far as I'm concerned, Christmas only truly arrives the moment BBC1 unveils its annual Christmas idents.

Last year's offering featured a group of kids on Christmas-pudding-shaped space-hoppers bouncing around a mock Arctic landscape. The idea for this was selected via a *Blue Peter* competition, which is about as warm and cuddly and all-round BBC as it gets. I've no idea what's in store this year, although I'd love to see any of the following: (1) Phil Mitchell fighting a reindeer; (2) Some baby Daleks building a snowman while a kindly grandpa Dalek looks on, smoking a pipe; (3) a claymation baby Jesus playing Swingball with Pingu; (4) Charlie from *Casualty* pooing into a stocking (hey, it might happen).

(I know what I don't want to see: a special Christmas edition of that nightmarish CGI-heavy advert the BBC started running a few weeks back to promote their range of digital services – you know, the one where a swarm of babbling human heads flies over the moors, forms itself into the shape of one giant face made up of hundreds of little ones, then squawks at you about how bloody brilliant the BBC is. Once seen, never forgotten, but not in a positive sense. Something about it makes me genuinely giddy: it's the sort of thing I'd expect to see in my mind's eye during brain surgery, or while fighting off a fever in a hot and airless room. Brrrr. I'd rather not even think about it.)

Whichever yuletide option the BBC decides to go with, chances are it'll be (a) as slick and sophisticated as being fellated by a butler, and (b) virtually omnipresent. Because that's the way all such TV 'furniture' seems to be heading. Gone are the days of the simple, garish BBC1 'revolving globe', or the Thames TV 'London skyline rising from the waters' ident – chunks of TV ephemera which look laughably amateurish compared to their modern equivalents, yet possess approximately seventy-eight times the charm. Where once a simple station logo would suffice, we're now offered polished widescreen mini-movies, smug optical haikus and, worst of all, intrusive little pop-ups telling us what we're currently watching, what's coming next, what we should think about it, and what docile pricks we are for sitting there and withstanding it all.

And in case mere visual spam isn't enough, in recent years all continuity announcers have been trained to butt in and start bellowing over the end titles of your favourite programme within 0.5 picoseconds of the first end credit appearing.

Not that it matters really – because the era of individual end-sequences is over anyway. Today, the precise length and layout of all closing credits is strictly controlled – Channel 4, for instance, specifies all dialogue or voiceovers must finish prior to the start of the credits (so their announcer can shout all over them), while text is kept to the left-hand side of the screen (so a big CGI bum can crap pictures of upcoming shows, spin-off books, holiday snaps, etc, all over the right-hand side).

Thus the branded furniture bleeds ever further into the programmes themselves, until individual shows start to feel more like strands in a single evening-long programme – the BBC show, the ITV show, the Channel 4 show, and so on. Good news for networks craving strong customer awareness, bad news for anyone who just wants to watch something decent on telly without being shouted at, patronised, or congratulated on the supposed 'lifestyle choice' some marketing prinkle insists they've just made.

If you want a vision of the future, imagine a C4 logo stamping on an end-credit sequence – for ever. Bah humbug.

Burned into the memory [31 December 2005]

Phew. Bang goes another thrill-packed year of sitting on the sofa staring at a box in the corner of the room. Usually, this *Screen Burn* awards ceremony round-up thing would explore some sort of overriding annual 'theme'. A while back, when Simon Cowell first appeared on our screens, the defining theme was 'cruelty'. The year John Leslie ran into difficulties, it was 'celebrities in trouble'. This time round, I'm jiggered if I can spot a theme. Looking back through the past 365 days, the shows that stand out are a pretty disparate bunch – so maybe the significant trend of 2005 was 'trendless incongruence'. Yeah. Because that makes tons of sense.

Enough quibbling. Let's dish out the awards. First up, the brand new Most Undeservedly Pleased With Itself award, which goes to the David LaChapelle teaser trailer for Channel 4's *Lost*, in which the cast danced around in slow motion while Beth from Portishead sang about feeling 'ever so lo-o-st' – almost impossibly, this managed to be even more pretentious and annoying than the series itself. If, upon seeing it, you turned to an equally moronic companion and said, 'Ooh, that looks interesting,' feel free to spend 2006 punching some sense into your own stupid face.

Lost also bags the Single Most Preposterous Episode award, for the edition portraying Charlie Junkie's rise to Madchester glory. Years ago the Comic Strip made a film called *Strike!*, which depicted a hilariously inaccurate Hollywood version of the miner's strike: *Lost*'s Driveshaft episode did much the same for the Oasis story. If you missed it, it's worth hunting down on DVD, just so you can point at it and laugh.

The award for the show Most Impervious to Criticism goes to *Jamie's School Dinners* in which Sir Flappy-Tongued Bumface himself saved the lives of millions of children – or so it seemed, given the orgy of self-fellating middle-class rapture that followed.

This was campaigning television all right, and while it's hard to disagree with the policy change it instigated, it's worth remembering that as a TV show it was merely preaching to the converted – a piece of entertainment laser-targeted at snobby plasma-screen dickwits whose Smeg fridges were already bursting with organic produce in the first place. These nauseating twats aren't trying to feed a family of five on a sink-estate budget: they wouldn't dream of feeding their precious Jake anything that hadn't come out of a Nigel Slater cookbook, and by Christ they're proud of it. For them,

Jamie's School Dinners merely heralded another golden opportunity to sit around smugly tutting at everyone else in the world. Well, up theirs. I don't want their kids to be healthy. I prefer them fat and wheezing. Large, slow targets are easier to hit.

The award for Most Utterly Stomach-Churning Person Imaginable is always a hotly contested category, and this year is no exception. An early candidate, bossy-gobbed Saira from *The Apprentice*, was soon overtaken by Maxwell from *Big Brother 6*, the mesmerisingly awful and overconfident bully-boy who managed to single-handedly evoke memories of every witless belching thug you've ever met. At least he did while he was actually in the house – the moment he stepped outside the *BB* crucible it became impossible to remember quite why he'd seemed so horrid. In fact, he's probably really nice – which means the winner, without a shadow of a doubt, is ITV's Jeremy Kyle, possibly the most disturbing morning talkshow host the world has ever seen.

Alternately bullying and then comforting his guests like a one-man Good Cop/Bad Cop routine, Kyle is one part Jerry Springer, two parts Nicky Campbell, and three parts Guantánamo Bay. I'm convinced he's genuinely insane, and wouldn't be at all surprised if I tuned in one morning to find him slapping a guest round the face with his dick. Well done Jeremy. You're Beelzebub's Man of the Year.

The award for the Most Giddying Afternoon of Television goes to the 21 July news coverage when, a mere fortnight after four wankers blew themselves up on the tube, an apparent copycat incident sent the news networks into overdrive. Press briefings, anxious shots of buses, armed officers ordering a man near Downing Street to lie on the ground . . . several times there was simply too much news all happening at once, so they had to go split-screen. It all resembled a hideous real-life version of *24*.

24 itself, incidentally, wins the Most Disgusting Thinly-Veiled Propaganda award for the way it suddenly started shoe-horning in all manner of unhinged neo-con bullshit into its fourth series, peaking with a shameful episode in which a lawyer representing a civil rights group called 'Amnesty Global' was depicted as a loathsome, shifty ne'er-do-well hell-bent on aiding and abetting terrorists – largely because he tried to stop CTU torturing someone for the 10 billionth time that series.

In the States, the series subsequently developed a cult following amongst dickless, tooth-gnashing Rush Limbaugh types. Co-creator Joel Surnow told the *Washington Times* that to label the show as conservative-leaning would be 'a fair assessment', adding that, 'doing something with any sense of reality to it seems conservative'.

Hello? Sense of reality? *24*? The show that opened with a gorgeous, pouting lesbian terrorist-for-hire blowing up and parachuting from a passenger jet – and grew steadily less plausible as it went along? The show in which Jack's wife got amnesia and his daughter got menaced by a mountain lion? In which Jack Bauer once literally came back from the dead? Someone's talking out of their backside, aren't they, Joel? Mind you, I still watched it from beginning to end, so what does that make me? (Answer: an idiot, obviously.)

Some quick and final honours now. Breakthrough Star of the Year has to be Sir Alan Sugar from *The Apprentice*, whose relentless curmudgeonliness was a joy to behold; the Most Awesome Plunge in Dignity award goes to *Big Brother*'s Kinga (who thinks an 'alcopop' is the noise you hear when you pull the bottle out); Most Hideous Single Image goes to the BBC's nightmarish 'jabbering heads' promo (eventually banned for being too damn weird); Daftest Postmodern Foray was Sky's daily Michael Jackson trial reconstruction.

Most Excellent Comedies Not Co-Written By Myself were *The Thick of It* and *Peep Show*; Best Dramas were *Deadwood*, *Bleak House* and *The Shield*; and the Best Overall Show of the Year was clearly, obviously and undeniably *Doctor* Bloody Brilliant *Who*.

As for 2006, my early tips are weirdy time-travel cop drama *Life on Mars* and warm, pant-pissingly funny sitcom *The IT Crowd*.

There. That's your lot. Auld Lang Syne, etc.

Reality itself has a hangover [14 January 2006]

Blech. Following the boozy snack-food excesses of the festive season, it takes about a fortnight to reorientate yourself with the sober normality of everyday life, so the sudden reappearance of *Celebrity Big Brother* (C4) on our screens can't possibly be a good thing. It's like staring through a porthole into an alternate universe where reality itself has a hangover.

So who's in and who's out? Here's your very own cut-out-and-lose primer.

First up, basketball star Dennis Rodman, a man about as famous in Britain as Bernard Matthews is in the States. Brooding silently like an Easter Island statue in a baseball cap, Dennis is so assured of his inherent coolness he scarcely speaks, communicating instead by running his hand over the nearest available female. Sexually speaking, he's constantly 'on amber', and I'm assuming by the time you read this he'll have shagged the arse off everyone in the house. Including, with any luck, George Galloway.

Galloway himself comes across much as he does in the outside world, i.e. as the sort of squat, shifty-looking human pepperpot you might cast as the chief villain in a children's programme about a dead-eyed maniac who secretly strangles cats in his bathroom. I wouldn't trust him as far as I could throw him (although if I was throwing him over the side of a ferry, that might be a fair old distance).

He's far less likeable than Michael Barrymore, a man whose own passport documentation lists his occupation as 'troubled comic'. His teary five-minute walk up to the house made for excruciating viewing, but once inside he struck me as refreshingly sane. Well, OK, not entirely – but a damn sight saner than the *Daily Mirror*'s hate-campaign coverage of his antics, that's for sure. Just for the record, his impersonation of Hitler was absolutely bloody hilarious.

My current favourite is Dead or Alive singer Pete Burns, who appears to have stepped straight from an episode of *When Surgeons Go Mental*. His face is astoundingly strange – neither ugly nor beautiful, yet endlessly riveting. If humans ever mate with cartoon characters, their offspring will look like this. Sometimes he resembles Lily Savage as reimagined by the Simpsons; other times Janice from *The Muppet Show* (Google 'Janice Muppets' and click on 'images' if you don't believe me).

Aside from all the work on his lips, cheeks and eyes, he's also undergone a tongue-sharpening procedure; consequently he's a fountain of caustic asides and inventive language, drawling gems like 'I've had insults thrown over me like a bucket of cum' without so much as blinking (come to think of it, he probably can't blink, not without his scalp snapping in two). He should win.

Finally, we'll skip past Rula Lenska, Maggot, Preston, Faria and Traci – because they're dull – and concentrate instead on the twin horror-show of Chantelle Houghton and Jodie Marsh. The former is a crashing nonentity suddenly afforded the chance to bask in the public eye; the latter doesn't seem quite so talented.

Chantelle, while thick, has enough sense not to strop around the place crying and bellowing, in the thickest manner possible, about how everyone says she's thick. Whereas Jodie hasn't quite worked out how the relationship between 'things you do' and 'things people say about you' works. Which explains why, if her time in the house is anything to go by, the poor girl's doomed to spend 50 per cent of her life complaining that the tabloids have labelled her a 'slag', and the remaining 50 per cent shoving her tits in people's faces and banging on about sex. It's not making her happy. With any luck she'll find love and snap out of it. She deserves some inner peace.

That's far too drippy a sentiment to end on, so I'll leave you by pointing out the tip of her nose, which looks like it's tried to grow in two different directions at once, and consequently resembles the business end of a chisel. She'll have someone's eye out with that. And catch it in her cleavage afterwards.

CHAPTER FOUR

In which George Galloway is examined again at close range, a terrifying face appears at the window, and Bono proves too annoying to inspire global salvation

Galloway to go   [27 January 2006]

I was at the *Big Brother* house on Wednesday night. Not to hurl bags of shit at George Galloway, you understand – I was there researching something I'm writing. And besides, security confiscated my bags of shit at the gate.

Anyway, once in, I was given the full tour. I got to go in the camera runs and everything. I peered through a window while Chantelle fixed her make-up. I witnessed Barrymore making a cup of tea in blistering close-up detail. I saw Maggot adjusting his balls. This was history in the making.

And it was also incredibly spooky: occasionally they shoot glances your way and you think they can see you – but all they're looking at is their own reflection, which, being celebrities, they never tire of.

Seeing Pete Burns's face-shaped surgeon's folly at close quarters sent a chill down my spine, but the most haunting sight was Galloway, pacing up and down in the kitchen, awaiting his inevitable eviction. It was like watching a polar bear losing its mind in the zoo, shuffling endlessly to and fro in a bid to silence the unhappy bellowing in its head.

He looked like a man on death row: a brightly coloured, Scooby-Doo kind of death row, but one with real doom lurking at the end of it. Or maybe that was just me, projecting what I knew of his utter public humiliation on to him. Maybe he was simply concentrating: picturing the mountainous stack of adoring fan mail from young voters he assumed he'd receive.

'Dear George – you is the best politician I has ever seen! I love the way you is so political with all your politics and that. Please can I have a signed photo because you is so sexy! Yours sincerely, a Nubile Fan Who Lives Within Driving Distance.'

But alas. About an hour later, he was out the door, to be greeted by what sounded like an explosion in a boo factory. Some crowd members shouted so hard their lungs exploded. Bits of splintered ribcage flew through the air. If Galloway wanted to make an impression, he succeeded. And if he wanted the impression to be that of a seething, swaggering, self-important bully, he succeeded spectacularly.

Because he could've ridden out all the cat stuff, all the dressing-up games. That's easily defused: just chuckle about it in your eviction interview, and hey, it's just a bit of fun. The humiliation would've been real, yet fleeting. What'll stick in people's minds, however, is his jaw-droppingly unpleasant behaviour in the days leading up to his eviction. Rounding on the nice-but-dim youngsters, taunting a recovering alcoholic, spluttering paranoid bile at every opportunity – I mean really. *What* a tosser.

In PR terms, it's hard to think of anything worse he could've done during his stay in the house. But I'll have a go. He could have (1) masturbated repeatedly on camera, staring the viewer straight in the eye; (2) pooed into a big bowl of flour in the middle of the kitchen; and (3) killed at least nine of his fellow housemates. But those are the only worse things I can think of. He's screwed.

Even so, you've got to hand it to him: when he shoots himself in the foot, he uses a cannon so big it takes his whole leg off.

The world's first satire war [10 February 2006]

So, then. Twelve cartoons appear in a Danish newspaper, prompting worldwide demonstrations and the occasional deadly riot, an Iranian newspaper hits back with a Holocaust doodling contest, and before you know it billions die in the world's first satire war.

Years from now, as survivors bury their dead, another Danish newspaper prints a satirical cartoon about the funeral service, sparking another round of riots and wars and people calling for the destruction of everything. And it all carries on until there's only one human left alive. Three hours of peace drift by, until he accidentally *thinks* about something satirical and offensive, and is so disgusted he burns himself.

At which point it's the turn of the cockroaches.

Tell you who I feel sorry for: one of the twelve Danish cartoonists, who clearly considered the whole thing a pretty fatuous exercise and instead of depicting Muhammad drew a schoolboy writing 'The editorial team of Jyllands-Posten is a bunch of re-actionary provocateurs' in Arabic on a blackboard. Right now he's doubtless quivering with the rest, knackered by a prank he never supported anyway.

He certainly won't be having fun. And I speak with a pinch of experience here, because in October 2004 I briefly considered going into hiding myself, when an extremely ill-advised joke I made at the end of a TV preview column in this newspaper's Saturday listings magazine prompted a wave of protests and death threats from several hundred people who took it very seriously indeed. The joke itself was based on an old bit of graffiti about Mrs Thatcher: 'Guy Fawkes, where are you now that we need you?' My version was updated, referred to President Bush, and in retrospect, didn't look as much like a joke as I originally thought it did, partic-ularly when it got passed around the internet under the heading 'UK Newspaper Calls for President's Assassination'.

The ensuing comments ranged from the comical ('If it hadn't been for the USA, your asshole would be speaking German right now' – what a party trick *that* would be) to the blood-curdling (such as the correspondent who advised me to stick close to build-ings and walk in a zigzag fashion if I wanted to avoid having my head blown off by his incredibly efficient sniper rifle). And it wasn't just me, no – almost everyone at the *Guardian* received similar missives, all thanks to me and my heeee-larious funny talk.

I was once asked to leave a dinner party on account of a tasteless joke I'd just made. That was pretty uncomfortable. Being asked to leave the planet feels considerably worse. Stewart Lee, co-creator of *Jerry Springer: The Opera*, does a nice bit in his latest stand-up routine about receiving threats: he says everyone's occasionally paranoid that other people don't like them, so it's jarring to dis-cover more than 50,000 people genuinely want you dead.

In this global media age, it's disconcertingly easy to infuriate everyone on Earth. We'll soon see the rise of a new field of coun-selling – dedicated support groups for people who've pissed off the world. Pariahs Anonymous.

The smoking gun [17 February 2006]

I wholeheartedly support the notion of banning smoking everywhere, for one entirely selfish reason: I've recently quit and don't
want to be tempted to start again. If no one else lights up around
me, I won't follow suit. Which means I'll live longer. And that's all
I care about. Sod freedom of choice for smokers. Sod their poxy
so-called 'human rights'. This is me we're talking about here. *Me*.

Mind you, I'm not convinced a simple ban is going to cut it. I've
got a far better idea – one that's firm, fair and pretty much final.
It's based on a scheme I originally conceived as an alternative to
London's congestion charge, and I offer it now, to the nation, free
of charge.

OK, so the congestion charge was supposed to reduce the number of cars in central London. Trouble is, it's far too complicated.
There's cameras and traffic zones and text-message payment systems and blah blah blah. It costs a fortune. And you'd get better
results if you replaced the whole thing with a sniper.

Yes, a sniper. Here's how it works: instead of charging people to
drive through busy parts of town, you simply announce that you've
paid a lone sniper to sneak around the city, hiding out on rooftops.
Every month he'll blow the heads off several random motorists: a
maximum of ten, say, and a minimum of five. You're free to drive
where you like, as often as you please – but you're taking a calcu-
lated risk each time you do so.

You'd announce the scheme, and at first no one would believe
you were serious. Indeed, you'd trade on that: perhaps nothing
happens for the first couple of days. People carry on as normal.
Then on day three: BAM BAM BAM. The sniper takes out not one,
but *three* separate motorists, in different parts of the city. Shock,
horror. Front-page news. Everyone's petrified. And the mayor
simply goes on TV, shrugs his shoulders and says: 'I told you so.'

Bingo. You're looking at a reduction in traffic of at least 40 per
cent, overnight. Problem solved. And whenever people start getting
complacent, you simply instruct the sniper to whack a celebrity or
two, just to keep the story in the public eye.

Flawless. Yet the cretins in charge never tried it. Now they've got a second chance. They can use it to end smoking.

We'll need more than one sniper, of course, because we're covering the entire country. And they won't just be stationed on rooftops; they'll be going undercover, like Jack Bauer – following people into bars, pumping lead into their backs when they request change for the fag machine (we wouldn't ban fag machines – they're bait).

And we don't want any perceived 'safe places' either. In the very first week, we should make a point of blasting the crap out of someone sparking up in a tent in the middle of Cumbria or something. Smokers need to realise there's nowhere to hide.

Let's change the warnings on the packs while we're about it. None of this wussy 'Smoking Causes Cancer' nonsense. Just a sniper, in silhouette, and the words 'HE IS WATCHING'.

And once we're done with the smokers, we'll start on the fatties. That's right, blobster, I can see you. Just try reaching for that doughnut. Go ahead, punk. Make my day.

The point of no return   [24 February 2006]

I was reading about the Singularity the other day, and apparently it's nigh. If you don't know what I'm talking about, it's a theoretical point in the evolution of technology: imagine we design an artificial intelligence smarter than ourselves, which in turn designs an intelligence smarter than itself, which in turn designs an even brainier entity, and so on and so on and so on until it's impossible for us to envisage anything smarter at all – at which point, TA-DA! Singularity! The point of no return.

(At least I think that's what it means. If you want a clearer explanation, invent someone cleverer than me and ask them about it, all right?)

Anyway, it sounds great. It takes the pressure off us. We never have to invent anything again. We'd leave all that to our android offspring. They'd just call us into the room occasionally to show us cool stuff they'd invented – disposable eight-bladed razors, holographic Xbox games, vibrating colours, soap operas set on the moon: that kind of thing. And that'd be it. We'd spend the rest of our lives sipping cocktails and getting our chins wiped by androids. Perfect.

Of course, our new super-intelligent robot masters might get fed up with us stumbling around like idiotic children, jogging their elbows while they're trying to write down equations. They might snap, inject us with paralysis drugs and use us as human power-cells in a *Matrix*-style battery farm – slurping life-juice out of our backsides while pumping a digitised caricature of reality into our brains. Whatever. Provided I never have to think ever again, I'm not that fussed.

Besides, there's always the possibility that five minutes after we switch them on, our super-smartarse descendants will develop nanotechnology, i.e. the ability to re-configure the molecular structure of absolutely anything – which means you could take a clump of soil and turn it into a delicious profiterole, or squirt extra synapses and knowledge banks and microchips into our brains, so we'd be as clever as they were; clever enough to carry the entire contents of Google around in our heads.

Or they could get really ambitious: take the entire population of the planet and knit us together into one single gigantic sentient being, with a billion arms and legs, an eye in the centre of its fore-head and a massive scrotum. Instead of starting wars, we'd simply sit around arguing with ourself, falling silent intermittently to admire the size of our balls.

Actually, if the nanostuff's really working, there'd be no point both-ering with a conventional physical form at all. We could become a wobbly cloud of gas that could float away and spend the rest of eter-nity exploring the universe, contacting far-off alien civilisations and flogging them ringtones. Or maybe we could go one better than that, and simply break down all our molecules and rebuild them as an endlessly reverberating sound wave. Something gentle would be ideal; perhaps the noise of someone breathing on a harp.

Whether that would be a good idea or not is totally beside the point – we're not making the decisions. We've delegated everything by this point, remember? Viva the Singularity!

Rubbernecker's Weekly [17 March 2006]

There are some bits of the media your brain filters out before they can even register in your consciousness. Certain types of advert, usually: don't know about you, but I'm almost completely oblivious to most dog-food or insurance commercials – the moment I clap eyes on them, my mind hits 'delete' and they fade into the background, like an unnoticed ticking clock.

But that's TV. On the newsstands, there's a particular strain of magazine I'm usually totally unaware of, but which I've just become obsessed by. I'm talking about those weekly women's mags, with names like *Chat* and *That's Life!*, which you often see cluttered near the checkout of your local supermarket (the sole exception being Waitrose, where you're more likely to see *What Servant?* or *Swan Recipe World*).

It's easy to ignore these mags because the covers are the same every week: a gaudy red logo in the top left corner, and a beaming non-celebrity model taking up most of the front page. Twee. Cosy. Harmless. You'd expect them to be full of word searches and knitting patterns.

But no. Take a closer look. Read the headlines. This is some of the most brutal stuff it's possible to buy. Take the latest edition of *That's Life!* magazine. The main headline is 'CUT OFF MY FACE' – a story about a deformed woman, replete with gruesome photos. Above that hover the twin delights of 'STRANGLED WITH HER OWN BLOUSE' and 'SO HUNGRY FOR A BABY I GORGED ON LARD TO FILL MY EMPTY WOMB'.

This week's *Chat* (slogan: 'WIT 'N' GRIT 'N' PUZZLES') isn't much rosier, with stories like 'I FORGOT I WAS GANG RAPED' jostling for position alongside tiny photos of a severed pig's head (which a nasty neighbour apparently deposited on someone's lawn) and a girl with a gruesome head wound, and a morbidly obese Scotsman. Oh, and a full-page photo of a woman laughing. Ha ha ha!

I think they're actively trying to drive their readers insane. And apparently it's working. Inside the same issue, Ruth the Truth

('*Chat*'s psychic agony aunt') doles out important advice such as: 'Janice from Pembroke – the squirrel in your garden has a message.' I'm not making this up. March 16 issue, page 36: it's right there.

There's also an ad for a spin-off mag, *Chat: It's Fate*, which looks even better, i.e. worse (sample: 'MY PHILIP MURDERED ME – SO I HAUNTED HIM UNTIL HE KILLED HIMSELF').

Anyway, when they're not urging their readers to talk to squirrels or torment their own murderers, they're filling their pages with the sort of extreme content normally associated with sicko websites aimed at snickering frat boys – grisly real-life murder stories, close-up photos of tumours and injuries, that kind of thing – the only real difference being that here the relentless horror is interspersed with heart-warming readers' letters in which Kids Say the Funniest Things. Somehow the juxtaposition only makes the nasty content seem worse.

In short, these are mainstream magazines aimed squarely at lunatics. And given their sheer number, they're a roaring success. The more I think about it, the more terrifying it is. But Christ, I'm hooked.

Night of the living follicles [7 April 2006]

Hair. Hair. Hair. Hair. Hair. It's a pain, is hair. It grows, you cut it off, it grows back again. It's bloody relentless, like a zombie. Which is exactly what it is, really – dead matter that just keeps coming. That's why hair can't be stopped – you cannot kill what does not live.

What's hair's beef, anyway? What's it trying to prove? It sprouts with enthusiastic urgency, sometimes in the most unexpected places, and then merely hangs around getting in the way. Think your job's pointless? At least you don't dangle off a scalp for a living.

Everything about hair is rubbish. Getting a haircut for instance. Hate that. It combines two of my least favourite things in the world: staring at myself in the mirror, and basic human interaction, both of which are guaranteed to leave me suicidal. I'm so barber-phobic I spent most of my twenties sporting a self-inflicted grade-one crop, which I generally administered with a set of clippers while hunched over my kitchen bin. This served me well until I reached thirty and my cheekbones started receding. A shaved head only really works on a bony face: pack a little extra weight and suddenly you're taking part in a Phil Mitchell lookalike contest in which the only contestants are you and Steve McFadden. And he finishes last.

So these days I brave the barbershop. And I mean 'barbershop'. I don't do hair salons – especially futuristic hair salons where the staff themselves sport fashionable asymmetrical haircuts that make them look like the cast of *Battle of the Planets*. You'd have to be mad to subject yourself to that. So no. I favour a down-at-heel local gents' chophouse: the sort of place where you simply go in, nod gruffly, and come out with a bit less fuzzy crap on your head than before.

Even this is fraught with complications. There's the stilted conversation for one thing. I have one lame joke I use with barbers – I ask them if it's possible to only cut out the grey hairs. Then I nod quietly while they go on about football or the weather, for ever and ever amen.

Since I'm incapable of describing what sort of haircut I want, I tend to end up with whatever they give me. Fortunately, this usually turns out agreeably bland, apart from the freak occasion when a suspiciously young, shifty guy cut my hair into a sort of Captain Kirk wave, then shaved a bare line down one side of my skull. I think he was having a breakdown. I just wish he hadn't had it on my head.

It's time science stepped in. We need a pill that controls hair growth to such a degree that, once taken, your hair 'locks' itself to a certain length and style, and simply stays there – until you change your mind, and take a different pill (there'd be one for every hairstyle, from afro to yohawk).

Better still, how about a special 'night barber' service – a private hairdresser who'll sneak into your home in the dead of night and stealthily cut your hair while you sleep. It might be a bit creepy, but hey: no more small talk about the weather. And if they go a bit mad and start playing with your bum or something – sod it. You're asleep. You'll never know. And your hair will look great in the morning.

Abort, retry or cancel?   [21 April 2006]

According to Parkinson's Law, 'work expands so as to fill the time available for its completion' – i.e. if you give me a maximum of seven days to tidy the house, even though it should only take two hours, I'll stretch those two hours across the week, tidying in slow motion and taking plenty of coffee breaks, because hey, that's human nature.

This is what happens if you work from home: you get trapped within a fuzzy prison of your own construction. 'Sorry, can't come out tonight. I'm supposed to be finishing this thing,' you say, but then you stay in all evening, pottering about, channel surfing, standing in a corner repeatedly rubbing your head up and down the wall like a depressed polar bear; doing anything apart from 'finishing this thing'. And this cycle repeats for days on end, until finally the deadline lurches up, grabs you by the scruff of the neck and forces you to knuckle down and complete it.

Like I say – human nature. Computers, of course, are far more efficient than humans. Nowhere is this more apparent than the field of time-wasting. You might blow a whole hour sitting on the loo reading a month-old Sunday supplement till your legs go numb, but that's nothing next to the swathes of your time your computer can piss down the drain.

I'm not talking about crashes, freezes, or hangs – but rather the endless stream of finickity little tasks a computer will set you without warning. The tiny hoops you have to jump through before it gives you what you want.

Install this driver. Now update it. Now update it again. Register to log in to our website. Then validate your membership. Forgot your password? Click here. Now there. Fill out this form. And this one. And this one. Please wait while TimeJettison Pro examines your system. Download latest patch file. Please wait while patch file examines own navel. Remove cable. Insert cable. Gently tease USB port with cable. Yeah, that's it, baby. That's the way. Now show us your bum or I'm deleting your inbox.

Maybe it's all deliberate. Maybe the computers are simply preparing us for the sort of life we can expect when they finally rise up and enslave us. They won't make us work in salt mines or use us as human batteries, no: they'll have us endlessly downloading and installing drivers for their own sick amusement.

My pet timewastin' hate is when two or more programs start fighting for your attention: when a bit of multimedia software repeatedly asks you if you want to make it the default player for all MP3 files or whatever, and you say 'no', but nonetheless each time you start it, it asks you again and again, like a toddler in a supermarket pestering mum for chocolate, until eventually you give in and click 'yes' – at which point another program sits up and says 'Hey! I thought I was your default player?' in a slightly wounded tone of voice, and embarks on a similar campaign of harassment, until you come to dread clicking on an MP3 file at all, or even going near your computer for that matter, for fear of being sucked back into the argument.

In any sane world, the people who wrote that software would be beheaded on live TV. In ours, they're trillionaires. I've said it before and I'll say it again: our world is bollocks.

Putting kids to good use   [28 April 2006]

I don't wish to brag, but I think I might have just solved the global energy crisis. Now don't all rush to thank me at once. You can form an orderly queue. In the rain. Like scum.

What happened was this: I was talking to someone unfortunate enough to have spawned a child, and they were describing how every weekend they get involved in daytime activities they'd never normally dream of – treasure hunts, fun days, face-painting parties, toddlercise classes etc – simply to knacker their damn kid out, so the shrieking little craphead willingly goes to bed early, leaving them to enjoy some tranquil quality time on their own.

What a waste, I thought: a bit like leaving a car revving in the driveway until the fuel tank's empty. Surely that energy ought to be harnessed somehow.

The next day I was trudging down the pavement, passing by a local school. It must've been playtime, because from the other side of a towering brick wall I could hear a large group of primary-schoolers running, tumbling and yelling their fat little heads off. And I thought, how dare they? Really – how *dare* they? Frittering away all that kinetic energy like that. It's shocking.

And then I thought, aha! Kids are thick, aren't they? I mean, really quite offensively thick. And that's nature's way of telling us to take advantage of them, isn't it? So instead of letting them fruitlessly scamper around like morons, why don't we build gigantic public treadmills instead, and encourage them to gallop on them for hours at a time. Think of all the lovely, environmentally-sound kilowatts they'd generate!

With global oil reserves running perilously low, we owe it to our children to exploit every ounce of their potential before it's too late. They'll thank us for those years spent on the treadmill later.

Speaking of which, if it's going to be a serious long-term enter-prise then maintaining their interest in the treadmill is crucial. Frustratingly, kids have independent minds and short attention spans. And they tire easily. So we'll have to control them through fear. Whenever they start flagging, you just get an adult to dress as a bear, leap on the treadmill and run behind them for a while, snarling and swiping at them with his claws.

And if they get too upset or too suspicious to continue, simply toss a load of brightly coloured foam spheres onto the treadmill, and pipe in some circus music. A few minutes of that and the kids'll be fooled into believing what they're doing is fun, the idiots.

Actually, the strategic deployment of brightly coloured foam spheres could be used to 'sell' pretty much any form of back-breaking manual labour to the nation's children. They'd happily work down a coal mine if you released some balloons and promised to hold a face-painting competition afterwards.

Look, it may all sound harsh, but come on: they're stupid, and we're much, much bigger than them. And honestly, right now they don't exactly serve much purpose. Take, take, take – that's their attitude. And it stinks. So why not put the selfish little shits to good use for a change? Is that really too much to ask?

Lies, all lies   [5 May 2006]

According to statistics, the average person lies 7,500 times a day. Or something. I'm not sure of the actual figure, but when you're writing a column it's essential to sound authoritative in your opening sentence, so I lied about it. The important thing is this: people lie a lot. We can't handle the truth.

I'm no exception to the lying-human-scumbag rule; in fact I probably tell more lies than most. Usually they are bog-standard white lies – compliments, mainly, although pretty much any statement that implies I give a toss about anyone other than myself is almost certainly untrue. I'd also class the majority of my facial expressions as white lies: occasional looks of concern, fixed masks of rapt concentration, smiles, you name it – all absolute bloody lies. If it were socially acceptable to do so, I'd walk around looking as blank as a Cyberman. Fuck the lot of you. Fend for yourselves.

My favourite kind of lie is the pointless but plausible lie: the odd nugget of needless fiction dropped into conversation just for the hell of it. For instance, whenever anyone I know returns from a holiday abroad and asks if anything interesting happened while they were gone, it amuses me to claim, for no reason whatsoever, that the actress Pauline Quirke died while performing a hang-gliding stunt on *This Morning*. In my experience, this is just conceivable enough for them to swallow it whole. They'll only discover the truth months or maybe years later, the next time they see her on TV, and by then they've forgotten who lied to them in the first place – the idiots.

It's a fun little game. Even though you rarely get to see the fruits of your labour first-hand (since you're long gone before the penny drops), pointless fibbing fleetingly makes your life seem 4 per cent more interesting than it actually is, so I wholeheartedly recommend it. To get you started, here are four brief examples for you to sow as you see fit.

1) Next time you go to the cinema with someone who knows nothing about the film, whisper, 'I bet I can work out which one's the android before you,' just as it starts. They'll spend the rest of the film studying the cast in completely the wrong way. I tried this out recently when watching the movie *Crash* with someone, and it improved it a thousandfold.

2) Text a friend at random saying: 'Wahey! I'm in a HELI-COPTER!' Someone did this to me once; it worked a treat. Try it now. Go on.

3) When passing a cemetery, nonchalantly claim Sherlock Holmes is buried there. The number of people who fall for this is frankly astounding.

4) You and a friend are listening to an unfamiliar song on the radio. Before it finishes, say, 'I can't believe this is Charles Dance – the man's lost his mind', then maintain that it is Charles Dance, it really bloody is, honestly, you read about it somewhere. Keep the pretence up as long as you can, despite their protestations, even if it's a woman singing. Say he's recorded it for a cow charity. Get angry if they don't believe you. They will eventually. They always do.

Anyway, there you go. Now get lying. It's good for you.

A face at the window   [12 May 2006]

It's late at night, pitch black outside, and you're in the house alone. You switch off the television. All is quiet. It's bedtime. You walk to the window to draw the curtains. And there it is!

Face at the window! Aaaaarrgh! A scraggy-haired lunatic with googly eyes! Maybe he's glaring, maybe he's grinning – whatever he's doing, this isn't good news. Because he's either actually there, in which case he's about to burst in, hack your face off and use it as a hanky, or you're hallucinating, in which case you've lost your mind, and you'll have to spend the rest of your life wandering shirtless into traffic, screaming about MI5 and geese and phantoms.

It's childish I know, but the terror of the face at the window plays on my mind whenever I draw the curtains at night. I even worry I've somehow jinxed myself by simply thinking about it in the first place: that since I've got the thought lodged in my head now, I might go crazy and imagine he's there.

How long does it take to go crazy anyway? Do you need a bit of a run-up, or is it possible to snap your mind in a nanosecond? And surely, once you've seen the face at the window, there's no going back. You don't just rub your eyes and forget about it.

And then I think: hang on, the fact that you're even having this debate in your head proves you've gone mad already. Seeing the face is simply the next logical phase. You'll *definitely* see it now! Argh!

So to safeguard myself, I end up drawing the curtains with my eyes shut. Which is the sort of thing a crazy person might do. I can't win – the face wins, whether it's there or not.

I'm not the only one. The other day, I was telling someone about my face-at-the-window paranoia, and she squealed and confessed that she often felt precisely the same. And then she said, 'You know what's worse? Face in the mirror. The lurking suspicion that you'll nonchalantly glance in the mirror one night, but it's become haunted or something, and there's a scary man there, staring back at you.'

I wish she hadn't said that. There's a giant mirror lining one wall of my bathroom. Going for a piss in the middle of the night has become a heart-stopping trial of nerves. My life's turning into an M. R. James story.

But then, that's the trouble with internal dialogue: it can send you round the twist. I once had an idea for a TV competition in which ordinary members of the public are hooked up to a futuristic computer, which reads their thoughts and displays them, in real time, on a monitor in front of them.

The contestants have to read their own thoughts aloud as they appear. So initially they'd read something like, 'I wonder if this is going to work?', shortly followed by, 'Bloody hell, it does!', and before long they'd be locked into a sort of consciousness feedback loop, reading aloud their own thoughts about reading their own

131

thoughts aloud. The last one to fall to the ground in a twitching, frothing heap is the winner.

And the host? There's only one candidate. A face at a window. Well, that or Chris Tarrant. Depends who's available.

Too annoyed to save the world   [19 May 2006]

Faced with a photo of a fly-encrusted child, the natural reaction should be to reach out and help. Instead, I start hearing Bono and Coldplay in my head. It's the most mind-mangling act of branding in history. I agree with what they are saying – I just wish *they* weren't saying it. How can I open my wallet while my fists are curled with rage?

Take Bono's special edition of the *Independent*. It's incredibly annoying. You're trapped in a windowless room with the usual tedious sods who apparently represent British culture, except suddenly they're wearing halos and pulling earnest expressions at you.

The front cover is by Damien Hirst. He's lobbed some clipart together in the shape of a cross. Across this runs a stark headline: 'NO NEWS TODAY'. You jerk with astonishment. No news? How can this be? Help us, Bono! We don't understand! Then you spot the footnote: 'Just 6,500 Africans died today as a result of a preventable, treatable disease.' You nod sadly. But before you can truly contemplate this harrowing injustice, you note that Damien Hirst's name appears on the cover not once, but twice – and suddenly the footnote takes on an even more tragic dimension. Because all those people died, yet Hirst still walks the Earth. You turn the page, weeping.

Inside lurk about 2,000 adverts for the new Motorola RED phone. If you buy one, an Aids charity receives an initial payment of £10, followed by 5 per cent of all further call revenues. This is clearly a good idea. But somehow, it's also annoying. For starters, the phone costs £149, of which £139 goes toward helping Motorola. Second, it's bright red and seems doomed to appeal to arseholes who want to add conspicuous compassion to their list of needless fashion accessories. I'm not just jabbering mindlessly on the phone in your train carriage – I'm saving fuckin' lives, OK?

Page 11: a piece of artwork by renegade graffiti artist Banksy, who has defaced a wall in Chalk Farm with a picture of a hotel maid. It's called *Sweeping It under the Carpet* and 'can be seen as a metaphor for the West's reluctance to tackle issues such as Aids in Africa' – or another example of Banksy's tireless self-promotion; take your pick. Banksy says the maid in question 'cleaned my room in a Los Angeles motel . . . she was quite a feisty lady'. Presumably his next portrait will depict some poor minimum-wage sod cleaning graffiti off a wall in Chalk Farm. Provided they're 'feisty' enough to appeal to him.

On it goes, with one Bonoriffic chum after another: noted philanthropist Condoleezza Rice picks her top ten tunes (including one by U2); Stella McCartney interviews Giorgio Armani, who has designed a pair of sunglasses for the RED charity range. These cost around £72 and will make you look like Bono: buy a ten-quid pair from Boots, bung the remaining £62 to an Aids charity and not only will you enjoy a warm philanthropic glow, no one's going to shout 'Wanker!' at you when you walk down the high street.

In summary: it's a worthy cause, rendered annoying – and that's annoying in itself. Bono genuinely cares, cares enough to risk ridicule, which is more than most people would do, myself included. It's just that, well, it's bloody *Bono*, isn't it?

CHAPTER FIVE

In which Noel Edmonds tests quantum theory, Doctor Who *turns pornographic, and Adam Rickitt pays tribute to disaster victims by pretending to eat them*

The dumbest story ever told   [21 January 2006]

Hooray! Hooray for *Prison Break* (Five), because it's wholly bloody stupid and doesn't care who knows it! In fact, it's *so* ridiculous, it might just single-handedly usher in an all-new golden age of inanity, thereby confounding anyone who thought society had reached its ultimate idiocy threshold a few years ago with the invention of novelty ringtones.

Prison Break is possibly the dumbest story ever told. It makes 24 look like *cinéma vérité*. It's as realistic as a cotton-wool tiger riding a tractor through a teardrop. I've played abstract Japanese platform games with more convincing storylines. And the American public recently voted it Favourite New TV Drama at the People's Choice Awards. Suddenly, the farcical tragedy of current world events makes perfect sense. I'm not saying the Americans are stupid. They're not. All I'm saying is a substantial number of them may well have lost their minds. Centuries from now, historians will cite *Prison Break* as the quintessential artefact of a civilisation sliding into absolute babbling madness. It's that good.

The set-up is as follows. Justin Timberlake has a problem – he's not called Justin Timberlake any more. He's called Wentworth Miller and he's a structural engineer. But that's not the problem. His brother's the problem. His brother's a Clive Owen lookalike with jawbones so square he looks like he's trying to hide a box in his mouth – and he's on death row for murdering the vice president. Except he didn't do it! He's the victim of a shadowy conspiracy! And only Justin Timberlake knows the truth!

Now, Justin loves his brother. Loves him with the kind of unquestioning intensity mere acting, dialogue and direction can't possibly hope to convey. So he cooks up a plan. Step one: he robs a bank – and gets caught on purpose!

Following the trial, Justin's lawyer (and close personal friend) can't work out why the previously intelligent, mild-mannered structural engineer would do such a thing. More perplexingly still, he seemed to actively welcome his prison sentence. 'This just isn't like him,' she muses. 'He just rolled over – he didn't put up a fight.' Two qualities that should prove handy in prison.

But he hasn't gone crazy. He's simply entering step two of his plan – because he's now in the same prison as his brother! And he's going to help him escape! It all sounds like the sort of scheme Elmer Fudd might dream up while drunk. It isn't. It's far stupider than that. You'd need a supercomputer to work out all the drawbacks.

But Justin has an ace up his sleeve – an ace that might, in our universe, be considered implausible: he designed the prison himself. Remember I said he was a structural engineer? For Whopping Contrivance, Inc? Well, he is. So prior to committing his armed robbery, he had the prison blueprints tattooed all over his body! Brilliant!

Hilariously, Justin is so certain of success, he actually enters the prison with a smirk on his face. This immediately irritates a guard, who asks him whether he's religious man. No, says Justin. 'Good,' replies the guard, 'because the Ten Commandments don't mean a box of piss in here.' The dialogue continues in this vein for the rest of the programme and, I hope, the entire series.

And so it begins – headlong we plunge, headlong into the very maw of folly. Gasp! as Justin has a fight with the tall scary bloke from *Fargo*. Coo! as Justin bonds with the absurdly cute female prison doctor! Cry! as the governor begs Justin to help him construct a matchstick model of the Taj Mahal for his fortieth wedding anniversary!

I'm not making this up. All of this happens in the pilot episode. It's like they took a two-year-old to see *The Shawshank Redemption*, asked him to recount the plot three weeks later, wrote down everything he said, and filmed it. It's flabbergasting.

Got the stomach for it? Then tuck in. But tread lightly. Because *Prison Break* is so astronomically dumb it could genuinely damage your brain.

Noel's red box party   [28 January 2006]

We've had gameshows based on card games. We've had gameshows based on pub quizzes. But never have we had a gameshow based on the Copenhagen interpretation of quantum mechanics. Until now.

I'm talking, of course, about *Deal or No Deal* (C4). In case you haven't seen it, I'll try to sum up the rules in a way that (a) makes sense and (b) isn't so boring you fall asleep halfway through and start dreaming up surreal, sexually charged rules in which Noel shaves parts of his body at random while you shrink to the size of a bee and lick specks of milk off them.

So. The game starts with twenty-two contestants, each guarding a sealed, numbered suitcase. Each suitcase contains a sum between 1p and £200,000. One of the contestants is chosen to play: the object of the game is for them to open the other suitcases in whichever order they choose, continually evaluating the likely value of their own suitcase as they go. So, if I open box number five and it contains the 1p, I know my own box doesn't. It might contain the 200 grand. Every so often, Noel takes a phone call from 'the Banker', a shadowy offscreen figure who offers the contestant a sum of money to make them stop playing. So, if the banker offers me £3,000 to stop, but I reckon there's still a chance my box contains the jackpot, I'll reject his deal. Hence the title.

In other words, my suitcase contains the financial equivalent of Schrödinger's cat: a sum that exists in a theoretical super-position, being both substantial and meagre until I open and observe it, thereby assigning it a quantifiable value in the physical universe.

Obviously, this raises complex philosophical issues about the nature of reality, which is why *Deal or No Deal* is hosted by Noel Edmonds. He's well into this shit. Did you know *Noel's House Party* was based on Hilary Whitehall Putnam's twin Earth theory of semantic externalism? Well it was. *Fact.*

Still, Noel's central task isn't to chinwag about collapsing wave functions or the viability of consistent histories. No. He's there to distract you from one glaringly obvious fact, which is that the game is actually a massively pointless exercise in utter bloody guesswork.

Because, hilariously, even though there's no applicable strategy whatsoever, Noel spends the entire show pretending there is. He continually says things such as 'What's your game plan?' and 'What drew you to that box?' and 'Ah, I see where you're going with this – I like your style', as though it's a game of 3D space chess between Einstein and a Venusian supercomputer.

In other words, the game largely exists in Noel's head. In fact, he's the only person in the studio with any game plan whatsoever, since he has to employ various cunning strategies to maintain the viewer's interest if the £200,000 prize is eliminated early on.

I say 'cunning strategies'. I mean 'different facial expressions and/or tones of voice'. Every afternoon, Noel's basically taking part in an improvisational drama workshop in which he plays the hysterical id of a man arbitrarily flipping a series of coins.

'Christ, I hope it comes up heads. If it doesn't come up heads we're in serious trouble. I do *not* want to see heads now. Not heads. Please God no . . . IT'S TAILS! HOORAY! Well played! How skilful! OK, time to flip the next coin . . .'

The weird thing is, it sort of works. Something about Noel's ceaseless interest in unpredictable events draws you in. Best of all are the moments when he lifts a telephone receiver to discuss proceedings with the Banker, who I suspect exists solely in his mind. In fact, he might as well do away with the prop phone, and instead simply roll his eyes up and have pretend conversations with God. While dressed as Peter Sutcliffe.

So there you go. It's all a figment of Noel's imagination. Maybe we all are. Maybe he's dreaming us now. And he's about to wake up and we'll cease to exist.

The average Nazi official   [4 February 2006]

You know what this country needs? More TV makeover gurus. There just aren't enough of them – only a few hundred or so, and between them they've got an infinite quantity of airtime to fill. The numbers don't add up, I'm afraid: unless we start teaching our schoolchildren the prerequisite skills (meddling with each other's lives, tutting disdainfully, delivering acid putdowns, etc) and unless we start teaching them now, the planet will suffer a chronic shortage of TV makeover gurus within our lifetimes – and millions could die.

Thank Christ then, for Anthea Turner, former GMTV presenter, confectionery promoter and unwitting star of a notorious health-and-safety instruction video almost everyone in telly has had to sit through (she appears in a touching sequence in which a motorbike backfires, setting her hair on fire). Now the gods have decided she's been away from our screens for too long, and they've reincarnated her as – hooray – a TV makeover guru.

Her vehicle is *Anthea Turner: Perfect Housewife* (BBC3), a 'light-hearted show' in which she 'mentors two hopeless housewives' and attempts to transform each of them into 'a domestic goddess – Anthea-style'. Trouble is, 'Anthea-style' apparently means 'in the manner of an uptight regimental harridan who's twice as organised and half as sexy as the average Nazi official'.

Cue an hour of relentless badgering in which everything has to be folded, ironed, steamed, pressed, labelled, filed, timed, polished and processed, lest it displeases Anthea. And when Anthea is displeased, she gets a face like thunder and looks like she's about to lamp you. It's genuinely scary. So you drop to your knees and you scrub and you scrub and you scrub, and all the time you know she's there – you know she's *behind you* and her eyes are boring holes in your back and she hates you, truly hates you, and her disgust is so palpable your brow starts to sweat, and it drips into your eyes and mixes with the tears and you're crying, you're crying so hard your eyes feel like they've been peeled, but you CAN'T STOP SCRUBBING because you KNOW SHE'S THERE and you MUSTN'T DISPLEASE HER AGAIN. It's like a nightmare vision of the future. They might as well replace Anthea with the Emperor Dalek and have done with it.

I mean really. It makes you wonder. How does someone this uptight achieve orgasm? At the sight of a neatly arranged linen cupboard?

Anyway, having weirded us out with Anthea's Tidiness Reich, the BBC continue to mess with our heads by broadcasting *Animal Winter Olympics* (BBC1), a programme so pointless it beggars belief. What they've done is take a load of *Walking with Dinosaurs*-style computertrickery, and used it to create a photorealistic sportscast in which animals compete with humans in a pretend winter Olympics – so there are ice-skating polar bears, toboggan-ing penguins and a ski-jumping leopard, all for no reason at all.

Sadly, it's not as good as it sounds: the polar bear isn't actually wearing skates, just running alongside a human who is. That's because this is an educational show, OK? Which is why, alongside the fancy CGI, we're treated to explanatory sequences which detail how polar bears' feet grip the ice, or what an emperor penguin's plumage is like, and so on.

Of course, cynics may scoff that the educational, fact-based content is somewhat overshadowed by the fact that we're watching these animals compete in the Olympic games, but so what? The important thing is that the BBC is dicking about with computer graphics for the sheer bloody hell of it. What next? The Eurovision Song Contest re-enacted with horses? 9/11 with cats?

And why stop with animals? How about a remake of *Butterflies* starring Winston Churchill and Marilyn Monroe? Or an edition of *How Clean Is Your Home* hosted by Joseph Goebbels? Oh hang on. They've already done that last one.

There's no Iranian bobsleigh team [18 February 2006]

Q: When is a sport not a sport? A: When it's part of the Winter Olympics.

Before aggrieved snowboarders start writing in to complain, let me clarify what I mean by 'not a sport': I mean something that doesn't feel like a sport in my head, as opposed to athletics or foot-ball or rugby or any of those other pursuits I can't stand and can't watch and would willingly drown in a sack if it were possible. I mean a sport whose presence on television I can actually withstand.

Yes, even though I'm not in the remotest bit interested in winter sports, and actively distrust anyone who is, there's something I find strangely watchable about the Winter Olympics. Perhaps it's all that soothing white space. Or the fact that most of the movement is so smooth and dreamy. Or because the contestants are dressed like Power Rangers. Or maybe it's the comforting repetition of events, many of which merely involve someone plummeting from one end of a slope to the other, over and over again.

Whatever it is, it works for me. It's much better than the regular summer Olympics, which is frantically hot and shouty and has far too many clashing colours for my liking (blue sky + green grass + magenta leotards = my eyes have just thrown up).

In fact, I'd be happy to see the Winter Olympics last a whole year because for the few weeks it's broadcast, it's a bit like having a cheerful screensaver channel at your disposal. An icy televisual lava lamp you can leave on in the background as you go about your business. Just don't ask me who's won what or which country they were representing when they did so. I haven't got a clue.

My favourite events are those which, to my ill-informed eyes, appear to involve no skill whatsoever beyond a demented willing-ness to take part; events such as the luge or the ski-jump, where the athlete is reduced to the level of a coin dropped into one of those seafront arcade penny-drop thingamajigs, bouncing off the pins of fate as they hurtle toward oblivion. It's all incredibly dan-gerous, yet somehow calming on the eye: a bit like watching an endless stream of people quietly jumping off an especially pic-turesque cliff. (That's another sporting event I'd be more than happy to watch all year round: in fact, I dare say it's already being televised somewhere in the former Soviet Union.)

Perhaps the sole event I don't really like is the snowboarding, and that's only because yer average gold-winning Olympian snow-boarder tends to be a gawky, iPodded nineteen-year-old cross between Napoleon Dynamite and the entire cast of *The OC*, and this makes me feel so impossibly old I can't watch them compete without experiencing an aching sense of loss that surely marks the premature onset of a mid-life crisis (is thirty-four too soon for one of those? No?).

Oh, there is one other inherent flaw – the Middle East is somewhat under-represented at the Winter Olympics. There's no Iranian bobsleigh team, for example, which is a crying shame because the world could do with a fun, globally inclusive gala at the moment, and I always thought that's what the Olympics were meant to represent. It seems a little unfair to base the whole thing around a single weather condition (i.e. snow), especially one that's going to become scarcer once global warming gets properly stuck in.

Still, with any luck, fifty years from now we'll have knackered the environment so comprehensively the Winter Olympics will have to take place entirely on sand. The upside: desert-based Arab nations get a fairer shot at gold. The downside: anyone coming off a sand-luge at 200 k.p.h. is going to get all the skin on the underside of their body sanded away in about 4.2 nanoseconds, then writhe around howling in agony, getting yet more sand in the wound. And that might prove a little less soothing to watch.

Slow down and watch the car crash [18 March 2006]

Real life's badly overrated. I mean, what does it consist of, really? Puddles. Grey skies. Stiff breezes. Boredom. Milk past its sell-by date. Empty carrier bags blowing round your feet. The Lord Jesus Christ urging you to kill that passer-by. It's mind-stubbingly mundane.

Little wonder we find solace in escapism. As Jarvis Cocker once sang, why live in the world when you can live in your head? And come to think of it, why live in your head when you can live in someone else's? Particularly when that someone else is fantastic, blazing US stand-up Chris Rock, and the part of his head you're living in is his memory sac.

'Memory sac' is the correct biological term for it, by the way. It's situated right beside the imagination kidney; the two organs are joined by a network of tiny veins, and sometimes there's interaction between the two, leading to the production of creative reminiscences, or 'fibs' as they're more commonly known. And that's pretty much what *Everyone Hates Chris* (five) consists of: embellished memories and obvious fibs, presented as a cross between an autobiography and a sitcom.

And it's good – really really good. Set in 1982, it tells the story of Rock as a thirteen-year-old, lumbered with an eccentric family and a full set of teenage neuroses, struggling to get by in a cruddy area of New York. It's sentimental (his parents wuv him) without being insipid (the school bully calls him 'nigger') and sharp and funny throughout.

'I'll beat your butt so bad, you'll need crutches in your sleep,' the young Chris tells his bullying nemesis. And when said bully responds, beating him up in slow motion, 'Ebony and Ivory' plays sarcastically in the background.

In other words, it's *The Wonder Years* meets *Crooklyn. Cider with Motherf***in' Rosie*, if you will. Chalk up yet another superb US import for Channel Five – their schedule's groaning with so many top-flight American shows, it's like visiting another country – one far more committed to quality than our own. Pretty soon you'll have to apply for a visa before tuning in.

Anyway, if *Everybody Hates Chris* presents a massaged, amusing take on reality, *My Reality TV Breakdown* (VH1) is the opposite: a warts-and-all look at former American child star Danny Bonaduce. Once a member of TV's Partridge Family, he's now a confused, self-obsessed, forty-five-year-old mess. Years of substance abuse have left him with a volatile temperament and a voice so gravelly it scrapes the skin off your ears on the way in.

As the series opens, Bonaduce and his wife are attending (tele-vised) therapy sessions with a creepy counsellor (one of those guys you only get in America, whose age is impossible to determine: he could be anywhere between twenty-five and eighty).

Initially the show documents their attempts to save their marriage; before long it becomes a portrait of a man free-falling into a hell of his own making – alcoholic binges, steroid abuse, paranoid confrontations and yes, even an apparent suicide attempt.

What happened to the days of the *nice* low-brow American import? You know – like *Scarecrow and Mrs King*?

Anyway, in the States, this was called *Breaking Bonaduce*. Since

Bonaduce – pronounced 'bonna-doochy', in case you're a stickler for correct internal elocution – since Bonaduce isn't exactly a household name over here, they've rechristened it *My Reality TV Breakdown* so viewers browsing the EPG get a sense of what they're in for.

God knows how many other alternate titles they rejected first – ten quid says they seriously contemplated calling it *The Adventures of Boozy Wrist-Slash Man* for an entire afternoon.

It's car crash TV, and proud of it. The 'star' himself even says as much during the opening titles. 'I'm a car crash, man', he growls, 'and you have every right to slow down and watch the car crash.'

Yeah, well. I have every right to stare up a cat's bum if I want to. That doesn't make it right.

Adam Rickitt's well of courage [25 March 2006]

Thirty-four years ago, Uruguayan Air Force flight 571 crashed in the Andes, leaving twenty-seven survivors fighting for survival in one of the most unforgiving, inhospitable areas on the planet. For seventy-two days they battled extreme cold, exposure and avalanches. Worse still, there was a complete lack of food. As starvation loomed, they made an agonising decision: to eat the flesh of those killed in the initial crash.

Using a shard of glass, they sliced strips of meat from the corpses, dried scraps of flesh on the fuselage, and gobbled them down between guttural sobs of despair. Sixteen of them eventually lived to tell the tale, only to be haunted for decades by the knowledge of what they'd done.

Now, I've got no idea what kind of thought zips through your noggin when you find yourself huddled on a mountainside, guzzling Brian from seat 24A in a desperate bid to survive – but I'm prepared to bet my shoes and spine that at no point would you think, 'Hey, this'd make a great Channel Five reality show!'

But that's precisely what's happened in *Alive: Back to the Andes* (Five): four celebrities find themselves stranded up a mountain with nothing but a few tents and a pile of raw meat for company.

I say 'celebrities', but to be honest, we're talking Adam Rickitt, Jean-Christophe Novelli, Carole Caplin and Lord Freddie Windsor – who, combined, are about 1900 per cent less famous than the Coco Pops Monkey.

Come to think of it, they're also less famous than the Andes survivors themselves, who at least had a Hollywood movie made about them. The only way Adam Rickitt's getting a film made about his life is if he devises a cure for cancer, becomes a serial killer, or blasts into space to defeat Zoltan the Mighty.

Still, at least he's taking part for a good reason. It's not about him. No. It's about honouring the survivors' ordeal. I know this because he says as much during the programme (he even uses the word 'honour', shortly before munching a load of raw meat) and on his website, Officially Adam Rickitt.

'We tried to manage even a millionth of what they suffered basically to highlight what an incredible group of men and women they were,' he writes, adding that it provided 'a real insight into the well of courage the survivors endured'.

There's a whole series in this, surely – *Adam Rickitt Honours the Well of Courage*, in which the former soap star pays tribute to survivors of various tragedies by re-enacting their plights. Episode one: Adam Rickitt honours the well of courage endured by survivors of the 2004 tsunami by smearing himself in mud and lying down in the bath. Episode two: Adam Rickitt commemorates 9/11 by setting fire to a napkin on the roof of a skyscraper. And so on and so on. It'd be the most moving television programme ever made.

(Actually, right now he's appearing in *The Games* on Channel 4, presumably in tribute to the eleven Israeli athletes massacred at the 1972 Munich Olympics.)

Anyway, the programme itself is easy on the eye (I suspect it's been shot in HD because it looks like a sodding movie) but disappointingly boring.

Remove the 'easy on the eye' bit from that sentence and you're left with a working description of the week's other celebrity chow-fest, *Eating With . . . Cilla Black* (BBC2), a stunningly pointless biography-cum-cookery programme.

During a seemingly endless half-hour, we learn that Cilla likes offal and bacon, and watch her cooking cheese on toast. Not much else happens, although at one point she rubs an Oxo cube on an orange and then eats it. Somehow, this is more disgusting than watching Adam Rickitt eat raw meat.

Still, Cilla isn't claiming to be a great chef. 'As my mother used to say, life's too short to stuff a mushroom', she says. 'And it all goes down the same hole, don't it?'

Just like telly, really.

Faintly baffling mini-movies [1 April 2006]

Here's a little project for you. Stroll up to someone in marketing, and after punching them square in the face because they bloody well deserve it, ask them to define the term 'branding'. Chances are they'll start babbling about 'consumer consciousness' and 'product personality', at which point you can punch them square in the face for a second time. Hey presto! You're getting a cathartic workout, and they're learning something valuable. Everybody wins. Apart from them, obviously.

But don't go feeling bad. After licking their wounds (with their lizard-like tongue) they'll drive off in a car so obscenely expensive the glove-box is worth nine times more than your house, and spend the rest of their lives dancing around in a shower of bank-notes, champagne and beautiful naked people, all paid for by their fat-bollocked marketer's salary. Because despite being utterly pointless, theirs is one of the most well-rewarded careers in exis-tence. Which is why you punched them in the face in the first place, remember?

Anyway, ever since there was more than one of them, TV stations have felt the need to brand themselves, just so you can tell them apart. And I have to admit, their efforts have provided some of my fondest telly memories since year dot. They may consist of little more than an animated logo and a tinny fanfare, but the lovely old bygone stings for TVS, ATV, Central or LWT still make me glow with nostalgia.

You can find these and many more on an excellent website called TV Ark (www.tv-ark.org.uk) which serves as an unofficial repository for all manner of broadcast ephemera (including continuity and adverts). It's a wonderfully evocative hall of forgotten memories, and an insanely addictive one at that. (I had to take a short break after typing the URL in just then, during which I repeatedly clicked-to-view the flowering ATV ident about sixteen times in a row, like a lab rat instinctively nudging a lever for sugar.)

Anyway, that was then. Right now, the trend for idents seems to have moved away from bold, stark logos in favour of quirky little films incorporating subtle corporate livery – the latest example being ITV1's faintly baffling mini-movies in which children cartwheel around, elderly men slap their tummies, and a couple stand in a cornfield hugging a tree, to a pseudo Sigur Ros soundtrack. Presumably it's meant to convey a sense of warmth, accessibility and fun, and to be fair, it pretty much succeeds – it's certainly less nauseating than past efforts involving ITV 'faces' such as Chris Tarrant larking around on a studio set. Trouble is, the other terrestrial channels are all doing something similar.

Five, for instance, has a series of nano-films in which the word 'five' doesn't appear at all: instead an alternate four-letter-word spelt out in the approved 'five' typeface is digitally woven into a piece of live-action footage (e.g. the word 'rush' appearing on the landscape below a plummeting skydiver). This in turn is similar to Channel Four's eye-catching stings in which a gigantic '4' suddenly looms over the landscape, sometimes made out of chunks of council estate, sometimes from pylons or bits of old hedge. Then you've got BBC1's cast of dancing, skateboarding, leaping, twirling, tumbling ninnies, decked out in pillar-box red.

In other words, they've all gone for the 'quirky idiosyncratic' feel, all at the same time – the end result being, ironically enough, that it's actually quite hard to tell them apart. They're like the crowd of followers from *Life of Brian*, shouting 'Yes, we are all individual' in unison.

The only terrestrial channel currently *not* substituting little live action epics for good old fashioned animated idents is BBC2, which means that's surely next in line to be assimiliated. Here's hoping they stick to their guns – actually, here's hoping they revert to a 2D cardboard-and-scissors kind of ident, just like the good old days. Something cold and distant and iconic and simple. A logo on a background. No slow-mo shots of jugglers. None of that bullshit. Or it's another yet smack in the face for your marketing chum, I'm afraid.

CSI: Jihad   [8 April 2006]

Terrorists! They're funny, aren't they? Those distorted belief systems and murderous schemes really crack me up. Actually they don't. They spook me to the core. We're always being told we shouldn't be afraid of terrorists because 'that's precisely what they want' – but since they'd never be classed as 'terrorists' if they weren't doing 'terrifying' things in the first place, that strikes me as a bit of pointless argument; a bit like expecting someone not to flinch when you shout 'boo' at them. Besides, take the 'terror' out of 'terrorist', and what're you left with? A 'wrist'. And what use is a wrist? Aside from providing you with a pleasant, fleeting distraction from encroaching global terrorism, I mean?

Scared and confused though I clearly am, I've nonetheless spent the last few days guzzling my way through *Sleeper Cell* (FX), a US mini-series about an FBI agent infiltrating a group of fundamentalist terrorists hell-bent on bringing death and destruction to Los Angeles. The first episode starts this week; unusually, I was sent the entire series for preview purposes, and sat through the whole thing in two marathon sessions.

Which isn't to say it's brilliant. It's actually rather jarring. *Sleeper Cell* resembles two entirely different programmes bolted together: one a complex and often intelligent look at Islamic fundamentalism, the other a dumb-as-a-box-of-rocks TV thriller. It's like an episode of *The A-Team* scripted by Robert Fisk.

The main character is undercover FBI agent Darwyn Al-Sayeed, who, as luck would have it, is also a devoted, peace-loving Muslim. He's also ridiculously good-looking – the sort of guy you normally see getting his shirt torn off in a Beyoncé video. Posing as an ex-convict, smoulderin' Darwyn is recruited by a terrorist sleeper cell led by Farik, a charismatic extremist who (somewhat cheekily) spends much of his waking life pretending to be a devout Jew.

Just to confound expectations, Farik's the only member of the sleeper cell from Arabic origins – the others being a Bosnian schoolteacher, a French ex-skinhead, an all-American blue-eyed bell-end called Tommy and Darwyn, who's black. Politically correct, maybe – but it's also straining credibility, especially since the French ex-skin is even more of a beefcake than Darwyn. This is the hunkiest group of would-be mass murderers the world has ever seen.

Plausibility levels continue to fluctuate wildly throughout the series: for every well-researched reference to contemporary global politics, there's a scene in which the sleeper cell swagger around as though they're in *Reservoir Dogs* – either that or we're treated to a dull, formulaic burst of love interest. Furthermore, it's glossy. So glossy they could've called it *CSI: Jihad* instead.

If there's one message the show is keen to hammer home, it's that Islam isn't inherently evil; that these guys, whilst understandably angry about global injustice, are psychotically misguided and unrepresentative of the whole. While that's a well-meaning sentiment, it frequently becomes downright patronising – especially during one scene in which Darwyn patiently informs a group of confused toddlers (i.e. us) that not every Muslim wants to fly planes into buildings. Well, no shit, Sherlock. What's on next week's *Did You Know?* Not all Frenchmen wear berets?

Anyway, purely on the level of a TV thriller, *Sleeper Cell* is a mixed success. Episode one is intriguing; then the series turns to mush for a while – until about two-thirds of the way in, when the sleeper cell's plan takes shape and it rapidly becomes as gripping as a good episode of *24* (and approximately 15 per cent more credible). The finale is pretty much non-stop thumping excitement (not to mention sodding terrifying, especially if you have nightmares about chemical warfare) although you'll have forgiven the show a multitude of sins if you make it that far.

But is it worth watching? Yes. I think so. If nothing else, it's different. Complex topical issues and cartoon-level drama don't really mix, but it's fun to watch them fondling each other's balls for a while.

Hardcore action   [29 April 2006]

Following a minor setback with this year's series opener, my love affair with *Doctor Who* (BBC1) is firmly back on: tonight's episode, in which K9 and Sarah-Jane return, brought tears to my eyes. Perhaps I'm losing my mind, or perhaps I'm just a sucker for a bit of bittersweet nostalgia, especially when it involves a ludicrous robot dog.

Since my burgeoning Whomania knows no bounds, I'm prepared to go to any lengths – or sink to any depths – to indulge it. And if that means covering a crappy pornographic spoof called *Dr Screw* (The Adult Channel), then so be it.

Last week's episode began with Dr Screw and his assistant Holly clambering inside 'The Turdis' (a time-travelling Portaloo), journeying to the medieval era, and getting into a laser-fight with some knights – all of which was realised courtesy of some surprisingly proficient CGI. This took about five minutes, which is just long enough for you to forget it's a mucky programme at all – until suddenly 'the Doctor' whips out a 'sonic dildo' and everything turns rude and stays there.

It's traditional for highbrow critics to feign ennui in the face of pornography. Sit Tom Paulin down in front of a cheery Ben Dover gang-bang or the latest hyper-explicit arthouse sexfest and he'll probably yawn himself into a coma so deep it makes death itself resemble a light snooze. That's because highbrow critics are made of sterner stuff than you or I. Not for them the simple call-and-response reaction of us simple apes. They only masturbate to harpsichords on Radio 3.

Well, I ain't highbrow: I be dumb. As such, I don't mind admitting I didn't find Dr Screw boring. No. I found it morbidly fascinating.

What got me was this: the pornstar cast are clearly having

genuine sex – yet thanks to our hopeless censorship laws both they and the programme's editors are forced to perform a bizarre game of mucky-pup peek-a-boo as they do so.

The end result is a nonsensical compromise. It's OK to see an erect penis, apparently, but you can't see it penetrating anything . . . except sometimes you sort of can. Cunnilingus is shown in fairly explicit detail, while blowjobs are hidden behind cupped hands or strategically posed thighs . . . except sometimes they're sort of not. It's like an orgy that can't decide how rude it wants to be.

I'm not complaining – just baffled. These regulations seem inherently pointless, like the American public drinking law that leads winos to swig cans of beer from within brown paper bags. At the end of the day they're still winos, still in public, still drinking beer. So what's the point?

Protection, presumably. Yet since the show is broadcast on a restricted-access post-watershed channel requiring PIN code entry (and a payment) to view, then who, precisely, are we protecting? The mugs prepared to pay to watch it? That's so circular it makes my head spin.

Hardcore smut has been legally available in Britain since the introduction of the R18 certificate six years ago. More recently, Michael Winterbottom's 9 *Songs* (which features more real sex than most marriages) was broadcast uncut on Sky Box Office (another PIN-restricted service). The other week, a leering C4 documentary on notorious bestial porn flick *Animal Farm* included a close-up of a man's face while he had sex with a chicken. Yet dedicated adult channels aren't allowed to show explicit consensual sex. Why?

Because porn's embarrassing and tawdry and we don't want that muck on our airwaves? Then ban it outright and have done with it. This present fudge just makes Ofcom look like bigger idiots than the pornographers themselves. And that's saying something.

In the meantime, I can live without seeing Dr Screw's high-jinks in their unexpurgated glory. As for porn channels per se – from what I can tell, their faux-moany erotic 'personas' are just a bit crap and condescending. If I want to see uncut hardcore action, I don't need a TV. Just a ladder and my neighbour's windows. Don't knock it till you've tried it.

The Badger hulks out   [6 May 2006]

'This is not a game! There is no "panel of judges" here! There's no "text-a-number"!' No 'text-a-number'? What sort of technophobic grandad-speak is that? Holy bleedin' cobblestones, Sir Alan, this is the twenty-first century! You run a technology firm for chrissakes! No 'text-a-number', indeed. I suppose you'd say it ain't a game of yer computerised Space Invasions, neither? None of yer Megadrive cassette tapes here, eh?

This series has seen an exponential coarsening of Sir Alan's already coarse demeanour; he now sounds more like a world-weary, misanthropic prison warden than a high-flying fat cat. Who the hell wants to work for that? A few weeks ago he used the phrase 'as sure as there's a hole in my bloody arse', and my brain filled with horrifying images – grisly close-ups of the aperture itself – which still play a starring role in my nightmares. Incidentally, is it just me, or is he starting to resemble Mrs Tiggywinkle from the Beatrix Potter books? You know – the hedgehog washerwoman? I swear he does. Especially if you squint.

No wonder he's looking for new blood. And this time around, said blood is lady-flavoured. Yes, *The Apprentice* (BBC2) shudders to a climax this week, with a live girl-on-girl finale featuring Ruth 'Haystacks' Badger and Michelle 'Eyebrow Pencil' Dewberry. If you haven't been watching the series thus far, suffice to say it should play out like a grudge match between Biffa Bacon's mum and a translucent, whining coat-stand.

Actually, that's horrifically unfair: both candidates have easily held their own over the past twelve weeks. I'm only being snippy because that's my job. As project manager of this column, petty unpleasantness is my number-one priority, and I'm proud to say I always meet my targets.

Yes, in reality, I admire them both – although admittedly, my admiration of Ruth is almost entirely rooted in fear; by the irrational suspicion that she might lunge through the screen at any given moment and squish my balls to paste in her fist. She's a cross between Lucy from *Peanuts* and a career-oriented Minotaur – pushy, stubborn and perpetually teetering on the brink of fury; Pauline Quirke meets the Terminator. If Sir Alan fires her on Wednesday, chances are she'll 'Hulk out' – punch her way through the wall, roar into the street and start tossing cars around like pillows.

And as for Michelle – well, I've developed an alarming crush on her, even if she does draw her eyebrows on with a pube-thin cray-on and speak in a voice so flat and off-putting I can only describe it as the aural equivalent of the taste of earwax. As I suspect most viewers did, I initially found Michelle a touch cold and distant – a spectral estate agent with a curiously expressionless fizzog.

Last week's 'job interview' special cast her in a new light, for the first time revealing her to be a tough little soldier who's overcome all manner of hinted-at hardships to forge a wildly successful free-lance career – without banging on about it every five minutes, like Syed.

Ah, Syed. He's like something out of *I, Robot* – a synthetic android sex doll with undiluted Microsoft Excel pulsing through his veins. And he's back this week, a phoenix from the flames, assisting with the gang's-all-here final task – so for God's sake savour your final minutes with him. Peppy bell-end businessmen are two a penny, but Syed's a special kind of peppy bell-end businessman, the kind whose peppy bell-endism is so relentless and blinkered it event-ually transcends annoyance and becomes hugely endearing. You'll miss him when he's gone, damn him.

Anyway, someone's got to win, and speaking as someone who always roots for the underdog, I favour Michelle. So there.

Oh, and BBC, if you're listening? How about a detective serial starring Margaret Mountford and Nick Hewer, in which they solve crimes in the city by lurking in the background and peering at the suspects one by one until someone cracks and confesses? It's got 'hit' plastered all over it.

Top-hatted warthogs [13 May 2006]

Panic! Scream! Kick the house down! Punch yourself in the fore-head! Because the Conservative Party's on the comeback trail and there's nothing we can do to stop them. You can see it coming a mile off – simperin' Prime Minister Cameron and a cabinet full of jowly top-hatted warthogs smugging their way through a four-year term. Arrrrgggh!

Thanks Labour. Thanks for cocking things up and handing the Eternal Enemy a second chance. We're doomed – doomed, I tells ya.

It's going to be like the 1980s all over again. What better time then, for *The Line of Beauty* (BBC2), a coming-of-age drama set in gaudy, salmon-pink Thatcherite Britain. It's been adapted from the Booker-prize winning Alan Hollinghurst novel by Andrew Davies, the one-man screenplay sweatshop whose annual workload would put a Cyberman to shame.

More on those later. Anyway, *The Line of Beauty* tracks the for-tunes of Nick Guest, a naive young gay guy lodging with the Fed-dens, a blisteringly posh, offensively loaded family living in a Notting Hill house the size of a flagship branch of PC World. Daddy Fedden is an aspiring MP, a personal friend of Mrs Thatcher and, most importantly, a thumping great git. The rest of the Feddens are more sympathetic, particularly their daughter Cat – a textbook beautiful mess.

Nick is soon drawn into a world of glamorous parties populated exclusively by chortling dinner-jacketed bluebloods with names like Toby and Jerome and Sebastian and Saffron and Camilla and Glyndebourne and Squiffy. Incredibly, rather than instinctively vomiting into his hands and smearing it round their tittering, privileged faces, he finds himself rather seduced by it all, and sets about becoming a professional hanger-on.

In the meantime, he's also exploring his sexuality with the demented zeal of an automated buggering machine. Early on, we're smacked in the face by a helping of enthusiastic al fresco sodomy which promises to send the BBC's homophobe hotline into meltdown, largely because it looks like jolly good fun. And that's by no means the end of it. Nick will have sex at the drop of a hat. Especially if someone bends down to pick it up.

Chuck in a blizzard of cocaine and the ever-lengthening shadow of Aids and . . . well, you can see the icebergs looming.

Appropriately for something called *The Line of Beauty*, the cast is preposterously beautiful. Nick, played by newcomer Dan Stevens, is a bit like a Muppet Baby incarnation of Hugh Grant, all limpid eyes and bewildered, stuttering smiles; while Hayley Atwell, playing Cat, starts out pretty and gets better-looking by the second. By the end of the first episode, she's so stupendously gorgeous, she's almost physically painful to look at. I had to rub an ice cube directly onto my heart just to sit through her scenes. That woman takes the piss.

Mind you, Mrs Thatcher turns up in episode two, and in this world even *she's* bloody beautiful. Honest. I damn near abased myself. To the Iron Lady. It'd take years of psychotherapy to undo that.

It's all sturdy, classy stuff, albeit slightly hamstrung by the passive presence lurking at its core – Nick's such an eager-to-please social chameleon he feels like more of an interested bystander than a lead character, and the Hugh Grant act starts to grate pretty quickly. A good watch nevertheless, even if it never really quite takes off the way you hope it will.

The Tories aren't the only heartless, blank-eyed, nightmarish, marching, mankind-crushing army of despicable automatons making a televisual comeback this week: the Cybermen return in tonight's *Doctor Who* (BBC1). Like the Tories, they last posed a serious threat back in the Eighties. Unlike the Tories, they can traditionally be killed by rubbing a lump of gold into their chestplates. If only real life was as simple as the world of populist fantasy.

This series is turning out to have some impressively hardcore sci-fi 'chops', and *The Rise of the Cybermen* is a prime case in point, with more ideas packed into its 45 minutes than most shows – and all Tories – manage in a lifetime.

A banana skin and an open manhole [20 May 2006]

My theory that 98 per cent of everything is absolutely rubbish doesn't quite hold water when it comes to the world of cinema. There it's more like 99.3 per cent.

I recently had one of those evenings where you sit indoors alone, so bored and lonely you teeter on the verge of gouging one of your own eyes out just so you'll have something to tell the grand-children. In desperation, I flipped through Sky Movies, desperate to find something interesting to look at. In the event, I might as well have stared up a cat's bum instead.

Modern cinema is downright embarrassing. It's all Adam Sandler this and Will Smith that. Ben Stiller and Owen Wilson smugging their shortarsed, bent-nosed heads off. *Ocean's Twelve. I, Robot. Garfield. Miss Congeniality 2. The Chronicles of Riddick. The Chronicles of Riddick. The Chronicles of Riddick. The Chronicles of Riddick.*

And what about *Crash*? Triple Oscar-winning *Crash*. Jesus. Have you *seen* it? It's the single most patronising film ever made: the characters might as well be walking around wearing sandwich boards with 'RACE IS A COMPLEX ISSUE' printed on them in massive, flashing letters. I half-expected 'Ebony and Ivory' to start playing over the end credits – but no: that might've been funny, thereby rendering the film 1 per cent less awful, and that would never do. Not when there's berks to feed.

Of course, mankind's been churning out terrible movies ever since the first motion cameras were invented; over time, our cul-ture simply forgets the really bad ones, like a repressed abuse memory. Curiously though, while the rare gems of brilliance get praised to the hilt, we rarely get a chance to actually see them.

Case in point: Buster Keaton. Since year dot I can remember being told that Buster Keaton was a comic genius; that he virtually invented 'deadpan' comedy; that he made audiences laugh so hard they'd cough blood all over the seat in front, which is why cinema seats are traditionally coloured red. I'd seen the famous clip from *Steamboat Bill, Jr.* in which Buster survives being crushed by a collapsing housefront by standing in the tiny gap where the window should be, and was suitably impressed, but the rest of his work blurred into a mass of speeded-up film and tinkling pianos in my head, none of which seemed the slightest bit amusing.

As a result, I wasn't particularly looking forward to the first edition of *Paul Merton's Silent Clowns* (BBC4), which examines Keaton's work in some detail. By the end of the show I was blown away, partly because Merton's unabashed love for his subject is infectious (and a delight to see), but mainly because the clips themselves are genuinely bloody funny.

I used to think people only *pretended* to like silent comedies in order to impress girls in glasses, but on this evidence I was wrong. And when you're not laughing, you're gasping. We're always told that the appeal of slapstick lies in its sense of *Schadenfreude*: the sickening delight of watching misfortune befall another, generally in the form of a banana skin and an open manhole – but on this evidence, you're more likely to experience the chair-clenching terror of watching a man genuinely dicing with death before your very eyes. Perhaps I'm stupid, but I'd forgotten just how perilous early slapstick could be. After witnessing clip upon clip of Keaton literally risking his life on camera, even the most demented excesses of *Jackass* or *Dirty Sanchez* look hopelessly tame.

But the best thing about the show is that it isn't just a load of clips. The first 35 minutes consist of a potted history and mini-lecture from Merton – and then just at the point where you start thinking 'this is all very well, but now my appetite's been whetted I wish they'd show us a whole Keaton film', they bloody well do: for the final 25 minutes we're treated to a 1921 short called *The Goat*, in its entirety. And suddenly an eighty-five-year-old silent film becomes the freshest piece of comedy you've seen in years. Tinkling pianos and all.

CHAPTER SIX

In which Sandi Thom is unmasked, romance is denounced, and Justin Timberlake is told to go and fuck himself

Time to get tough on flags   [26 May 2006]

Rejoice! Thanks to the national obsession with football, the cross of St George has finally been reclaimed from the racists. Nowadays, when you see an England flag on a car, sprawled across a T-shirt or flapping from a novelty hat, you no longer assume the owner is a dot-brained xenophobe. Instead you assume he's just an idiot. And you're right. He is.

It's a great piece of visual shorthand. Imagine the outcry if government passed a law requiring the nation's dimbos to wear dunce's caps in public. No one would stand for it. There'd be acres of newsprint comparing Blair and Co. to the Nazis. We'd see rioting in the streets – badly organised rioting with a lot of mis-spelled placards, but rioting nonetheless.

Instead, every numbskull in the land is queuing up to voluntarily brand themselves. They even pay for the privilege! As brilliant ruses go, it's the most brilliant, rusiest ruse you could wish for. I can't wait for stage two, when they're persuaded to neuter themselves with safety scissors.

The only problem I have with this berk-demarcation scheme is the design of the flag itself. Personally, I'd jettison the big red cross/white background malarky in favour of a black rectangle with the word CRETIN printed in the centre in stark bold text.

Traditional flags are hopeless. A few weeks ago, I took part in a pub quiz. In round three you had to match countries to their national flags. It was impossible. With a few notable exceptions, most flags are more or less identical. A different colour here, a thicker line there, but on the whole they all just look like . . . well, like flags.

Perhaps I'm wrong, but I always thought that the whole point of flags is to make it easy to tell which country you're dealing with. Instead, thanks to a rash of uninspired design choices, they do the precise opposite. Flags have become a tedious puzzle, a tosser's clue. What next? Replace the names of countries themselves with anagrams? What is this, *The Da Vinci Code*? The system's in chaos.

Who decides what can and can't go on a flag anyway? Is there a worldwide flag council overseeing this stuff? Presumably drawings are permitted – the Welsh flag's got the right idea with that lovely dragon – but what about photographs? If, say, the Dutch decided to replace their boring tricolour with some hardcore pornography, would they still be allowed to hang it outside the UN?

Or what about sarcastic flags? If I was prime minister of Iraq – which I'm not – I'd commission a parody of the Stars and Stripes and insist on using that. Replace the stripes with missile trails and the stars with skulls. And a little cartoon of George Bush pooing into a bucket or something. It wouldn't cost much and it would make literally everyone in the world laugh out loud. And perhaps all that laughter would bring us all together as one, and we'd spend the rest of the century hugging each other and tumbling around in a great big bed. Or perhaps not.

Anyway, in summary: those protesters who burn flags outside embassies have got the right idea – but they shouldn't be burning them because they disagree with something the country in question has done. They should be burning flags just because they're flags. And flags are rubbish.

The great online dick fight   [2 June 2006]

Last week I wrote a load of nonsense about flags and idiocy; as well as appearing in print, it also turned up on the *Guardian*'s 'Comment is Free' blog-o-site, where passers-by are encouraged to scrawl their own responses beneath the original article.

Some people disagreed with the piece, some agreed; some found it funny, some didn't. For half a nanosecond I was tempted to join in the discussion. And then I remembered that all internet debates, without exception, are entirely futile. So I didn't.

There's no point debating anything online. You might as well hurl shoes in the air to knock clouds from the sky. The internet's perfect for all manner of things, but productive discussion ain't one of them. It provides scant room for debate and infinite opportunities for fruitless point-scoring: the heady combination of perceived anonymity, gestated responses, random heckling and a notional 'live audience' quickly conspire to create a 'perfect storm' of perpetual bickering.

Stumble in, take umbrage with someone, trade a few blows, and within about two or three exchanges the subject itself goes out the window. Suddenly you're simply arguing about arguing. Eventually one side gets bored, comes to its senses, or dies, and the row fizzles out: just another needless belch in the swirling online guffstorm.

But not for long, because online quarrelling is also addictive, in precisely the same way Tetris is addictive. It appeals to the 'lab rat' part of your brain; the annoying, irrepressible part that adores repetitive pointlessness and would gleefully make you pop bubblewrap till Doomsday if it ever got its way. An unfortunate few, hooked on the futile thrill of online debate, devote their lives to its cause. They roam the internet, actively seeking out viewpoints they disagree with, or squat on message boards, whining, needling, sneering, over-analysing each new proclamation – joylessly fiddling, like unhappy gorillas doomed to pick lice from one another's fur for all eternity.

Still, it's not all moan moan moan in NetLand. There's also the occasional puerile splutter to liven things up. In the debate sparked by my gibberish outpouring, it wasn't long before rival posters began speculating about the size of their opponent's dicks. It led me to wonder – has the world of science ever investigated a causal link between penis size and male political leaning?

I'd theorise that, on the whole, right-wing penises are short and stubby, hence their owners' constant fury. Lefties, on the other hand, are spoiled for length, yet boast no girth whatsoever – which explains their pained confusion. I flit from one camp to the other, of course, which is why mine's so massive it's got a full-size human knee in the middle. And a back. A big man's back.

Anyway, if we must debate things online, we might as well debate that. It's not like we'll ever resolve any of that other bullshit, is it?

Click. Mine's bigger than yours. Click. No it isn't. Click. Yes it is. Click. Refresh, repost, repeat to fade.

On wishing one was a punk rocker
(with flowers in one's hair) [9 June 2006]

I've not heard that Sandi Thom single all the way through yet, but I've seen the TV ad about six billion times, and the short, poxy burst on that is more than enough to convince me that if her sudden rise to stardom *wasn't* the end result of a shrewd marketing campaign, the implications are terrifying. Because to believe the official story – that thousands of people voluntarily subjected themselves to this shit online, then recommended it to their friends – is to lose your faith in mankind completely.

There's a simple way to settle this once and for all, and that's for the huge crowd of people who apparently watched Thom's inaugural bedsit webcasts to step forward and make themselves known. Come on. Hands up. I want to see your faces. And then I want you smacked to death with brooms. You people are the enemies of fun. Your bland emissions pollute the atmosphere, threaten the environment. For the sake of humanity, you must be stopped.

I don't know. Maybe I'm wrong. Maybe Sandi Thom genuinely touches some people. Whoever they are, I can't relate to them. Woody Allen once marvelled with horror at 'the level of a mind that watches wrestling', and I'm the same with Sandi Thom fans. All I hear is that telltale, indefinable something that immediately marks it out as something that's bypassed the soul completely: consumable noise for people who don't like music but know listening to it is 'the done thing' – like mutant imposters mimicking the behaviour of humans. I can't relate. It doesn't go. I'm being alienated by the replicants.

There's a word for this sort of thing. It's not 'art', it's 'content'. And it's everywhere, measured out by unseen hands, mechanically dangled over the replicants' flapping gobholes: flavourless worms for android hatchlings.

Sometimes I can *almost* see where content is coming from. Take 'Angels' by Robbie Williams. It's a massively popular piece of content, beloved by millions. If I strain really hard, I can just about make out some genuine emotion. Just a speck or two – but enough to make its huge success at least vaguely explicable. Compared with anything that has any semblance of balls whatsoever, 'Angels' is a bowl of cold mud – but next to most content, it's a towering emotional epic. It almost makes you feel something. No wonder it's become the official theme tune for thick people's funerals.

Anyway, back to Sandi Thom. As luck would have it, while typing this article, I've just heard 'I Wish I Was a Punk Rocker (with Bollocks in My Mouth)' on the radio, and the real brain twister is the lyric, in which she yearns for a time 'when accountants didn't have control and the media couldn't buy your soul'. It's a bone-headed plea for authenticity, sung in the most Tupperware tones imaginable: a fake paean to a pre-fake era. It's giving me vertigo.

Wait. It gets worse. I've just looked it up on Napster – oh Christ. I didn't realise how far this had gone. The B-side is a cover of 'No More Heroes' by the Stranglers. 'Whatever happened to the heroes?' she warbles, knowing full well she's replaced them. She's the musical Antichrist.

This is too creepy to be mere coincidence. Someone's messing with us. The replicant kings are trying to mangle our minds. Plug your ears. Block the signal. Final phase. They're taking over.

Plucky little England   [16 June 2006]

Thanks to the magic of newsprint lead times, I'm writing this yesterday, before Great Britain's soccer match against Trinidad and Tobago in the World Trophy competition, so I'd like to take this opportunity to retrospectively wish them all the best. Good luck Britain! Here's hoping for straight sets!

Ha ha. I'm hilarious. Enough of the lame sarcasm. Yes, I'm a member of the apparent minority that dislikes football most of the time and grows to actively despise it during the World Cup. But this year, I've decided not to moan about it.

It's quite simple. I've finally realised that loudly and repeatedly complaining that the World Cup is a whopping great pain in the arse ultimately achieves nothing. Us haters can't win. We're either accused of adopting a contrary position for the sake of it, or told to just ignore it (which we can't, because it's bloody everywhere). Sometimes fans yawn and say they're bored by us killjoys moaning about it, even though they can't possibly be as bored as we are, bored with every flag and cheer and news report and rebranded chocolate bar: the kind of boredom that gnaws at your bones till you don't want to live any more. They just don't understand.

And sometimes people look genuinely upset, and implore you to stop having a go at the World Cup on humanitarian grounds. 'Leave it alone, it's just a bit of fun . . . it's done nothing to you,' they whine through their disgusting football-loving faces, as though the World Cup were a defenceless nine-year-old girl you're attacking with a hammer, instead of an overhyped money-spinning festival of tedium in which the world's thickest millionaires kick a rubbish ball round a poxy field to the wonderment of an audience of foghorning cretins. In my pathetic opinion.

Anyway, like I say, I've decided this time round I won't gripe about it in the slightest. If it gives pleasure to millions, who are we to quibble? The fans are right: we're killjoys. Besides, I've just read about an exciting development in World Cup technology that just might entice me to start taking an interest. I've just read about the Robot World Cup.

RoboCup is now in its tenth year. It's a tournament (held in Germany) in which boffins from around the world organise football matches between teams of specially designed robots. Each year, as both the mechanical designs and the artificial intelligence powering them improve, the players grow more lifelike and proficient. It even has two robotic commentators, called Sango and Ami, who narrate the proceedings in synthesised voices and pump their arms in the air when somebody scores. By 2010 the players should be turning up with an entourage of absurdly spindly robotic wives in tow. By 2014, the first act of robotic football hooliganism. And so on.

But the really exciting bit is this: the organisers reckon by the year 2050, the robots will be good enough to compete in – and win – the 'real' World Cup. Now that I want to see: plucky little England taking on the might of an emotionless army of steel. The tabloid coverage would be priceless.

I'd support the robots, obviously. Especially if they're allowed to eviscerate their human opponents using extendable buzz-saw arms. Because they're robots – that's what they do. Do us proud, robolads! Come on you rivets!

On having a nice day   [23 June 2006]

Greetings from America, where everyone's so bloody friendly and laid-back and nice it makes you want to puke blood in their faces. Earlier today I found myself sharing an elevator with one of the bellboys, and, to make conversation, I asked him whether they had any celebrities staying in the hotel.

'Every guest is a celebrity to us,' he replied, without pausing. And then he smiled.

A few minutes later I'm standing in a corridor, when an engineer walks by.

'Hello there,' says the engineer. 'My name's Frank.' He taps his nametag. It is indeed. He smiles. 'You need anything fixing, any trouble with the TV in your room, computer problems, anything – just call the front desk, ask for me.'

'Um, OK,' I say. 'Thanks, Frank.'

'You're welcome', says Frank.

'Have a great day now.' Then he taps his cap and ambles away, whistling.

I almost have to pinch myself. I've just experienced precisely the sort of benevolent human encounter that only occurs in pre-school children's programmes, except it was real.

In the afternoon I visit a high-street clothing store. Nothing posh; part of a chain. I examine a pullover, but I'm not sure if it's my size. XXL appears to be the only one available. I turn to look for an assistant, and discover one's already beside me, standing at precisely the right distance – close enough to be of use, not so near as to seem invasive.

'I think we still have those in other sizes,' he says. 'Want me to check?'

A few minutes later, I'm buying the pullover. While he's folding it perfectly, the assistant (whose name is Milo) asks if there are any cool bands in England he should know about. He'd been holding out hope of seeing the Libertines, but they split up, which sucked. I rack my brains, but can't think of any cool new bands. Not one. Lamely, I offer the Arctic Monkeys. It turns out Milo's heard them, and thinks they're pretty good, but something about his manner implies he's a touch underwhelmed.

In an excruciating bid to curry favour with my new friend, I say I hear there's this new girl called Lily Allen who's been getting a lot of coverage. Milo writes her name down on a piece of paper and tells me I'm awesome. I walk out of the shop feeling young and fashionable. But I've never heard Lily Allen. What I just did was almost unbearably pathetic; somehow Milo made it seem OK.

Everywhere I turn, members of the service industry are smiling at me, holding doors open, straining to help. I know most of the time they're angling for tips, but I don't care. Sometimes they're just being nice. In London, Frank the engineer would've told me to piss off. The clothes shop guy wouldn't have said anything. I'd be nothing. I'd be less than dirt. Here I'm treated like Sir Lordship of Kings.

Now it's getting late. I'm in my room, typing this. There's a problem with the TV. But I don't call reception and ask them to send Frank up. We've already built a rapport in the corridor. Now he's my buddy, I'd feel uncomfortable expecting him to do chores for me. So I don't call him. He doesn't fix the TV. He doesn't get the tip. Spin on *that*, Frank.

Too old for MySpace   [30 June 2006]

It had to happen, and it has. Age has crept up on me. I'm becoming resistant to technological change.

It used to be so different. I've always been a geek, and proud of it. In my twenties, I lived in a chaotic mangle of keyboards and wires. I was the person people would phone up when they had a problem with their computer. I wrote for video-games magazines, making up jokes about polygon counts and cel-shading.

Then the internet roared up. I ran a website called TV Go Home, which was essentially a fortnightly pisstake of the *Radio Times* with lots of unnecessary swearing in it – just the sort of thing that's been a staple of comedy spin-off books since year dot, except because it was on the internet it was somehow seen as the shiny sharpened bleeding edge of new. My career prospects suddenly changed. Traditional media came calling – TV, newpapers. They wanted me. As far as 'they' were concerned I was someone who 'got' the 'modern' world and all that went with it. For about nine seconds, I felt vaguely cool.

Fast forward to now. I'm looking at MySpace and I'm a fumbling old colonel struggling to comprehend his nephew's digital watch.

Because I don't 'get' it. I mean, I know what MySpace is and what it's supposed to do and how influential it is. It's just that whenever I've visited a MySpace page I've thought 'Is that it?' and wandered around the perimeter looking confused, like a blind man patting the walls for an exit he can't find.

So users create a page and upload their music and photos and videoclips; they post blog entries and links to other stuff and leave witty little messages for one another. And it all meshes together to form a thriving social network. Okey dokey. On the surface it all makes sense.

Yet it's not for me. I mean, I could go and create a page myself, but somehow I'd rather scrape my retina off with a car key. At thirty-five, I'm too ancient for MySpace – I'd look like a school-gate paedo – but that's not really the issue. No. It's simply bloody-minded 'olditude' on my part – the same sort of fusty grumbliness that made greying musos boycott CDs in favour of vinyl in the 80s because they *just didn't want to know* about this new-fangled whatchamathing.

Last week, in the US, I saw an advert for a handheld gizmo using the slogan 'It's not a cellphone: it's MySpace on the go'. It's a terri-fying first – a new gadget I know I'll never want to buy. I've never felt so lost.

Or perhaps it's MySpace's 'social' element that disturbs me. I'm a misanthrope. Everyone on MySpace seems young and happy and excited and flip and approachable, and this upsets me. Still, at least the teenage MySpacers are getting on with the business of being young and alive, unlike the fustier elements of the 'blogosphere', who just waste the world's time banging on and on about how important the 'blogosphere' is and how it spells the end of every old notion ever, when the truth is that, as with absolutely every form of media ever, 99 per cent of the 'blogosphere' is rubbish created by idiots.

Especially the word 'blogosphere'. A word I refuse to write without sneery ironic quote marks either side of it. Because I hate it and it's crap and *i just don't want to know.*

Rise of the invisibles [14 July 2006]

According to clever scientists with spectacles and calculators and pipettes and blackboards and brains the size of beanbags, only 4 per cent of the total energy density in the universe can be accounted for. The rest consists of 'dark energy' and 'dark matter', which basically means they don't have a clue what it is. But you've got to hand it to the scientists – 'dark matter' is such a cool term, it distracts you from accusing them of ignorance . . . although if I was in charge, I'd have called it 'magic space blancmange', because that's even better.

Anyway, dark matter doesn't just exist in space. There are millions of people who essentially consist of dark matter; unknowable swaths of the population I have never encountered and will never understand.

People who watch *Emmerdale*, for example. *Emmerdale* is Britain's third most popular soap opera – second, actually, when *EastEnders* is having an off day. It attracts something in the region of 5 million viewers, which means approximately one in twelve Brits regularly tunes in. Yet I've never actually met anyone who watches it. If you add up the number of people I've met in my life, divide it by the percentage of people who should watch it, then multiply the result by the number of *Emmerdale* episodes broadcast during that period, you end up with a number that definitively proves two things: firstly, that I'm hopeless at maths, and secondly, that the *Emmerdale* audience consists of invisible dark matter whose presence can be detected only in viewing statistics, not the everyday physical world. What are they? Spirits? Ghosts? I haven't the foggiest. It's scary.

Then there's the Red Hot Chili Peppers. They're one of the most popular bands in existence. They play sell-out gigs all over the world and regularly top the album charts. They even get good press. But have you ever met a single, actual fan? I mean, everyone can name *one* Red Hot Chili Peppers song they kinda, sorta like – usually 'Under the Bridge', or that other one (that no one ever knows the name of) – but where the hell are all these adoring fans? Clearly, they're lurking out of sight, in an alternate dimension that exists somewhere between the atoms of our world, where the Chili Peppers are considered acceptable rather than simply annoying. This magical alt-Earth only intrudes on our reality when the Chili Peppers release an album or put tickets on sale. The rest of the time it's invisible.

Fry's Turkish Delight. That's another one. I can't remember if it was me or someone else who once described it as 'a refrigerated human organ dipped in chocolate', but whoever it was, they were on to something. It's been on sale since 1914 and is still going strong – but do you know anyone in their right mind who'd voluntarily eat one? It's a mystery on a par with the continued success of Fisherman's Friend (a cross between menthol and earwax in tablet form) and Kendal Mint Cake (urinal bloody cake more like).

Perhaps people just consume all these things on the sly. Or perhaps I just move in limited circles. But no. I prefer to think there's a phantom population: invisible people, invisible consumption. Dark matter with shoes.

Plan Z   [11 August 2006]

If you ask me, the most terrifying sound in the English language is the word 'plan'. I don't plan. I can't plan. The merest whiff of a plan fills my head with fog and makes me jittery. When someone's outlining a plan, especially one that involves me, my mind refuses to hold the details in focus; instead I nod and frown and pull my best 'listening' face, while inside, my brain's shrieking 'Concentrate on the plan! Concentrate on the plan!' in such a high-pitched squeal it's impossible for even the most basic instruction to register.

Way back in the mists of time, when I wrote about video games for a living, every so often I'd be handed a point-and-click war game to review. Generally, these involve lightning-speed military deployment, informed by an adaptable battlefield strategy you've formulated while studying a map at the start of the game. In theory, anyway. To me it was all blind panic. Every game consisted of several minutes of increasingly desperate mouse gymnastics followed by a crushing defeat. My brain isn't wired to cope with this stuff. A dog could thrash me at chess.

The reason, apparently, is that I'm a 'present-dweller'. I'm incapable of envisaging any kind of future whatsoever, even one that begins in five minutes' time. My life consists of a single, gigantic 'YOU ARE HERE' arrow, pointing directly to now. Which makes things pretty simple. I don't have to worry about fulfilling my long-term goals, for instance, because I don't have any.

Furthermore, I can leave teetering piles of bills unopened, because I simply can't imagine the consequences of not paying them. Instead I walk around in a woozy real-time bubble in which my sole concern is instant gratification. Can't be arsed to fill out that pension form? Then don't bother! Tomorrow never comes. Tomorrow was never there in the first place.

Trouble is, this is all very well when you're fifteen years old, but when you're in your thirties it starts to look pathetic. It's hard to tidy up after yourself, for example, when you repeatedly fail to understand that an unwashed mug on the bedside table will stay there for ever unless you take it away and clean it. It's especially hard when you find yourself glancing at said mug every so often, actively thinking, 'I should take that to the kitchen, wash it, and put it away' – and then still not doing anything about it because that's crazy future cultist talk.

The bigger picture ain't so grand either. I don't own my own property, simply because the thought of all those viewings and negotiations and twenty-five-year contracts makes my head throb like a hammered thumb. And when people tell me this is crazy, that 'everyone feels like that but they just get on with it', it makes no sense to me. I mean, what's their motivation? I don't get it.

What's required, I think, is a time machine. If I could skip forward to my own future, preferably one in which I've put the mugs away and bought my own home, then maybe, just maybe, I'd finally feel like a fully qualified adult. But could someone else invent one, please? Because I can't imagine where to begin.

Down with parties   [18 August 2006]

Here's an amusing game for all you coal-hearted misanthropes out there. Next time you find yourself lurking in the corner at a party, watching the disgusting fun unfold around you, start saying the word 'despair' out loud. Begin the incantation at conversational level, then increase the volume incrementally until someone asks you to leave. I guarantee you'll be bellowing at the top of your lungs before anyone even notices. If you're lucky, someone else'll join in, and then you've made a new friend. I know; I've tried it myself.

Don't get me wrong. I'm a fun guy. There's nothing I enjoy more than a bit of pointless dicking round. It's the single most life-affirming activity in the world. But I have a problem with parties. Parties are supposed to be the last word in devil-may-care enjoyment, yet they fill me with an infinite sense of sadness, so vast and gaping that shouting 'despair' seems like the only sane course of action. After years of pondering the subject, I've worked out why.

Parties somehow represent the rationing of fun, and that very concept depresses me. You're allowed to act like a tit at parties; therefore, by implication, you're not allowed to act like a tit the rest of the time. I consider that a serious infringement of my human rights. It's like society is blowing a whistle and shrieking, 'Attention drones – your allotted enjoyment period starts now.' Talk about enforced bonhomie. It takes the joy out of joy itself.

Consequently I'm suspicious of parties, and all who sail in them. Experience confirms my aversion. For example, when people refer to someone as a 'party animal', you can guarantee what they really mean is 'a loud, unimaginative, overbearing cretin who just about gets away with it when everyone around them is too drunk or stupid to complain'. If there are any self-proclaimed 'party animals' reading this, I hope the ink rubs off on your fingers and poisons you – and if you're online, I hope your monitor shatters, firing white-hot LCD shards into your dimwit, party-loving eyes.

Come to think of it, just hearing the word 'party' makes me angry. In addition to wishing misfortune on 'party animals' every-where, I firmly believe that anyone who uses the word 'party' as a verb – as in 'Hey everybody – let's part-ay!' – deserves to die shack-led in rags while a masked torturer pours a saucepan of their own boiling blood down their throat. 'Let's party' is a pathetic phrase. It really means, 'Woo hoo everybody – we're allowed to enjoy our-selves for a moment! Aren't we ker-razy!?' Ugh.

The only solution, as I see it, is to swap the fun/no fun balance in everyday life. I'd prefer it if the entire year consisted of one long party, punctuated by bursts of compulsory stony-faced toil, prefer-ably doled out in the most fascistic manner possible: two hours of serious work a week, overseen by jack-booted stormtroopers who'll thrash you into a coma if you so much as chuckle before the all-clear sounds. Global efficiency levels would sky-rocket. Better still, our quality of life would improve dramatically. And that'd give everyone real cause to celebrate. Not party. Celebrate.

It's time to smother romance in its sleep
[25 August 2006]

Hands up anyone who's had a great experience with romance. Now put your hands back down and stop lying. Romance never works. Romance never does what it says on the tin. Romance, ultimately, is bullshit.

If I sound jaded, it's because I am. I'm so sick and tired of love and its pitfalls I can scarcely lift my fingers to type. If love were a product, the queue at the faulty goods desk would stretch right round the universe and back. It doesn't work properly. The seams come apart and it's full of powdered glass.

Each fresh romance has two potential outcomes: (1) one of you falls heavily, and quickly, until this helpless, unattractive neediness sends the other running for the hills; or (2) by some miracle your desperate neediness levels balance out, and you stay together for several years – until the love between you withers and dies, at which point one or both of you will stagger away, howling like a wolf with a hook in its gut, wounded beyond reason.

When you're smitten, romance is a thrilling high-wire act over a looming lake of woe. Your head's full of music; the first few steps are a joyful scamper. Then the skies darken, the breeze picks up, the tightrope shudders and you fight to retain your balance. In your heart of hearts, you know you're heading for a tumble, but you're out and exposed and there's no turning back – and who knows, maybe you'll make it?

Imbecile. Of course you won't. Instead, the rope snaps and suddenly you're plunged back into the monochrome workaday reality of flowers in the dustbin and dogs being sick on the pavement.

At this point, wandering in a post-romantic shock, things get even worse. Being numb and distant somehow renders you magically attractive to others. It's sod's law in action, and before you know it you're abusing the privilege. Hungering for another go on the tightrope, you hurl yourself at the nearest admirer, but since the love canary's recently flown your cage, you're selfish, robotic, and doomed to wipe your arse all over their soul. Congratulations: you've become an emotional vandal. And you'll do it again and again until you meet another special someone – only this time the tightrope's higher up and more precarious, and you're so scared of falling that your feet shake the moment you step aboard.

On and on and on it goes, and there's no end to it. This madness must be stopped. We can medicate depression into oblivion; why not romance? A preventative tablet, perhaps, or an adhesive patch that suppresses the relevant endorphins, which you can slap on your skin at the first sign of attraction, killing romance dead, stopping you in your tracks before you make a fool of yourself or a hapless Aunt Sally of another.

And sizzled on the back of every packet, embossed on every patch, just to keep things melancholic and swoonsome, you'd find the last line from Graham Greene's *The End of the Affair* – the battered protagonist's final plea, which sums up the absolute aching awfulness of romance so eloquently it makes your heart nod along with tears in its eyes: 'O God, You've done enough, You've robbed me of enough, I'm too tired and old to learn to love, leave me alone for ever.'

Anyway. Next week: some jokes.

The war on boring terror [1 September 2006]

Guns and bombs, guns and bombs – boring, boring, boring. I'm sick of things going bang. Listen: if the world *must* slide into unbridled chaos and savagery, if we really *are* doomed to splutter our last lying face-down in individual pools of our own viscera, can't we be dispatched more creatively?

Take massacres. It's been ages since anyone went berserk with a firearm in this country, and obviously that's a good thing, mainly because insane machine-gun rampages are just so Nineties. Even so, it won't be long before we see crazed terrorists scampering through the streets toting AK-47s, drilling pedestrians to sausage-meat with big beatific grins on their faces. Well, where's the challenge in that, you pussies? It's far too one-sided. Obviously, harbouring belief in any kind of religion whatsoever betrays a crushing lack of imagination, but really, that's pathetic – like stamping on ants.

If you're hell-bent on wiping us out, at least put some effort into it. Arm yourself with nothing but a frying pan and a saw, and if you manage to score a body count in double figures, then maybe I'll respect you. Otherwise, up yours. You're boring.

Bombs are equally lazy. There's nothing you can do about a bomb going off, short of psychically foretelling the blast and running away. There's no sport to it. I'm getting bored of being frightened of bombs. Give me something new to fret about. Here's an idea: an ankle-height laser beam that sweeps across densely populated concourses in the blink of an eye: a sheet of light slicing everyone's feet off simultaneously. Imagine the chaos! It'd be more humane too, since there's a good chance you could surgically reattach the feet later – although matching each foot to its rightful owner would be a logistical nightmare. Chances are you'd end up with a size ten and a size three. Still, it'd break the ice at parties.

Actually, even foot removal is too violent. The thing I don't grasp about terrorism is why it has to involve violence at all. Detonating a gigantic bag of manure in a crowded space would make the same point far more eloquently – and the victims would still be around to put pressure on the government to do something to ease the crisis. Indiscriminate slaughter isn't just barbaric and selfish – it's immature and idiotic. Any budding terrorists reading this now: toss those detonators in the bin and try being man enough to change people's minds via some other method for once. Girls will respect you. Only wankers kill people. Whether you're a head of state or a disgruntled fanatic, the moment you get blood on your hands, you've become a massive wanker.

Come to think of it, that's how the news should be reported. 'Thirty people were killed today when a massive wanker blew himself up in a busy marketplace' has quite a ring to it, as does 'President Wanker', or 'Prime Minister Wanker'. In fact, why doesn't every bloodthirsty cretin prolonging this sorry dispute simply paint the word 'Wanker' on their forehead and piss off to a remote island somewhere, where they can fight it out with pans and saws while the rest of us settle our differences using non-violent means? We've got the imagination to succeed. What've they got? Hairy palms and firearms, and that's about it.

GPS for life [8 September 2006]

Like the hapless manchild I am, I can't drive a car. I have no licence. Most of the time, that doesn't matter, because I live in London, where it's easy to get about using public transport and you can find most of life's essentials – from groceries to crack cocaine – freely on sale within walking distance, wherever you are.

The taxi is my favoured mode of transport: they're expensive, but overall cheaper than owning and running my own car. As a result, I spend a lot of time sitting in minicabs, an experience that's undergone a huge shift in recent years, thanks to the advent of GPS for all. Your driver no longer needs to have the faintest idea where he's going, because the magic smartarse box does it all for him. I recently got in a cab and the driver literally couldn't speak a word of English; at the start of the journey he passed me the GPS gizmo and expected me to input the destination address myself. The pixelated arrow did the rest. At first this struck me as pretty shoddy, but the more I thought about it, the more convenient it seemed – it was one step away from having a robot chauffeur. The transport equivalent of an automated vending machine.

And while I sat there it occurred to me that I'd quite like a GPS system of my own. Not for geographical directions, but for simple real-life instructions on what to do next. It'd cover all the basics – telling you to pay your bills and tidy up, helping you locate your house keys, telling you to switch the Xbox off and go to bed, etc – just like an electronic organiser, except it would be plugged directly into your brain; a soothing yet insistent inner voice you can't switch off.

And once the everyday stuff was taken care of, it could help you tackle more complex goals. Just as a GPS system asks you to type in your destination before calculating the quickest route, the 'Life GPS' system would let you input a goal (becoming prime minister, perhaps, or having a hit record, or getting off with someone you've taken a shine to), and would then work out the best way to achieve it, in tiny, incremental steps, voiced by someone inherently trustworthy – Kiefer Sutherland in the guise of Jack Bauer, say.

Instead of bleating 'turn right at the next junction', Jack would say something like 'wipe the fridge door', and you wouldn't understand why, but you'd have to do it anyway, because he'd worked out that a clean fridge door is somehow hugely important in the grand scheme of things, an essential branch of the flowchart.

And just as a GPS system will recalculate its suggested route on the fly if you take the wrong turn, so the Bauer GPS would revise his instructions whenever life threw a random event your way. If, on an important first date, you were suddenly struck by a violent attack of diarrhoea, Jack would leap straight into damage-limitation mode and guide you through the next few hours with such skilful grace you'd not only maintain your dignity, but appear ten times more attractive than you did before your bowels started churning. He'd be the best friend you ever had.

OK, so you'd be little more than an obedient puppet, wandering through life with no free will – but by God, it'd be simpler. Bauer always knows best.

On Justin Timberlake [15 September 2006]

Who the hell does Justin Timberlake think he is? I've only just heard his recent single (several weeks after every idiot in the world ran out and bought it, it seems), and according to the lyrics, he's bringing sexy back.

That's what he says, bold as brass. 'I'm bringing sexy back,' he moans, with a meerkat grin on his fizzog, like he's in charge of the world's sexy resources, the cheeky bastard.

I mean Jesus Christ, Timberlake: sexy isn't something you can withdraw from the market then subsequently revive, like Texan bars or *Prime Suspect*. No. It's an amorphous concept which means different things to different people. There's no regulatory body monitoring its supply, Opec-style – and even if there was, no one would put you in charge of it anyway, you snide, self-satisfied, stink-arsed, jigging little stoat.

How dare he? Genuinely – *how dare he*? How *dare* this dot-eyed, crop-haired, fun-sized, guff-tongued, pirouetting waif-boy scamper on to the world's airwaves and loudly proclaim to be the sole global administrator of all things sexy? You'd think it takes massive balls to do something like that, but given the shrill, squeaking vocals cheeping through his ghastly little gobhole, it's safe to assume he's got testes the size of capers. He's practically a human dog whistle, the shrieking, high-pitched, mosquito-lunged ponce.

And wait, it gets worse. Having declared himself the Lord of All Sexy, the lyric goes on to decry the rest of us mere mortals as being somehow not up to scratch. And he calls us bad names while he's doing it!

First he says 'them other fuckers don't know how to act' – which translates as 'everyone in the world, with the sole exception of myself, is a clueless fornicator'. Then he threatens us, using language so offensive it pains me to reproduce it here (and while I apologise for any offence it may cause, I think it's important to quote him in full, if only to bring home the full import of his disgusting slurs). 'You motherfuckers, watch how I attack,' he says. Out loud, right there, on the record.

Yeah, that's right: Justin Timberlake just called *everyone listening to his song* a motherfucker! It could be you, it could be me, it could be your four-year-old nephew – he treats us all with the same high-handed revulsion. Can you believe the nerve of this jumped-up bitch?

Incredibly, he's not through with us yet. In the very next line, he clearly states his intention to meddle in the private affairs of others. 'If that's your girl you'd better watch your back,' he tweets. Why, Justin? What are you going to do? Knife me in the spine and rip her dress off in front of me? I wouldn't put anything past you by now, you hateful, preeping maniac. Sod putting out a single – our mere existence evidently sickens you to the bone, so why not just kick our doors in, burn down our homes, blast us with a shotgun as we crawl pathetically from the flames, and have done with it?

He should be jailed for saying stuff like this. Gagged and manacled and hurled in the deepest, dankest dungeon imaginable. A cell so small they have to snap his skeleton in half to fit him in. And the moment the door slams shut, the whole thing should be soundproofed, sealed and bombed into a million bits.

Justin Timberlake? Justin Piss, more like.

On Banksy   [22 September 2006]

Here's a mystery for you. Renegade urban graffiti artist Banksy is clearly a guffhead of massive proportions, yet he's often feted as a genius straddling the bleeding edge of now. Why? Because his work looks dazzlingly clever to idiots. And apparently that'll do.

Banksy first became famous for his stencilled subversions of pop-culture images; one showed John Travolta and Samuel L. Jackson in a famous pose from *Pulp Fiction*, with their guns replaced by bananas. What did it mean? Something to do with the glamorisation of violence, yeah? Never mind. It looked cool. Most importantly, it was accompanied by the name 'BANKSY' in huge letters, so everyone knew who'd done it. This, of course, is the real message behind all of Banksy's work, despite any appearances to the contrary.

Take his political stuff. One featured that Vietnamese girl who had her clothes napalmed off. Ho-hum, a familiar image, you think. I'll just be on my way to my 9-to-5 desk job, mindless drone that I am. Then, with an astonished lurch, you notice sly, subversive genius Banksy has stencilled Mickey Mouse and Ronald McDonald either side of her.

Wham! The message hits you like a lead bus: America . . . um . . . war . . . er . . . Disney . . . and stuff. Wow. In an instant, your world-view changes forever. Your eyes are opened. Staggering away, mind blown, you flick V-signs at a Burger King on the way home. Nice one, Banksy! You've shown us the truth, yeah?

As if that wasn't irritating enough, Banksy's vague, pseudo-subversive preaching is often accompanied by a downright embarrassing hard-nut swagger. His website is full of advice to other would-be graffiti bores, like: 'Be aware that going on a mission drunk out of your head will result in some truly spectacular artwork and at least one night in the cells.' Woah, man – the cells!

He goes on to explain that 'real villains' think graffiti is pointless – not because he wants you to agree with them, but because he wants you to know he's mates with a few tough-guy criminal types. Cos Banksy's an anarchalist what don't respect no law, innit?

One of his most imbecilic daubings depicts a monkey wearing a sandwich board with 'lying to the police is never wrong' written on it. So presumably Ian Huntley was right then, Banksy? You absolute thundering backside.

Recently, our hero's made headlines by sneaking a dummy dressed in Guantánamo rags into Disneyland (once again fearlessly exposing Mickey Mouse's disgusting war criminal past), and defacing several hundred copies of Paris Hilton's new album (I haven't heard her CD, but I'm willing to bet it's far superior to Blur's god-awful *Think Tank*, a useless bumdrizzle of an album, whose art-work was done by Banksy – presumably he spray-painted it on a brick and hurled it through EMI's window, yeah?).

Right now you can see some of Banksy's life-altering acts of genius for yourself at his LA exhibition *Barely Legal* (yeah? Yeah!), including a live elephant painted to blend in with some gaudy wallpaper. This apparently represents 'the big issues some people choose to ignore' – i.e. pretty much anything from global poverty to Aids. But not, presumably, the fat-arsed, berk-pleasing rubbishness of Banksy. We're all keeping schtum about that one.

– *To be fair to Banksy, the 'murdered phonebox' sculpture he once dumped in Soho Square was genuinely great.*

On pissing like beasts [29 September 2006]

Ours is an increasingly polarised world, with a population separated by one yawning partition after another: racial differences, the generation gap, the rich/poor divide, interfaith squabbling – in fact everyone's alienated from everyone else in some way. It's the only thing we've all got in common.

Actually, it isn't. We've also got our bodily functions. When Michael Stipe sang 'Everybody Hurts', he might as well have sung 'Everybody Empties Their Bum' instead – because it's true (admittedly the song might have felt a bit less poignant with those lyrics, but on the plus side the video would've been funnier).

Our bowels are a great leveller. Angelina Jolie is the most beautiful person on earth, but even she's suffered the odd badstomached scatological interlude, the kind that turns the bathroom into a tropical stink-chamber powerful enough to necrotise your face the instant you open the door. Yeah. She's done that, too. It's a comforting thought.

Bodily functions may be universal, but that doesn't mean they have to be performed in a disgusting fashion. I, for one, am grossly offended by 'performance farters', for example – witless bozos who think it's acceptable to break wind for comic effect. In my book, that's assault; it's particles of their excrement wafting up your nose, for heaven's sake. It should carry a prison sentence of at least five years. I'm not joking.

Annoying though they are, such chuckling guffers are at least comparatively rare compared with the everyday horror of the gents' toilet – a place where time's stood still since the Dark Ages. It doesn't matter where or who you are: even a chortling, dinner-jacketed toff swapping bon mots at a glittering soirée becomes a grunting dehumanised beast the minute he steps into the gents.

Men's bogs are disgusting, and our tolerance is baffling. Take urinals. It's the twenty-first century – why are we still standing in a row, sloshing piss around like animals? It may come as a shock to delicate female readers, but a huge proportion of men, on taking position at a urinal, immediately perform the following ritual: (1) loudly clear phlegm from nose and throat; (2) spit said phlegm directly into urinal; (3) use personal stream to chase phlegm down plughole; (4) vigorously shake self dry while breaking wind, clearing throat and sniffing; (5) leave abruptly without washing hands. (Look, I know it's disgusting, but it's true – every man reading this knows it.)

I'm more genteel – i.e. I'm one of the ones who often can't 'go' when someone else is standing there. Not because I'm a wuss, but because I'm a civilised human being who believes it's the sort of thing you should do behind closed doors. In silence. With no ladies present. Usually.

Surely I'm not alone in this. Gentlemen of Britain, it's time we held a secret ballot. Let's vote to make private urinals compulsory by 2008. Oh, and working hot taps would be nice too. Together we can do it. All we need is the guts to say 'no more'. That and 'now wash your hands'.

You aren't what you eat   [6 October 2006]

On a street near my home there's a gigantic poster depicting a grisly photograph of a young girl glugging a five-litre bottle of cooking oil. The oil is pouring down her chin and over her shirt. It looks disgusting and is designed to put you off eating crisps. 'What goes into crisps goes into you,' shrieks the tagline. Do you see?

Beside the fact that it'd be bloody weird if what went into crisps didn't go into me, but somehow leaped inside the nearest bystander, what's really annoying about the advert (paid for by the British Heart Foundation) is that it's a hysterical exaggeration, the equivalent of a shrieking idiot telling you you'll have someone's eye out in a minute if you don't put the cap back on that pen.

What their stupid poster is trying to say is this: if you eat a large bag of crisps every day for a year, you're effectively 'drinking' almost five litres of cooking oil. But so what? Drinking five litres of cooking oil would indeed be awful, but only if you necked it in one go. Sip it in tiny quantities over a full year and it might be quite pleasant. Or you could drizzle it over some crisps. That'd be even nicer.

You could create an equally sickening campaign attacking organic brown rice. Run a cinema ad showing a year's worth of excrement emerging from someone's backside in one endless, unbroken go, accompanied by a voice-over saying look, if you eat organic brown rice every day for a year, here's how much waste you'll jettison. And then to underline the point you'd show some-one vomiting over it. You know: just to argue your case subtly, like the British Heart Foundation does.

It's not just them. Wizened, infuriating, oatmeal-and-bracken guru Gillian McKeith creates unappetising food mountains in the kitchens of blobsome paupers in an effort to fuel their self-disgust. Look, you hopeless waddling gluttons: look how revolting it is when we take all the cream cakes and sausages you ate in a week and stack them on top of each other! Watch how the tomato sauce from Thursday's spaghetti hoops congeals with Monday's choco-late milkshake. Weep! Weep, you fat fools!

St Jamie Oliver pulled the same stunt on his recent *Return to School Dinners*, mixing chips and cakes and fat into an almighty steaming lump in front of horrified onlookers. As a spectacle, it's stomach-churning; as dietary advice, it's meaningless. Churn a ton of pesto, scallops, muesli and yoghurt together and it'll look just as grim, especially if the camera intermittently pans up to take in St Jamie's increasingly well-fed face gurning over the top of it.

Still, who cares if the shock tactics make sense – this is about saving lives, right? Well, yeah, maybe – that and snobbery. But where does this demonisation end?

Tip junk food into a trough and you're effectively saying the people who eat it are pigs: greedy ignorant livestock, who perhaps deserve pity, or perhaps scorn, but clearly don't deserve freedom of choice. Because left to their own devices, look what they'll do: they'll happily drink a five-litre bottle of cooking oil, like the woe-ful, indolent scum we think they are.

The decoy doomsday [13 October 2006]

I always wondered what the end of the world would look like. Now I know. Let's face it – we're doomed. Each time I pick up a paper or catch a bulletin, the news is 15 per cent worse than before. Serious-ly, if I switched on the TV and they were showing live footage of an army of fire-breathing pterodactyls machine-gunning people to death on the streets of London right outside my door, I'd be horri-fied, but not entirely surprised, nor any more scared than I already am. I'd probably just shrug and wait for them to smash the door down.

We're so screwed, I don't even know what to worry about first. Terrorist extremists? Yeah, they're frightening – but what about those North Korean nukes? Or global warming, come to think of it? I need a personal bloody organiser to sort it out – a gizmo that'll set me a 'timetable of concern' just so I can break down my overall sense of creeping dread into manageable, bite-sized flurries of panic. Otherwise, I'm in danger of forgetting to worry about some things – like bird flu, for instance. I haven't seriously crapped myself about that since, ooh, February? Whenever it was, a top-up's long overdue.

I'm not the only one. I was reading a George Monbiot piece about climate change on the *Guardian* website the other day, and it painted such a bleak vision of our potential future, I swear I physically felt my will to live draining through the soles of my feet, as though it were being flushed out of me and replaced with a sort of heavy, porridge-like despair.

Below the article, in the comments section, a passer-by remarked, 'I have two pieces of advice for anyone reading this: (1) Keep an overdose-sized supply of sleeping pills stashed away that is sufficient for yourself, your family and anyone else you care about. (2) When things start getting bad, use them.' And this was one of the cheerier entries.

Still, the news isn't always violently upsetting. No. Sometimes the bad headlines turn out to be a false alarm – like the other day, when early reports of a second 9/11 happening *right now* turned out to be a comparatively minor accident involving a light aircraft. Can't be much fun being one of the victims, of course – for one thing, you've just been killed, and for another, your death was announced by an anchorman mopping his brow, and drowned out by a worldwide sigh of relief – but for the rest of us, it was the closest we've come to hearing good news in ages.

With this in mind, perhaps news journalists everywhere would like to make our lives a little more bearable by running several deliberately petrifying and utterly fabricated stories a week, just so the genuine terrifying stuff feels a bit less terrifying by comparison. And at the end of the week, simply reveal which stories were true, and which were fake. That way, we'll spend our last few years on Earth feeling like we've lived through a string of lucky escapes, rather than a protracted, dispiriting meltdown.

Start with the pterodactyl example. A week later, invent a health scare – some new hyper-contagious disease that makes your eyes boil and burst and run down your cheeks. The gorier the better. Then invent some bogus knuckle-whitening bullshit about a maniac on the Korean peninsula who's got hold of a nuclear bomb and . . . Oh. Oh bugger.

One night in paradise [20 October 2006]

You're whisked to a top London restaurant for an expensive bloody meal. Before eating, you slurp drinks at the bar: a three-dimensional diagram populated by the cast of *Star Trek*. The ceiling is high, the lighting is low, and everything looks supernaturally rich, as though a high-definition 'cinematic' visual effect is being applied in post-production. All the laughter and hubbub sounds posh or strangely accented. Surely you're in a commercial.

One of your party orders a vodka and cranberry. 'That's a Belvedere,' says the barman with a smile. So from now on, a Belvedere it is. Shortly afterwards, a woman from the future arrives to tell you your table is ready. She practically curtsies as she does so. The Belvedere is gently taken from you, placed on a silver platter and spirited away to your table, to greet you on arrival, thus sparing you the bicep-snapping ordeal of lugging it all the way there yourself.

Orders are taken and a meal is served; each dish is whispered into position under your nose and unveiled like a precious gem being offered to a sultan. At the table beside you sits a preposterous man sporting a cravat and moustache, each straining to out-ridiculous the other. He's of indeterminate age – anywhere between twenty-five and forty-five – yet no matter how old he is, his companion is clearly twenty years younger.

In between silky mouthfuls, you scan the room, playing the 'escort/daughter' guessing game as you alight on various couples. A bullish man with a fat thigh for a neck is dining with an underfed beauty in a backless spun-gold drape. She's a supermodel; he's a burly Greek fisherman crossed with Tony Soprano.

The bill arrives; it's large but it's worth it. Your laid-on taxi is late. As you stand outside, a bodyguard built like a gigantic iron bell ushers a group of Russian businessmen into a people carrier. Then Tony the Fisherman and his superwaif date emerge and clamber into a tarmac-hugging supercar, so shiny on the eyes it's like being stabbed in the iris with a pin. The seats are low; as she dips to get in, her entire compact bum pops out the back of her backless drape. Tony roars away with a hand up her skirt.

Eventually your car arrives. The driver apologises with so much forelock-tugging deference, he might as well invite you to beat him. 'Would you like some music?' he asks as you pull away. You say that'd be nice, and suddenly the air's filled with some bullshit bounce-wid-me R&B, all glossy beats and, genuinely, a lyric about 'feelin' ready to squirt'. The car is the size and shape of a riverside apartment. You could comfortably stage a threesome in here without awkwardly banging your elbows.

Outside on the street, pavement scum queue for night buses. Suddenly, part of you feels like winding down the window and giving them the finger. Because compared to you, they're just clueless, staggering crudsacks. You've spent the night in an expensive Bond movie, pampered at every step, ferried home like a prince. Those laughable bozos wind up howling incoherently like cows in the rain.

Eventually you're dropped home. This special cab cost three times the usual. You've spent a fortune. You get what you pay for. You pay to feel superior. It works. The rich do this nightly. They must be insane.

CHAPTER SEVEN

In which millions come to bury Sezer, Billie Piper is praised to the skies, and Gillian McKeith attempts to murder music

Berks the size of hills   [27 May 2006]

Christ almighty. Hellzapoppin'. Where on God's Earth do you start? *Big Brother* (C4) has shovelled some berks our way in the past, but this time – for round seven – they're using nuclear-powered shovels and berks the size of hills. It shouldn't be possible, but clearly it somehow is.

By now, everyone in Europe will be aware that one housemate has stood out for all the wrong reasons: I speak, obviously, of Shahbaz. Shahbaz – a children's party entertainer created in a madman's laboratory, set loose on the world minus an 'off' switch. Shahbaz – an episode of *Crackerjack* with an erection down its shorts, running, sobbing and shrieking, right in your direction. Shahbaz the All-frighty. Fear him. Pity him. Just for God's sake don't encourage him.

Shahbaz spent his first few days in the hellhouse bouncing round the linoleum shrieking, blubbing, squealing and bear-hugging anyone within grasping distance. That was disturbing enough. But when, for some mad reason, this failed to win anyone over, he really went into meltdown – deliberately provoking arguments then playing the victim: behaviour that's not so much attention-seeking as attention-kidnapping. By the time you read this he'll be conducting a dirty protest in tears – and all because he just wants to be loved. Unsettling in a none-too-entertaining way, he should've been pulled out days ago, and unless he's an actor, I fear for his stability following the inevitable eviction. Here's hoping for a soft landing and a happier tomorrow.

Of course, there's one bit of knowledge Shahbaz can comfort himself with: whatever his faults, at least he isn't Sezer. Sezer: yuk. Just what we need on our screens: a pint-sized, pixel-eyed, mono-tone, priapic, hair-gelled rodent, so in love with himself he proba-bly masturbates to videos of himself masturbating. And it's misplaced adoration, because sculpted torso aside, he's got pre-cisely nothing going for him. He'll never say anything you haven't heard expressed by someone less objectionable before. There are a million identical dullards in the capital alone – hurl a bag of shit into any bar in central London and the chances are it'll burst over four or five of them. (Footnote: infuriatingly, at the time of writing, Tuesday morning, Sezer has behaved entirely reasonably for a full 24 hours. If he doesn't start pissing me off again, I'll have to revise my kneejerk opinion of him. And that would never do.)

Most of the remainder are relatively dull. There's Mikey (sexist Vernon Kay/Owen Wilson cross-splice whose punchably dumb face probably adorns the banknotes in Thickland); George (near-silent posho with the head of an Easter Island statue and a severe case of Portillo lips); Nikki (spoiled chimpette who throws tantrums like Geoff Capes throws fence-posts) and Grace (skinny dance instructor apparently played by Peaches Geldof).

Who else? Think hard now. You can do it. Ah yes: Lea (planet-boobed sometime pornstar who's surgically enhanced her way out of the human race altogether – she now resembles Samantha Janus as described by a lunatic); Dawn (an 'exercise scientist' who believes in chakras – so not a scientist at all then); Imogen (cute but flavourless; a passable human vacuum in a thong); and Richard (catty Right Said Fred diplomat clearly doomed to spend the rest of his natural life lifting heavy objects on daytime DIY makeover shows). Apparently, there are two others, called Bonnie and Glyn. But I don't think they've been on camera yet. Still it's not all bad news. Lisa (Lucy Liu channelling the spirit of Bez), for instance, is vaguely tolerable.

But the clear victor, by ten country miles, is Pete – the Tourette's sufferer whose frequent uncontrollable spasms turn him into a cross between Rik from the Young Ones, Keyop from *Battle of the Planets*, a Tex Avery cartoon wolf, and Klunk, the chirruping inventor from *Dastardly and Muttley in Their Flying Machines*. Funny, charming, intelligent, talented, modest and utterly even-handed, he's by far the most likeable contestant in the programme's lengthening history. And if he doesn't win, I'll eat Shahbaz.

The twat amplifier [3 June 2006]

I used to quite like my ears. Not visually, I mean, but notionally. I admired the way they were content to hang around on the side of my head ferrying noises into my brain. Selfless. Reliable. Steadfast.

This week, however, our relationship changed forever. They turned on me. They forced me to listen to *X Factor: Battle of the Stars* (ITV); specifically, they forced me to listen to Gillian McKeith singing.

I still can't believe I just typed that. I'll type it again: Gillian McKeith singing. Gillian McKeith singing. Gillian. McKeith. Sing. Ing.

I won't get over that in a hurry: my least favourite atrophied Hazel McWitch lookalike in the world, singing 'I just want to make love to you', right there on primetime telly. She has to be the only person on Earth who can take a lyric like that and make it seem like a blood-curdling threat without changing any of the words. It was so horrible, I felt my brain straining to repress all memories of the event before they'd had a chance to form. I almost blacked out.

At the time of writing, there's only been one edition of this 'celebrity' song contest – an unending howlfest culminating in Paul Daniels getting the heave-ho – but if the inaugural broadcast was anything to go by, I fully expect rioting in the streets by the time tonight's final rolls round. It's cacophonous to the point of avant-garde – beyond the point of avant-garde, in fact, all the way into 'sonic weapon' territory. You can't submit an entire population to this kind of punishment. It just isn't right.

Speaking of horrendous affronts to humanity, perhaps it's a bit early in our collective timeline to make rash statements like this, but I strongly suspect future scholars may judge Sezer from *Big Brother* (C4) to be the single most objectionable man in the history of civilisation.

At least, that's how it feels to me right now. I know it's a passing illusion. Ten minutes after he leaves, my pulse will slow and I'll feel nothing. But while he's in there . . . Jesus. It's not healthy, hating someone that much. My heart's turned to carbon. Whenever he appears onscreen, I twist in my seat, agonised. And I've started hallucinating rat ears, poking out the top of his tosser's hairdo. He's not even human any more.

The *BB* house works as a kind of twat amplifier, you see. Once harnessed within, someone who in normal life would merely strike me as a bit of a git quickly swells in negative stature, eventually coming to symbolise everything I hate about our cruel and godless universe.

Last year it took Maxwell three weeks to reach the pitch required for optimum hatred. Sezer managed it in nine days.

And you know who's close behind? Grace. Bug-eyed bloody Grace: the sanctimonious, hoity-toity, stick-thin, Michelle Fowler-faced, I-Know-Everything, plummy, bummy, passive-aggressive Sloane whose blithe faith in her own even-handed worthiness is an absolute gut-churning bollock to behold. Ugh. Hate her too.

Actually, they're all leaving a sour taste all the way from the throat to the backside this year (apart from, say, Glyn, who doesn't count – he's merely a hair in the lens). Once again, I'm writing this on Tuesday morning, so who knows – maybe the new housemates will turn out to be lovely. But so far? It's a big bunch of tossers without exception. Apart from Glyn.

And Pete, obviously. Pete doesn't really count as a housemate either. He's far too agreeable, like someone who's accidentally wandered in from another show. It's the *BB* twat-magnifier working in reverse, I think; making him seem almost saintly. In the real world, he's the sort of person who'd suddenly spring from nowhere to completely do your head in at a gig – offering you a go on his whistle and asking disjointed questions at breakneck speed.

But his main drawback is . . . well, he's just a bit too nice. Come on, Pete. You're a decent guy. Hoof Sezer in the nuts. For us. Just once. You can do it. Please. You can.

Added tit shots [10 June 2006]

Some things in life are permanent. Others are fleeting. And a precious few are ostensibly fleeting, but feel permanent anyway. The DFS half-price sale is perhaps the clearest example of this. The gap between individual DFS sales seems shorter than the average sneeze; all but imperceptible.

Still, that's nothing compared to the microscopic delay between individual Channel 4 documentary seasons examining the world of sex and bums and people with nothing on. Right now, the theme is 'Sex in the 80s', which must've been an exceptionally hard sell round Channel 4 towers. Mullets! Tits! Duran Duran! More tits! Bigger mullets! Ha ha ha! All you need is a few seconds of voice-over babble about 'changing attitudes' and 'social upheaval' laid over the top and hey presto: you've justified everything. It's not just a load of tit shots – it's a sociological investigation. With tit shots.

Anyway, the randy nostalgia reaches an end this week with *The Story of Club 18–30* (C4) – a nudge-wink documentary essentially consisting of hee-larious archive footage intercut with soundbites from people who once got their end away on holiday. There's also a thuddingly pointless thread in which two former Club 18–30 reps return to the Portugal resort they once ruled in their prime . . . and walk around a bit. The contrast between their 1980s snapshots (gangly youths drooling over sunburned knockers) and the pre-sent-day reality (waddling middle age) is a disturbing testament to the ravages of the ageing process. One now resembles Ben Dover, while the other's blobbed out and looks like a cross between a tortoise and a mayor.

By the end of the show you've been mildly entertained, but learned nothing. A bit like an actual Club 18–30 holiday really, but with fewer unwanted pregnancies. Next week on Channel 4: a season of documentaries examining the complex shift in sexual attitudes during the 2001 foot-and-mouth crisis. With tit shots.

In many ways, *Big Brother* (C4) is the present day equivalent of a 1980s Club 18–30 Holiday – flirting, sunbathing, silly little organised games, and lots of people you'd like to remove from the gene pool with a cricket bat.

Over the past fortnight, I've managed to establish a pattern whereby whichever housemate I've ranted about most has been magically evicted by the time the article makes it into print, leaving me feeling even more pointless and impotent than usual; an idiot shrieking at a shadow. Still, I won't let that stop me having another pop at Grace, the poisoned twiglet – even though I secretly hope she survives the jinx because I rather enjoy hating her. She single-handedly redefines the word 'snob' for the twenty-first century: a new, self-deluding breed of snob that considers itself not just superior but inherently cooler, more compassionate, and more down-to-earth than everyone else.

Last week I said she looked like Michelle Fowler, but that's not quite accurate enough. She actually looks more like Howdy Doody, the popular American kiddy show mascot – do a Google image search (go on) and you'll see what I mean. Then pass it on.

Howdy Doody was a puppet, so it's fitting that Grace's current squeeze is the spectacularly wooden Mikey – a man so profoundly thick he can scarcely form sounds, let alone words.

He's hardly even sentient. Lord knows what he's using in place of a brain. Presumably there's some low-wattage internal organ wired up to his nervous system, providing just enough kick to make his eyes blink twice an hour and push shit through his arse when required. A kidney perhaps. Or a liver. But not a brain. Push him into a burning building and he'd simply wander into the flames with a cow-like expression on his face. And when his clothes caught fire he'd spend his final moments trying to swat out the embers with his tail, never quite realising he doesn't have one.

The spectacle of Grace repeatedly binding her spindly frame to this semi-mute humanoid log, breaking off occasionally to bitch about anyone within mindshot, is making this year's *Big Brother* a grinding, masochistic, darkening trial. With tit shots.

Goodbye, England's Rose   [8 July 2006]

Goodbye, England's Rose. Yes, tonight's the night Billie Piper exits *Doctor Who* (BBC1) following her two-year tenure. When it was first announced that the revived Doctor's travelling companion was to be played by Piper, a former kiddywink popstar, I rolled my eyes so violently I found myself staring backward into my own skull. It's Bonnie Langford all over again, I figured.

How pitifully wrong I was. Anyone who thinks she's been anything other than excellent is a brick-hearted stump of a being.

Effortlessly balancing feistiness and charm, vulnerability and goofiness, Billie Piper out-acted almost everyone else on television.

Out-sassed them too. She's extremely good-looking in a most peculiar way: her eyes, mouth and nostrils all seem to be competing to see which can look biggest on her face. At times she resembles a *Spitting Image* caricature of herself. It shouldn't work, but it does. You'll miss her when she's gone.

As for how she's gone, I've no idea – at the time of writing, no preview tapes of tonight's finale were available. I like that. Makes for more of an event. Not enough of them these days. As for series two as a whole . . . well, it's been bumpy. My series three wish-list runs as follows:

1) Curb the zaniness. David Tennant's Doctor alternates between 'boggle-eyed schoolroom wacko' and 'concerned intergalactic statesman' almost without warning. There's too much of the former, not nearly enough of the latter, and precious little in between. A bit of mucking about is fine; too much and it all starts to resemble *The Adventures of Timmy Mallett in Space*.

2) Enough déjà vu, already. Too often, the Doctor seemed scripted as a seen-it-all-before smartarse hell-bent on greeting every creature, artefact, space station and gizmo with a loudly over-familiar 'Oh, it's *you*' bordering on camp. At its worst, this is a bit like going on holiday with someone who's visited your destination before, and behaves like a squawking tourist guide the whole time you're there, pointing out the best cafés and choosing from the menu on your behalf until you feel like ramming their digital camera up their arse, just so they'll be able to take home a picture of something they haven't seen before. I know the Doctor's been exploring the universe for aeons, but a touch more humility would be nice.

3) More two-parters, please. Several three- and four-parters wouldn't go amiss either. Partly because it'd be nice to give some of the stories more space to breathe, and partly because I'm presuming the economies of scale involved might make it possible to do away with the occasional 'cost-cutting' talky episodes altogether.

4) More episodes directed by Euros Lyn. Not only were his

episodes the most visually interesting, but his name sounds like a space station and therefore looks really cool in the credits.

5) My suggestions for next companion: Bez; Wayne Rooney; the entire cast of Channel 4's *Coach Trip*; a purple CGI blob with a retractable anteater's proboscis, voiced by Tim Westwood; Lisa Simpson; Chloe from *24*; Charles Kennedy; Pink.

6) More scary monsters. OK, so tonight we're being treated to an all-out bundle between Daleks and Cybermen. That's great. But some new regular nasties would be nice. Not the Slitheen; they're just silly. I want to see an all-new race of humourless, fascistic bastards worthy of ranking alongside the old favourites. Oh, and they should be armed with drills. Not lasers. Drills.

7) Stop the continuity announcers talking over the end credits so we can hear the theme tune properly.

Anyway, that's my two pennyworth. Said gripes and suggestions are, of course, born out of love. Although I found myself in the uncomfortable position of utterly hating one episode this series (the Love and Monsters wack-a-thon starring Peter Kay), and although it's a series aimed primarily at an audience yet to experience puberty, it's still the most consistently inventive, lovingly-crafted British drama on TV. Fact!

Punishing the viewer at home   [15 July 2006]

The world is full of unexpected comebacks. Lazarus. Elvis. Noel Edmonds. Whooping cough. And now *Love Island* (ITV1), which has returned to our screens despite being the butt of every single topical joke cracked during 2005. Back then, of course, it was known as *Celebrity Love Island* – ITV have since dropped the C-word from its title, partly because the word 'celebrity' had become a talisman of failure, and partly because this year's cast are so shockingly unfamous they make last year's bunch look like the line-up for a new Ocean's Eleven movie.

Here in London, there's a man who hangs around Oxford Circus preaching with a loudhailer. He's popularly known as the 'Be a Winner Not a Sinner' guy, because that's what he tends to shout at the thousands of tourists and shoppers who scurry past each week. With the possible exception of Sophie Anderton, I can comfortably state said Sinner/Winner guy is 10 million times more famous than anyone on *Love Island*. And I for one would love to see what he'd make of it. Let's have a whip-round: we could have him choppered out there by this time next week.

Two of the *Love Island* inmates – namely Gazza's stepdaughter and Pierce Brosnan's son – have been included simply because they're related to famous people. This generous widening of the fame net is an exciting development for all of us. Soon you won't need to share genetic information with a star to be considered a celebrity yourself – sharing a postcode should suffice. I'm pretty sure the woman who presents *Ten Years Younger* lives round the corner from me, therefore I automatically qualify for *Love Island* 2007, during which I intend to enjoy a steamy romp with a woman who thinks she once sat a few seats down from Adam Woodyatt on a train.

Still, famous or not – and they're not – at the time of writing, it's too early to say whether the show itself will turn into a car crash or just a debacle. It's designed, of course, to become an entertaining version of the former – and let's face it, since no one there's got much status to lose, they might as well throw caution to the wind and really get the nation talking. Here's hoping by the time you read this they've decided to simply gather on the beach and rut like dogs in full view of the cameras, pausing occasionally to dig holes and crap in the sand. Fearne Cotton's face should be a picture.

Meanwhile, this year's glaringly butterfingered *Big Brother* (C4) thunders on with its recent House-Next-Door recruits on board. Of the four, two are boring (Michael and Jennie) and one's a walking joke (Spiral – picture a member of Goldie Lookin' Chain impersonating Dougal from *Father Ted*). The inclusion of Jayne, however, marks an important milestone in the programme's history: for the first time, *Big Brother* has decided to abandon its usual housemate-torturing antics in favour of directly punishing the viewer at home.

An entire Trisha studio audience condensed into one bellowing chub-armed fishwife, even in the self-obsessive wilds of the *BB* house Jayne stands out as an unusually raucous attention-seeker, which is saying something. Something bad. In real life she must be unbearable: truly military-grade awful. Her voice is so jarring, each time she opens her gob I feel like someone's cracked a paving stone over my head and danced around cackling. What's next, *BB*? How you going to top this Jayne experiment? Fire metal spikes directly into our eyes?

The remaining housemates, meanwhile, are starting to look like hopelessly institutionalised prisoners. Pete's just dull, Nikki's endless tantrums have ceased to be amusing and now border on *Exorcist*-level disturbing, while Richard's on the verge of talking all the bullshit out of his body – soon there'll be nothing but a hollow whistling sound whenever he tries to speak. The only one I've got any time for is Aisleyne, who I find trashily endearing. So let her win. Why? Because she'll have to do.

Bastards' Hole [5 August 2006]

The trouble with dumb names is they tend to stick. Snickers. P. Diddy. Snakes on a Plane. Absurd the first time you hear them, through repeated use they become as commonplace and boring as words like 'cup' or 'pen'. I reckon I could even walk into a shop and ask if they had any Cillit Bang without feeling preposterous, such is the extent of my exposure to the advert. Bang and the dirt is gone. Of course. It all seems so normal.

Dragons' Den (BBC2) represents the latest example of this phenomena. You could comfortably write everything I know about the world of finance on the side of a coin, but even I'm aware that the word 'dragon' is not standard city jargon for 'potential investor'. A 'dragon' is a mythical lizard that breathes fire and chases knights around in old paintings.

The first time I saw it, I simply couldn't come to terms with Evan Davies's dogged insistence on casually using the word 'dragons' in every other sentence throughout the show. He kept saying things like 'Mike's onion-dispenser has impressed the dragons', or 'The dragons seem angered by Sue's belligerence', and I kept falling about laughing.

This time round, I scarcely noticed. They're dragons now, and that's that. Normality has shifted to accommodate it. Congratulations, Evan Davies: mission accomplished.

Mind you, I can't help wishing they'd called it Bastards' Hole instead. After all, it's far more fitting, and even after three series I'd still hoot my face to snot whenever Davies said 'The bastards have spotted a flaw in Simon's business plan', or 'Two of the bastards are still interested', or – well, each time he used the word 'bastards', basically.

There are two new bastards this series: Deborah Meaden and Richard Farleigh. Deborah's a furious-looking, middle-aged, disapproving matron type, which means Davies has to be careful not to use the word 'dragon' when the camera's pointing her way. She's far sourer than her female predecessor, simperin' Rachel Elnaugh, who looked like she'd invest in any old new-age shit dangled in front of her. You wouldn't catch Deborah Meaden hanging a dreamcatcher over her bed. A burglar, perhaps, but not a dreamcatcher. If the first episode's anything to go by, she (a) hasn't smiled since the *Belgrano* went down, and (b) could chew the tin balls off a Cyberman. Fuck with the Meaden and you're getting *owned*, bitch.

Nor, it seems, would fucking with Richard Farleigh be a sensible option. He's clean-cut and sports a head shaped like a cube – in fact, he vaguely resembles a slightly squashed Dolph Lundgren, although his accompanying Australian accent automatically makes you think he used to be a regular cast member in *Home and Away*, even when you know he wasn't, because you actually went and looked it up on the IMDb. He seems to be filling the role Doug Richard played in previous series: the firm but fair technology expert who knows his stuff. He's slightly more annoying than Doug ever was, mind. In his 'bit' of the show's title sequence, Davies's voice-over explains how mind-bombingly wealthy and successful Farleigh is, while we watch him winning a game of tennis, and somehow this grates more than the footage of Duncan Bannatyne waterskiing.

Apart from that, nothing seems to have changed: as ever, the budding entrepreneurs are a mix of the inept, the deluded, and the occasional level-headed player, and most of the fun comes from watching them having their dreams pissed on – although disappointingly, Peter Jones, traditionally the most heartless dragon, shows signs of mellowing. At one point this week, he virtually begs someone not to sell their house and jeopardise their family's future to finance the production of a insanely rubbish-looking 'multimedia table' the dragons have just scoffed at.

Come on, Jonesy. Compassion is for wimps. Two series ago, you'd have laughed in the guy's face. You're a dragon! Breathe fire! Keep this up, and it'll be renamed Pussies' Corner before you know it.

Pointing away from the problem [12 August 2006]

So, as *Big Brother* (C4/E4) staggers to an end like a beaten hound tottering in the vague direction of an exit, what has it taught us? Is this simply an exercise in mindless entertainment, or is it something deeper than that? When we look at *Big Brother*, do we grasp what it means to be alive in the early part of the twenty-first century?

No. It's a gaudy circus act in which apes get goaded with sticks while the public throw rocks at them. As the world floats ever closer to a third world war, TV shows like *Big Brother* are essentially little more than brightly coloured, lightbulb-studded arrows, pointing away from the problem.

Ah well. We've all got to die some day. So without further ado, let's dish out the gongs for this year's Screen Burn *Big Brother* Awards.

The Instant Star award goes, obviously, to Nikki, the unstoppable tantrum machine. A bit like a female Tasmanian devil with the face of Ruth Gordon from *Harold and Maude*, Nikki's already been signed up for a post-show series in which she 'attempts to hold down a job'. If that isn't a comment on the frothing cauldron of madness into which we've all been plunged, I don't know what is. What next? Someone who can't wipe their own arse?

Speaking of arses, the award for Most Forehead-Gnawingly Objectionable Git goes to Sezer, the single most self-regarding housemate *Big Brother*'s ever seen. Strutting round the house with a face like a perineum with tiny black dots drawn on it for eyes, he was the human equivalent of a cock-shaped novelty pen with ego problems. I can say no more about Sezer for legal reasons – i.e. I'll get up and kill an innocent bystander if I have to think about him much longer.

The Most Irritating Voice award goes to Richard, whose pseudo-psychological babble filled the house like a radio tuned to Bullshit FM. On entry, Richard described himself as a 'sexual terrorist', which was one of those wacky soundbites auditionees like to bung in to improve their chances of selection – an unfortunate choice in this instance, since the phrase 'sexual terrorist' conjures up images of indecent assault and violent death, both of which would've been preferable to what he actually delivered – weeks of tedious mono-tone burble.

Most Misunderstood Housemate was Aisleyne, who I stubbornly continue to admire, even in the face of close friends bellowing that I'm wrong. I refuse to believe she isn't quite a nice person, actually.

The Biggest Suckbowl Award goes to Mikey, the do-nothing Scouser with a brain of wet mud. Mikey was little more than a docile, incomprehensible sloth, who spent half his time accusing other people of 'arse-kissing' and the other half slumped by the bridge to nowhere emitting a low hum. Watching him was like sitting through a 15-hour fly-on-the-wall documentary about the world's thickest shop-window dummy.

Finally, the Butterfingers Award for Clumsiest Housemate goes to *Big Brother* himself, who punctuated this year's show with one thumping cock-up after another. The 'rigorous selection process' threw up unstable housemates, hunger strikers and a sulky posho who didn't want to be there in the first place; the 'Golden Ticket' contest delivered a boring silicone-titted ghost who'd been audi-tioned and rejected several times in the past; and the 'soundproof' Secret House had walls made of atom-thin toilet paper.

Even when the twists worked, there was something unfortunate about them: as the 'prison' task took place, the news broke that a former contestant had been arrested on suspicion of rape; suddenly the sight of housemates trudging around in cartoon jail rags felt downright haunting.

Anyway, *Big Brother 7*: that was that. *Big Brother 8* is scheduled to take place in the glowing centre of an irradiated war-torn wasteland formerly known as Earth. See you there.

No one loves the ugly   [26 August 2006]

Mirror, mirror on the wall – please stop throwing up. Yes, it's a hard life being ugly. People stop and stare, then wish they hadn't. You ruin photographs just by being there. And worst of all, no one ever truly loves you. Oh, they pity you, sure. But love? Hah! Love's the sole preserve of the slender, symmetrical ones. No one loves the ugly. And even if they do, they're just being patronising – like girls who squat down and chat to the tramp by the cashpoint for five minutes to make themselves feel better.

Actually, that's nonsense. Despite our obsession with looks, anyone with an ounce of sense realises the old 'it's what's inside that counts' cliché is true – although you have to learn it the hard way. Years ago, I had a girlfriend who was so beautiful I once burst into tears simply watching her sleep. From the outside, an angel. But inside? Cold to the point of inhuman. I might as well have fallen in love with a shoebox.

So sod looks. Besides, unprettiness has its advantages. I could, if I so chose, grind a broken bottle into my face, then punch all the shards in, safe in the knowledge that I couldn't be any more hideous than before. How liberating is that? Sometimes I can scarcely contain the joy.

But not everyone's as comfortable with their own grisliness, even when they aren't grisly in the first place. Witness the poor bastards scattered throughout BBC3's Body Image season, paying particular attention to the lost souls showcased in *Too Ugly for Love* (BBC3) and *My Small Breasts and I* (BBC3).

The former is a documentary following three people with body dysmorphic disorder – a mental condition whose victims become obsessed with their own imagined ugliness. Convinced passers-by are recoiling in horror, they resort to hiding indoors or behind a mask of make-up. In reality, they look fine: in their heads, they'd make the Elephant Man sick up through the hole in his bag.

The whole thing would be comic if it weren't for the obvious agony involved. One man is so convinced he has gruesome dark circles under his eyes (which he doesn't) he spends his entire life wearing opaque sunglasses. A woman despises her face so much her family virtually bankrupt themselves paying for repeated nose-jobs – which naturally, she's never satisfied with. Eventually, she's had so much surgery her conk is in danger of collapse. Yet she presses on, convinced she's disgusting. Which she absolutely isn't.

My Small Breasts and I, meanwhile, follows three beautiful, little-titted women on a mission to improve their busts. One obsessively pumps them up using a terrifying suction device; another contemplates surgery; the third undergoes a bizarre 'photo therapy' which basically involves a photographer talking her into stripping off for some pictures.

Now, speaking on behalf of all heterosexual males for a moment, no man worth his salt gives a sailor's tug how big a lady's chest is. We could get aroused simply glancing at a crude charcoal sketch of a single boob scrawled on the side of a shed. Place an actual, live pair of boobs in our immediate proximity and you've already fulfilled our every waking dream. Who cares how many atoms they're made out of? THEY'RE BOOBS, FOR CHRIST'S SAKE! CAN'T YOU GRASP THE SIMPLE SOARING MAJESTY OF THAT?

Anyway, it's not hard to see where much of this dissatisfaction stems from. Celebrity twat mags circle patches of cellulite and run away cackling. TV is a warped slideshow of false perfection, backed with an alarming tendency to pillory anyone who doesn't match up. It's acceptable, for instance, for Simon Cowell to tell a homely wannabe that they're simply too plain to be famous – we meekly shrug and accept that he's just being honest. And in today's stinking world, he is.

Kurt Vonnegut once compared television to the lead in the water pipes that slowly drove the ancient Romans insane. But then what does he know? He's only some ugly old bastard, after all.

Brian Conley: irritant or genius? [9 September 2006]

Stealthily, by degrees, contemporary daytime TV has transformed itself into a bizarre cover version of 1980s primetime TV. There's lightweight celebrity chat with Sharon Osbourne instead of Wogan; Noel Edmonds hosting conservative gameshows on Channel 4; and now, brilliantly, *Let Me Entertain You* (BBC2), an old-school talent and variety show that doesn't just beggar belief but bugger it – with all the frenzied passion of Heath Ledger in *Brokeback Mountain*.

It works like this: every day, a fresh bunch of excruciating amateur entertainers performs before a live studio audience. Each member of said audience has a button to push when they've had enough of the act: the moment 50 per cent of the audience are fed up, a klaxon sounds and the performance is halted. Simple. It's *The Gong Show* minus the irony.

You know you're in for a treat the moment the host bounds on stage because it's Brian Conley. Hosts don't come more 'showbiz' than that. He's a goddamn showbiz machine. For starters, he opens each edition with a song – a *song!* – punctuated with cheeky winks to the camera. Then he tells some thrillingly creaky *Crackerjack* jokes and engages in nudge-wink banter with the old dears in the front row. It's cruise-ship hell all the way, which feels hugely refreshing for some mad reason.

In fact, if you're anything like me you'll appreciate it on two opposing levels at once – the ironic, cynical part of your brain has a sneery guffaw, while the cuddly, human part simply enjoys a warm chortle. It's confusing. I genuinely can't decide if Brian Conley is an irritant or a genius.

Psychologists have a term for this state of mind: 'cognitive dissonance' – the act of trying to hold two contrasting viewpoints at once. Left unchecked, it can drive people crazy. Which is bad news, because the moment Conley makes way for the amateur entertainers themselves, a self-perpetuating cognitive dissonance feedback loop starts to build in my head.

There are singers. There are dancers. There are people who

balance saucepans on the end of their nose . . . you name it, they're on it – and they're bloody awful.

Throughout each performance, a timer ticks away in the bottom left and a 'disapproval rating' percentage score builds in the bottom right, and it's this that renders the show oddly hypnotic. If a contestant makes it to the three-minute mark, they've 'won' and automatically go through to that week's final. But that rarely happens. Most performances are abruptly murdered somewhere round the two-minute mark: the klaxon sounds, the lights go out, and the bewildered, humiliated performer staggers away.

Some acts barely get a chance to open their gobs before people start hammering their buttons. Even kids – and yes, *Let Me Entertain You* features *loads* of child performers – don't always scrape by on a sympathy vote. Since the audience is voting anonymously, they're remarkably unsentimental, particularly when faced with a creepy young performer (i.e. all of them).

Ethnic minorities don't seem to fare much better. This is unfounded speculation on my part, but I suspect if you were to compare booting-off times, you'd find white acts get a significantly easier ride, thanks to some degree of subconscious prejudice on the part of the (largely Caucasian) audience. Mind you, the quickest dunking I've seen thus far was dished out to a bald white guy who'd painted himself orange.

And occasionally, an abysmal performance enjoys a mystifying degree of approval. Some don't even qualify as a 'performance' in the first place: last Monday, a man made it through to the final by incoherently discussing his love of *Only Fools and Horses*. It's unfathomable. You could piddle into a teacup and there's a good chance you'd beat a pubescent dance troupe who'd sewn their own costumes and travelled 5,000 miles just to be there.

In summary, then: It's brilliant. It's awful. It's brawful. I don't know what it is. But I know that somehow, it's worth bloody watching.

I hate you. We all hate you. God hates you

[16 September 2006]

Last time I checked, the Nazis didn't win the Second World War – not that you'd sodding notice. After all, the Third Reich was pretty big on issuing orders and demanding cold, robotic obedience from the populace, and that's pretty much what we're saddled with today. But the way the orders are delivered has changed. Instead of being barked at in a German accent through a loudhailer, they're disguised as concerned expert advice and floated under your nose every time you switch on the TV or flip open this newspaper.

There's a continual background hum, a middle-class message of self-improvement, whispered on the wind. 'You eat too much. You eat the wrong things. You drink. You smoke. You don't get enough exercise. You probably can't even shit properly. You'll die if you don't change your ways. Your health will suffer. Have you got no self-respect? Look at you. You sicken me. I pity you. I hate you. We all hate you. God hates you. Don't you get it? It's so sad, what you're doing to yourself. It's just so bloody sad.'

That's the mantra. And it goes without saying that the people reciting it are routinely depicted as saints. Last year, the media dropped to its knees to give Jamie Oliver a collective blowjob over his *School Dinners* series, in which he campaigned to get healthier food put on school menus. Given the back-slapping reaction, you'd be forgiven for thinking he'd personally rescued 5,000 children from the jaws of a slavering wolf.

Anyway, the series was a huge success. In fact in telly terms there was only one real drawback: it wasn't returnable. After all, when you've saved every child in the nation from certain death once, you can't really do it a second time. The only solution is to find a new threat, which brings us to *Ian Wright's Unfit Kids* (C4), a weekly 'issuetainment' programme in which the former footballer and renowned enemy of grammar forces a bunch of overweight young-sters to take part in some extracurricular PE.

It's essentially a carbon copy of the Jamie Oliver show, with more sweating and fewer shots of pupils mashing fresh basil with a pestle: an uplifting fable in which Wrighty shapes his gang of mis-fits into a lean, mean, exercisin' machine – combating apathy and lethargy, confronting lazy parents, and attempting to turn the whole thing into a nationwide issue that'll have Range-Rover mums everywhere dampening their knickers with sheer sancti-mony in between trips to the Conran shop. Oh, isn't it simply terrible, what these blobsome plebs do to themselves? Not our Josh, you understand: he eats nothing but organic spinach and attends lacrosse practice six hundred times a week.

Bet he does, the little shit.

It's cleanly executed – we even get glimpses of Ian's temporarily bleak home life, just to ram home what a self-sacrificing saint he is – and yes, it is heartwarming to watch flabby, unconfident kids transforming themselves with a bit of simple activity . . . but there's something about the underlying eat-your-greens message that really sticks in my craw, in case you hadn't guessed.

What happened to the concept of *choice*, you fuckers? So a bit of jogging might increase your life expectancy – so what? That just equates to a few more years in the nursing home – whoopee-doo. And besides, I'd rather drop dead tomorrow than spend the rest of my life sharing a planet with a bunch of smug toss-ends trying to out-health one another.

In episode two, video games and the internet are singled out as villains in the war on flab: they make kids too sedentary, you see. Oddly enough, TV, which is equally sedentary and, unlike those two activities, actively encourages you to let your mind atrophy along with your physique, escapes without a bollocking. Funny, that.

Well listen here, Channel 4 – instead of forcing kids to eat bracken or do squat-thrusts, how about teaching them to think more expansively, so they reject the sly, cajoling nature of programmes like this? Or would that be a campaign too far?

Pin sharp   [23 September 2006]

You'd think, as a globally influential writer of unprecedented cultural import, I'd be offered freebies, perks and trinkets round the clock. Free DVDs. First-class flights. An all-expenses-paid stay at that sail-shaped hotel in Dubai where visitors wipe their bums on gold leaf and swan's wings. VIP passes to the opening of Lindsay Lohan's blouse. Yeah. That's what you'd think.

In practice, the only freebie I've ever received is a tray of sausage rolls from Gregg's the bakers, delivered unexpectedly to my desk after I mentioned them in print. And I had to give most of those away. There's only so much mashed pig you can eat in one sitting before your tear ducts start leaking yellow fat.

Anyway, all that changed the other week, when an email arrived offering me a free top-of-the-range HD television and a Sky HD box. Should I accept it? Wouldn't doing so make me a bought and sold whore, blackmailed into praising Murdoch's empire by the promise of free gadgetry? I agonised over the ethical implications for three whole seconds before emailing them back with directions to my flat and a comprehensive list of times I'd be in.

So now I'm an early HD adopter, albeit one who hasn't had to shell out for it. And let me tell you, the picture's so sharp you could cut your face on it. And the colours are so vibrant, your eyes over-heat trying to process them all. Watch a documentary on coral reefs and it's just like being there (in two dimensions and with far less moisture).

Yes, the picture *is* far better, obviously, but there's not really anything to watch yet. You get a couple of documentary channels, Artsworld, a HD version of Sky One (which means 24 and *Dead-wood* in HD, so that's good), a few movies, some football (boo), and a BBC 'preview' channel that loops HD footage from *Bleak House* and Jools Holland and full-length repeats of *Planet Earth* (the world's most expensive screensaver). If I'd paid for it, I'd be dis-appointed. It'd be like spending a fortune on a flying car, only to discover that under current regulations you're only allowed to fly it to Gwent and back. On Sundays.

In fact the main impact this fancy HD set-up has had on my life is to make anything that isn't broadcast in HD – i.e. almost every-thing – look hopelessly shit by comparison. At the weekend, I tuned into *The X Factor* on manky old lo-fi ITV1, and it was like staring through the holes in a wet Hessian sack: blurry, muddy, and seemingly out of focus. Louis Walsh became a chuckling smudge, Simon Cowell an arrogant cloud. You couldn't even see the contestants cry properly.

Select one of the bargain-basement satellite channels dedicated to old repeats and things get even worse. The combination of old video and huge compression rates transforms them into incoherent, jumbled collections of fuzzy multicoloured blocks. You might as well squint into a bowl of Lego soup.

In short, my freeloading glimpse of the crystal-clear future has spoiled everything. It's like trying to eat a Fray Bentos pie in a tin the day after dining in a Gordon Ramsay restaurant (not that I'm planning to visit one – unless his PR company send me a free invite).

Worse still, common sense dictates that by the time every channel's taken the leap into HD wow vision, some other new technology will be waiting in the wings to annoy you: perhaps some new broadcast system that enables you to feel a cool breeze whenever Inspector Lynley winds his car window down. And a hot one when Keith Miller blows off.

It's trad TV's attempt to fend off the internet, of course; just like the cinematic gimmicks of the 1950s (such as 3D) which tried to stave off the threat of TV. Except there's nothing to stave off, really – it's obvious we're heading for some kind of YouTube-structured future in which channels no longer exist and individual programmes get emailed directly into your mind's eye. By robots.

Robots owned by the wonderful Murdoch family and their beautiful, talented colleagues.

Rubbin' the hooded man   [14 October 2006]

Life expectancy was poor in medieval times. There were wars all over the place – not nice clean modern wars, with laser-targeted superbullets that dock points from your Nectar account instead of killing you but sweaty, close-combat wars in which boggle-eyed beardos with hardly any teeth battered you with clubs or hacked bits of limb off you with swords, leaving you thrashing about in the hay squirting blood from your stumps like a shrieking Bayeux tapestry bitch.

If you managed to avoid that, lack of hygiene would get you. All the food was germ-flavoured, and the plates were discs of dried cow shit, hammered flat and baked in the sun. You get the picture. Things weren't nice.

Anyway, this is the world *Robin Hood* (BBC1) doesn't even try to bring to life. Instead, the BBC's new interpretation plays like a cross between a low-budget *Pirates of the Caribbean* and an Arctic Monkeys video. And clearly this has offended a sizeable section of the viewing public, who are flooding message boards with complaints that the show is 'too modern', and 'too crap', but mostly 'too unlike the ITV version'.

Well, I was never a fan of the ITV version; I couldn't abide the mystical Herne the Hunter guff, thought the Clannad theme tune sounded like they were singing about 'rubbin' . . . the hooded man' (far too rude for Saturday teatime), and hated the stupid hair. (Bizarrely, many of the people citing ITV's Michael Praed as the definitive Hood find the haircuts in the new version outrageous – as though Praed's flowing Timotei ladylocks represented the last word in hard-edged realism.)

Anyway: Hood 2006 is a curate's egg. On the one hand, it's heartening to see another ambitious family drama in the family teatime slot. On the other . . . well, it's all over the place, isn't it? At its worst, it's like watching someone else playing an RPG full of lengthy cut scenes, in which you trek between three different locations ad nauseum. (Incidentally, the way the location names pop up accompanied by a twanging arrow sound effect is so video-gamey; I keep trying to press the start button to find out where I am on the map.)

Like many video games, it looks like it's been rush-released with too many rough edges intact. The script often sounds like a first draft in need of a polish, and some of the editing is downright bizarre, with dialogue bleeding too far into the next scene, and repeated shots of so-so stunts from a variety of angles and at different speeds, which always feels like desperate shorthand for

'Look! We can afford stunts! Please be impressed!' Tonight's episode just seems to end at a weird, arbitrary junction, as though a final scene was cut at the last minute.

And Robin's archery skills are so superhuman, there's no sense of peril; when he gets into a tight spot, you know he'll simply do something impossible with his arrows, then smugly waggle his eyebrows around like Robbie Williams. And he's too young. The repeated references to him spending 'five years away' fighting in the Holy Land are supposed to imbue him with gravitas, but instead make you think he must've still been a foetus when he set out.

The remaining cast largely consists of people who look distractingly like other people: Marian looks like Rachel Weisz, Much resembles a cross between Paul Giamatti and Leigh Francis, and Alan-a-Dale could easily play Alun Armstrong's son (largely because he is).

Despite the avalanche of flaws, I can't bring myself to entirely hate Hood '06: Grand Theft Sherwood because (a) I suspect it'll improve, and (b) it does have intermittent flashes of thumping good Saturday-night fun about it, even if they are few and far between.

Robin should be able to properly kill people though. I know it's pre-watershed, but the bloodless A-Team panto-fighting is ridiculous. This is Ye Olden Days! Life was brutal! And if we don't see an arrow puncturing an eyeball before the end of the series, I'll be furious.

CHAPTER EIGHT

In which words are replaced by faces, psychics are thrown in jail, and Barclays Bank wants to be your friend

The best a man can get   [30 October 2006]

Damn the news, damn it to hell and back. It used to be so exciting: sieges and streakers and balaclavas and Fred West and all that. There were good guys and bad guys. It was cute. And quite funny. Not any more. Now no one's in the right and we're all going to die. It's so depressing, the only sane course is to ignore it completely until it goes away.

That's why we're so hooked on distraction, which is available in more forms than you can shake a stick at (stick-shaking being just one example). TV provides distraction, as do sport, fashion and coloured lists of Chantelle's top ten favourite cuddles.

The internet is an incredible distraction: the equivalent of one of those Pavlovian training machines that dispenses pine nuts to lab rats when they nudge the correct lever – except instead of nuts, the internet dispenses porn, chit-chat, 9/11 conspiracy theories and YouTube footage of kittens falling over.

The greatest form of distraction, however, has to be the pursuit of swanky material goods. Nothing staves off that gnawing sense of dread quite like a spending spree. Maybe I won't get my legs blown off by terrorists if I buy enough aspirational bullshit? That's the spirit.

This being space year 2006, you no longer need to visit Harrods to experience the kind of opulent extravagance usually associated with billionaires and sultan's daughters. A trip to Asda will suffice. Almost every product you can think of is available in a toffee-nosed aristocratic version, all the better to mesmerise yourself with.

Fancy some crisps? Don't scoff bog-standard Walkers; indulge in some hand-cooked balsamic and sea salt Kettle Chips instead. You'll still end up fat as a whale, but at least you'll have taken the posh route.

Clothes a bit mucky? Forget ordinary washing powder. Use new 'Crushed Silk and Jasmine' Bold 2-in-1. That's right: crushed silk and jasmine. Make sure your butler programmes the spin cycle correctly when he's using it.

Need a shave? Toss out your Bics and grab the Gillette Fusion, which single-handedly represents Consumer Product Event

Horizon by combining 'the comfort of five blades' (on the front) with 'the precision of one' (on the back). The main cutting surface is about the size of a sheet of A4; so large you can't get it under your nose without shearing off your top lip, which is why you need the blade on the back – it's the only bit you can enjoy a reasonable shave with.

There's also a battery-operated 'Power Handle' option that makes the whole thing buzz like a wasp in an envelope – not to help you shave, but to offer yet more fleeting distraction from the *unremitting misery of life*.

The Fusion Mk2, out next year, features 190 blades, a 30GB hard drive, a pine nut dispenser and a synthesised voice telling you everything's OK, even though the mere existence of such a razor proves otherwise. I've pre-ordered mine already.

The bank that likes to say any old shit

[6 November 2006]

So the other day I'm using an ATM, and while I'm tapping in my PIN number, trying to perform an obfuscating contemporary dance with my fingers so it looks like I'm typing different numbers to the ones I'm actually using, my eyes momentarily alight on the top of the cashpoint and I notice it isn't a cashpoint at all. Not officially, anyway.

It's been renamed The Hole in the Wall. Right there on the machine itself. Barclays has taken the unofficial, slang name for the ATM and legitimised it. It is co-opting the language of the people. It is trying to pretend it is 'one of us'. It can piss off.

It gets worse. Next to the door, there's a sign reading 'Through these doors walk the nicest people in the world' – which strikes you as monumentally nauseating, until you realise it's a little gag: beneath, in smaller lettering, it says something along the lines of '. . . as voted by their mums'. Tee hee, Barclays! Tee hee!

When I get home, I do a bit of Googling and discover this japery has been going on for a while; I just hadn't noticed until now. Apparently, it's all part of a rebranding exercise.

Barclays felt it was perceived as being too stuffy, too formal, so it decided to replace traditional banking jargon with chummy, colloquial language. The ATM became The Hole in the Wall, the customer-service desk has a sign saying Can I Help? over it, and the Bureau de Change has been rechristened Travel Money.

Why leave it at that? If you're hell-bent on making your bank look and sound like a simpleton, a desk labelled Travel Money is still a bit too formal. Why not call it Oooh! Look at the Funny Foreign Banknotes! instead? And accompany it with a doodle of a French onion-seller riding a bike, with a little black beret on his head and a baguette up his arse and a speech bubble saying, 'Zut Alors! Here is where you gettez les Francs!'

Actually, why still call yourself a bank at all? 'Bank' sounds boring. Call yourself 'Barclays Money Circus' instead.

Don't know about you, but I feel like vomiting myself inside out whenever big businesses try to cute themselves up this way – all lower-case brand names and twee little jokes and overuse of the words 'you' and 'my' and 'we' and 'us' as though we're a bunch of cuddly-wuddly pals and hey, we're all in this crazy world together, so let's have some fun with it, right guys?

It's the modern equivalent of someone who uses multiple exclamation marks to denote how ZANY!!!!! they are. It's desperate. Anyway, one solution is to come up with new colloquial terminology they can't co-opt. Sod The Hole in the Wall. They've absorbed that one. Let's start calling ATMs Coinshitters instead. See how long it takes Barclays to start using that. My guess is quite a while.

World War II: the domestic version

[20 November 2006]

Video games are great. Vibrant, addictive and continually evolving, they beat TV hands-down on almost every count. Video games don't pause for an ad break every 15 minutes. There has never been a video game hosted by Justin Lee Collins. You can't press a button to make Phil Mitchell jump over a turtle and land on a cloud (unless you've recently ingested a load of military-grade hallucinogens, in which case you can also make him climb inside his own face and start whistling colours).

Yes, games are great. Trouble is, they've become so sophisticated, some are no longer content to provide simple fun, and instead aim to immerse you in a world of their own devising – and not always in a good way.

Earlier this year I played a game called Condemned, in which you had to trudge around a dingy underworld desperately fighting off psychotic tramps using virtually anything that came to hand: planks, crowbars, shovels, you name it. Between scuffles, you had to collect dead birds and bits of old tin. I soon gave up, not because the game was rubbish, but because I was too depressed to continue.

And now there's Call of Duty 3, a first-person shooter which takes the mournful contemplation and harrowing violence of *Saving Private Ryan* and applies it to a video game. 'Brings you closer than ever to the fury of combat,' screams the back cover, and it isn't bloody kidding. Previously, the closest I've ever been to the fury of combat is wrestling with a tough-to-open ketchup sachet in a motorway service station. Now I've got the Second World War in my living room.

Press 'Start' and you're plunged headlong into a bedlam of gunfire and screaming, replicated in HD visuals and 5.1 surround-sound. You're firing wildly in the vague direction of Nazis, out of your mind with terror, while battle explodes all around you. It's enough to make Donald Rumsfeld as stiff as a flagpole.

For extra immersion, the game simulates blurred vision and tinnitus whenever a blast goes off at close range. When you're injured, the controller vibrates in your hand, imitating a faltering heartbeat. And when you inevitably drop dead, the screen pretentiously displays a sombre quote about war, such as 'All wars are fought for money – Socrates', presumably because a simple 'Game Over' might appear somehow disrespectful, what with the Second World War being a real event that killed millions and all that.

But don't get me wrong. I'm not saying it should be banned or put on a high shelf where humankind can't reach it. I'm saying it's a good thing. Because eventually I realised the experience of playing it was so relentlessly horrible, I'd rather go and do the washing up, just for some harmless escapism.

That proved so relaxing, I wiped the oven clean too. Later I might do some paperwork I've been putting off. The war was too real for my liking. I'm a deserter now, and real life is paradise. Hooray for pixels.

If I didn't do it [27 November 2006]

This week, I was originally going to write about If I Did It, OJ Simpson's notorious hypothetical 'confession' to the hideous murders he definitely didn't commit with a knife that wasn't his in a jealous rage he never experienced. Then my editor pointed out that since the OJ story had already been covered in exhaustive detail elsewhere in the paper, for days, the publication of yet another article on the matter might just smack of overkill – fitting, perhaps, given the subject at hand, but tiresome for anyone who had already had their fill of the story.

So I reluctantly agreed not to write about it. And I haven't.

But if I had (which I haven't), I'd have started by asking whether OJ (who is innocent) was the best choice of narrator in the first place. After all, once you remove the murders from his CV (murders which shouldn't be on there in the first place, since he had nothing to do with them), he's kind of boring.

If you must get a famous person to explain how they'd have carried out a murder they didn't commit, cast someone more surprising, someone less likely. I'd prefer to hear, say, Norman Wisdom speculating about how he'd have done it. Chances are he'd have made a hilarious bungling mess of things – accidentally ripping his trousers as he struggled to pull on that undersized glove, tumbling over a hedge on his way to the getaway car. It'd be a scream.

Come to think of it, this could form the basis of a great Christmas novelty book – a 500-page compilation in which celebrities describe precisely how they'd have committed various appalling crimes throughout history, in blistering first-person detail.

Shriek! as Tim Henman explains how he would have stalked London's East End in the late nineteenth century, killing prostitutes. 'I reckon I acted alone,' he writes. 'I'd possibly had some kind of surgical training and perhaps heard voices in my head urging me to kill.'

Gasp! as Lorraine Kelly recalls the chilling moment she stood in the Texas School Book Depository watching John F. Kennedy through her rifle sights. 'As my finger tightened on the trigger,' she explains, 'I'd definitely have wished I was back on the sofa at GMTV introducing an item on rollerblading, or sandwiches, or shuttlecocks . . . anything really, instead of standing there, preparing to assassinate the world's most powerful man.'

Get confused! as Kelly Osbourne imagines how Tony Blair might have single-handedly carried out the Sharpeville massacre – in a series of crayon illustrations by Pete Doherty.

If any celebrities are reading this now, email me your confessions and we'll have it in the shops by Christmas. All proceeds go to charity. Or rather they would, if you'd read this request and I'd written it – which you haven't and I didn't.

When it comes to psychics, my stance is hardcore: they must die alone in windowless cells

[4 December 2006]

If I walked into a single mother's house and said I could read her baby's mind, then started shouting four-letter words, claiming I was simply voicing her offspring's thoughts, I would expect to be arrested the moment I stepped outside.

And if, during my 'psychic reading', I also speculated about the mother's sex life, and a potentially abusive relationship with a former boyfriend, claiming her toddler was concerned about 'men who want to touch Mum's privates', and I went on and on in this vein until the mother burst into tears, there in the living room, in front of her child, I'd expect to be arrested, sectioned, and beaten in the back of the van.

And if I allowed a TV crew to broadcast what I was doing, I'd expect to be attacked by a mob, who'd pull me apart and kick my remains around the street, pausing only to spit on any bits of my face that got stuck to their shoes.

But no. In fact the outcry would be muted at best and Ofcom would turn a blind eye – as it did last week, while clearing Channel 5's unbelievably disgusting Baby Mind Reader of any wrongdoing.

I've never fully understood the public's docile acceptance of psychics, or why, when it comes to their supposed abilities, the burden of proof is assumed to lie with the sceptic, as opposed to the sort of shrieking idiot who claims to be able to contact the spirit world (or in Derek Ogilvie's case, communicate telepathically with kids too young to talk).

I'm quite hardcore on this. I think every psychic and medium in this country belongs in prison. Even the ones demented enough to believe in what they're doing. In fact, especially them. Give them windowless cells and make them crap in buckets. They can spend the rest of their days sewing mailbags in the dark.

The audiences that psychics prey on are equally infuriating, albeit less deserving of contempt. They're just disappointing, like a friend who's let you down. Often, they're simply grieving and desperate.

I mean, if you want to believe in psychics, fine. You're a danger-ous idiot and I wouldn't trust you to operate a spoon without putting an eye out . . . but fine. Your choice. Delude yourself silly. Your world is probably more fun than the real one. There's no death, just an afterlife filled with magic spirits who like to commu-nicate with eerie, ugly, otherwise-unemployable bottom-of-the-barrel 'showmen' back on Earth.

But don't accuse anyone with the temerity to question your sad supernatural fantasies of having a 'closed mind' or being 'blind to possibilities'. A closed mind asks no questions, unthinkingly accepting that which it wants to believe. The blindness is all yours.

(If you want to feel your eyes pop rudely open, swot up on the 'cold reading' techniques fake psychics use – a combination of guesswork and sly conversational tics which give the impression that the 'psychic' is magically receiving accurate information from the ether. A fantastic (albeit pricey) step-by-step guide is available from ianrowland.com.

Anyway, back to my psychic prison fantasies. The problem with trying to jail all the mediums in Britain is they'd see it coming and (a) escape overseas to somewhere even more gullible, like Narnia, before you'd passed the legislation, or (b) call on their ghostly friends in the spirit world to whisk them from harm's reach.

Except they couldn't because ghosts – unlike scumbags and conmen – don't exist. Pity. But that's the real world for you. Often disappointing. But real. At least it's always real.

Faces not words [8 January 2007]

I read a magazine yesterday and suddenly truly understood in my bones that human civilisation will die screaming in our lifetime.

It happened on the toilet. I was reading a copy of the free magazine Sky send to all their subscribers. Visually inhaling crap at one end, rectally exhaling it at the other; my corporeal self a mere conduit for the elemental crapforce that binds the universe together. I have all the spirituality of a doorframe. This is as close as I get to a religious experience.

Anyway. The Sky magazine is one of those *Heat*-a-like graphical holocausts where every millimetre of the page is plastered with rowdy colours and exclamation marks that crane their necks to squeal at you. I say I was 'reading' it, but in reality you don't 'read' magazines like that. There is too much visual noise, so instead you simply 'look at' them, having first disengaged your temporal lobe so you don't feel like you are being stabbed in the mind by an over-zealous Christmas lighting display. Even though that is precisely what is happening.

And I was dumbly gazing at the bit that tells you which films are coming up on the movie channels, when I noticed that at the bottom of each synopsis sat a group of tiny faces. Celebrity faces. Nestling at the end of the paragraph, like part of the typography, as though the editors had done some research and discovered their readers had devolved to the point where their brains can no longer parse text unless it is broken up with miniature photos of their famous imaginary friends grinning back at them. I slapped myself awake and tried to make sense of what I was seeing.

Slowly it dawned on me: this was a rating system. I flipped back a few pages, and sure enough, there was the key: a brightly-coloured box full of little celebrity faces, accompanied by a brief description of what they stood for. 'It's fast, easy, and practical,' lied the subhead. This is what each face meant:

- Brad Pitt – 'Eye Candy'
- Peter Kay – 'Laugh Out Loud'
- Michael Jackson – 'Thriller'
- Sarah Jessica Parker – 'Get the Girls Round'
- Christopher Lee – 'Scary'
- Victoria Beckham – 'Star Spotting'
- Chico – 'Guilty Pleasure'
- Ant and Dec – 'Family Fun'
- Vicky Pollard – 'Real-Life Shocker'

Sure, it would insult the intelligence of a cod. Under this system, *Schindler's List* = Vicky Pollard.

But I knew it was worse than that. I just didn't know why, not yet. So I looked at it again. Somewhere in my head, a camel's back splintered beneath a straw. And I understood: this is madness. Genuinely: this is madness. Concepts replaced by faces. Grinning faces. It is not evidence of 'dumbing down'. It is the disjointed thought process of madness. That this is even vaguely acceptable is the most dizzying madness of all.

I wanted to run into the street, without even pausing to wipe, and hurl myself, boggle-eyed, at passers-by, flapping the magazine around, screaming: 'HELP! WE'VE LOST OUR MINDS! I HAVE PROOF! I HAVE PROOF.'

But I didn't. I stayed put; pooing and afraid.

And I thought: Our leaders lie, and we know they have lied, and there is war in our name, and the world kicks and boils itself to death and we do nothing but stare into the tiny grinning faces of people we don't even know; faces that are, apparently, more 'fast, easy and practical' than language itself.

I give us six years, tops.

On recognition   [15 January 2007]

There are four problems with having a byline photograph hovering over the top of a column, like the one you can see up there on the right (unless you're reading this online or between the covers of a book, in which case you're spared the misery).

Problem one: the average writer has a face like a bloodhound's funeral. Problem two: in most byline shots, the writer is making eye contact with you, which automatically makes the column itself faintly unnerving to read, because you're dimly aware someone's staring at you – someone who wrote it, and is probably scanning your face for clues as to what you make of it, even though logically you know that can't be true, because all they are is a photo and . . . Hang on – what was it they were writing about again? Oh, forget it.

Problem three is that, as a writer, you're stuck with whatever expression your face happened to be pulling when the photo was taken. That's the face you're making as you say all this stuff, no matter what 'all this stuff' happens to be. If you smile, you smile for ever. From now on, every word you write will be interpreted in the context of you enjoying a great big smile, so if you write about the twentieth anniversary of the *Zeebrugge* ferry disaster in which 187 people died, it'll look as though you're pretty chuffed about the whole thing and don't care who knows it.

Problem four is that you're no longer anonymous, so if you call Geoff Capes an idiot and Geoff Capes reads it, and then two days later you bump into Geoff Capes in the street, there's a good chance Geoff Capes will hit you, especially if, thanks to the byline photo, he thinks you were smiling while you slagged him off. Since Geoff Capes has fists the size of microwave ovens, this is bad news (or it would be, if he *was* an idiot, which I'm certain he isn't – although I hear Richard Littlejohn believes otherwise).

For years I was without a byline photo, and had no desire to get one, because I knew they were intrinsically wrong. But I never fully appreciated the luxury of anonymity until it was taken away from me. Thanks to a combination of the byline photo and a low-budget BBC4 show during which my face repeatedly pops up onscreen, I now get recognised about once a week. In terms of celebrity, that puts me 40,000 rungs below the bloke in the elephant.co.uk commercial, but nevertheless it's weird.

I'm still geared toward assuming that anyone who unexpectedly introduces themself to me in a pub or nods at me in the street is either someone I've met before but failed to recognise, or a kindly stranger who's about to warn me I've left my flies undone. Instead, now, they're occasionally people who know who I am but first have to ask me to confirm that I am who I am, before going on to explain that they thought I was who I am, but they weren't sure. By which point, neither am I.

It's not always pleasant attention, either. One man stomped over in a newsagent's to call me a 'telly cunt', which struck me as hilarious two days later when I finally stopped shaking.

Still, it could be worse. While I was going out with my ex-girlfriend, she landed a part in ITV1's erstwhile women-in-prison schlockfest *Bad Girls*, playing a lesbian murderer – which meant van drivers wound down their windows to shout 'lesbian!' or 'murderer!' at her when we walked down the street. Generally, this was done with affection, but that's hard to explain to passers-by who by now are regarding the two of you with open suspicion.

Burqas for all. Only way forward.

CHAPTER NINE

In which the MacDonald Brothers provoke war an Anglo-Scottish war, Jeffrey Archer hurls pennies at beggars, and Shilpa Shetty meets some new friends

Up the Eton Road   [21 October 2006]

If you're looking for proof that there's a large number of knee-jerk racists lurking among the Great British Public, surely the outcome of last week's *X Factor* (ITV) vote is it.

Maybe you didn't see it because, like many a caring, sharing *Guardian* reader, you prefer the unbearably cruel early audition shows in which one no-hoper after another gets a big bum wiped all over their dreams. The tacky live studio finals, which are essentially more about celebration than denigration, leave you cold. And who can blame you? Most of the acts are mediocre at best, and some of them are downright rubbish.

Louis Walsh's selection is especially poor. He's already lost The Unconventionals, a sort of doo-wop amateur dramatic society known round these parts as A Cappella Irritant Squad, who last week delivered a performance of 'Dancing in the Street' which sounded like six clumsy cover versions playing at once. The audience couldn't wait to ignore them.

And they were his most likeable act. The rest are saddled with absolutely unforgivable band names; names so shitbone awful, you hate them before they've even opened their mouths. There's a flavourless quartet called 4Sure (4FuckSake would be more appropriate), and an ethereally skinny boy band called Eton Road (which sounds like a euphemism for an illegal underage sex act to me – as in 'the police arrived just as he was taking one of the prefects up the Eton Road'). But worst of all, there's the MacDonald Brothers.

And this brings me to my point. The MacDonald Brothers are a pair of characterless twins whose startlingly dreadful performance somehow managed to veer from cheesy to flat to eerie to nauseating and all the way back to cheesy again before finally settling on outright rubbish. There's something indefinably creepy about them – they're the kind of act a child killer might listen to in his car. And yet somehow, they were spared elimination by the viewers at home.

Meanwhile, a twenty-six-year-old called Dionne, whose voice is so good it could advertise heaven, was left at the bottom of the pile alongside The Unconventionals. Why? Well, it can't be her singing. Perhaps it's the gap between her front teeth, but I doubt it. That's sort of endearing.

No, the only reason I can think of is that she's black, and there's still a sizeable section of the audience that's either threatened or dissuaded by that. There's no way a rational person could choose the MacDonald Brothers over her. It's like choosing a kick in the balls instead of a cuddle. The programme's not at fault here. The viewers are.

Anyway, what I'm getting round to is this: if you watch *The X Factor*, it's time to stop doing so in a detached, ironic, I'm-above-this-shit kind of way. It's time to muck in and get voting. Yes it is. Stop arguing. So what if it's a rip-off? You want the MacDonald Brothers to win? You sicken me. Vote Dionne.

Anyway. *The X Factor* isn't the only live, over-long reality spectacular. Last week, Sky unveiled *Cirque de Celebrité* (Sky One), which . . . well, you can guess what it is from the title. Yes, in an apparent bid to strip the word 'celebrity' of its last remaining atoms of glamour, the famous are now desperately performing circus tricks for your amusement, like starving dogs at a medieval banquet.

Sadly, it's not as much fun as you think. Yes, you get to see Syed from *The Apprentice* dangling from a trapeze, and Zammo dancing on a large, brightly-coloured ball, like a bear in a bad cartoon, but the show lasts 90 minutes – approximately 60 minutes longer than its novelty value. Still, at least it's given Grace from *Big Brother* a chance to rehabilitate herself (she came first last week). More importantly, if the look of concentrated terror on Syed's face is anything to go by, it's only a matter of time before he shits himself live on air – and in those tight spandex tights, that's going to look absolutely hilarious. It's surely worth recording just for that.

Touch wood   [28 October 2006]

Lots of things designed to be used by children end up appealing to adults too. Harry Potter. Jelly babies. Kids' bums. The list is endless.

TV's *Doctor Who* is a good example. Originally conceived as an educational drama for 1960s kiddywinks, it attracted a devoted adult audience from the very beginning. They knew they were watching something that wasn't, strictly speaking, 'for them' but they loved it anyway.

The trouble with *Who*'s freshly-minted anagrammatic 'sister' serial *Torchwood* (BBC2) is that it's not really clear who it's aimed at. It contains swearing, blood and sex, yet still somehow feels like a children's programme. Thirteen-year-olds should love it; anyone else is likely to be more than a little confused. Which isn't to say *Torchwood* is bad. Just bewildering. And very, very silly.

The central presence of Captain Jack Harkness, one of the most pantomime characters ever to appear in *Doctor Who*, doesn't exactly help. He's like Buzz Lightyear, but less realistic. The moment you see him running around being all larger than life, you think 'aha – so *Torchwood*'s a camp space opera? Fair enough.'

But then the storyline goes all dark and unpleasant and people are getting their throats torn open and shooting themselves in the head, and suddenly you don't know where you are. Not in Kansas any more, maybe – but where?

Cute and dark, sweet and sour, up and down. It's like tuning in to watch *Deadwood*, only to discover they've replaced Al Swearengen with the Honey Monster. Or sitting through a 're-imagining' of the Captain Birds Eye commercials, in which the white-haired skipper traverses the oceans in a raging thunderstorm, ruling his child-crew with an iron fist, tossing dissenters overboard into the rolling, foaming waves – but dances the hornpipe with a big cartoon haddock while the credits roll. Or stumbling across an episode of *Scooby-Doo* in which Shaggy skins up on camera.

In fact *Scooby-Doo* (more than, say, *The X-Files* or *Buffy*) is probably the show most analogous to *Torchwood*, in that both series revolve around a fresh-faced team of meddling kids tackling an ever-shifting carnival of monsters in a world of childlike simplicity. The *Torchwood* gang even have their own version of the Mystery Machine, although theirs is a spectacularly ugly SUV with two daft strips of throbbing LED lights either side of the windscreen whose sole purpose is to make the entire vehicle look outrageously silly –

they might as well have stuck a big inflatable dick on the bonnet, to be honest.

The inside's not much better – LCD screens embedded in every available flat surface, each urgently displaying a wibbly-wobbly screensaver . . . it must be like driving around in a flagship branch of PC World.

There are other glaringly daft touches: the countless overhead helicopter shots of Cardiff (what is this, Google Earth?); the ridiculous severed hand-in-a-jar (straight from the Addams Family); the protracted sequence from episode one in which Captain Jack stood atop a tall building surveying the cityscape like Batman *for no reason whatsoever*. Oh, and the team's insistence on using the silly invisible elevator that slowly, slowly ascends through a sort of 'magic hole' in the pavement – even though there's a perfectly reasonable *back door* through which they can enter and leave the Batcave at will.

And on top of all that, there's a bizarre emphasis on bisexual tension thrown in for good measure. You half expect the *Torchwood* gang to drop their slacks and form a humping great daisy chain any moment. It's *Shortbus* meets *Goober and the Ghost Chasers* meets *X-Men* meets *Angel* meets *The Tomorrow People* meets *Spooks* meets Oh God I Give Up.

Still, the act of jotting down some of *Torchwood*'s thundering absurdities has put a big dumb smile on my face. Whatever the hell it's supposed to be, there's nothing else like *Torchwood* on TV at the moment, and that's got to be worth something. I just don't have a clue how much.

Haunted porcelain dolls [4 November 2006]

Told you so. Last week Dionne got the boot from *The X Factor* (ITV1), despite having far and away one of the best voices in the contest. Originally, I put this down to racism on the part of the voting audience, but maybe I'm doing them a disservice. Perhaps the average ITV1 viewer isn't that shallow. Perhaps they voted her out because of the gap in her front teeth.

They also ousted Kerry, the sexy wheelchair-user (who the tabloids would've dubbed 'Hot Wheels' if they had any balls), which is just as well because she wasn't the greatest singer.

Anyway, all the remaining acts deserve their place on the stage, with three notable exceptions – the first being Ray, an unsettling cross between Harry Connick, Jr, Chucky from *Child's Play*, and a boy raised by wolves. Ray needs to stop grinning. Whenever he smiles it's like watching Jack Nicholson leering through that shattered door in *The Shining*. And he's got a weird cold-yet-needy look in his eye, which screams 'STAGE SCHOOL!' so loudly it almost drowns out his actual singing voice.

I say 'almost', because in practice his be-bop transatlantic slur is too infuriating to ignore. (Why do some people think it necessary to sing Rat Pack numbers with a voice so slack it mushes all the consonants and vowels, so a simple lyric like 'She gets too hungry/ For dinner at eight' becomes 'a-she gess a-too hunnnryyfoh/ a-zzinner-a-eighh'? Sinatra's diction was crisp as a bell, you morons.)

Exception number two: the MacDonald Brothers, whose continued presence in the competition is proof that a large proportion of the British public have no idea what they're doing. Seriously, no sane mind could possibly enjoy their performances, which combine piss-weak crooning with an indefinable sense of creeping dread. They're sinister and horrible, like a pair of haunted porcelain dolls who've suddenly come alive on the sideboard. Each time one of them gets close to the camera, I imagine he's going to slither out of the screen and calmly strangle me in my living room. Please make it stop, Lord.

The third and final notable exception is Eton Road, the emaciated boy band who look like they've staggered on stage to beg for basic rations. I keep expecting the UN to start dropping food parcels in the middle of their act. One of them's so thin he sometimes stands between the individual pixels on my LCD television and completely disappears from view.

Anyway, those are the three acts that need to be sent home first. Oh, and the producers really need to cut down on the amount of unnecessary lighting in *The X Factor* studio before George Monbiot shows up to kick their arses. There must be 10 million bulbs in there: it's like the whole of Las Vegas crammed into one hangar. That show's costing us an iceberg a week.

Perhaps they should follow the lead set by *Unanimous*, Channel 4's new who-gets-the-money reality show, which leans in the other direction, being so gloomy and underlit it's like venturing into the underground realm of Fungus the Bogeyman.

Curious show, this: nine contestants are locked in a bunker until they can unanimously decide which of them deserves to win the jackpot (which starts at a million, and drops by a pound a second). The whole thing's harsh and downbeat, with oppressive walls and no natural light, and it revolves around a group of people who grow more ruthless and greedy by the minute.

It's not a barrel of laughs. In fact, it's a bit like the aftermath of a nuclear war. Bet they're catching and eating rats by week five. Hungrily wolfing them down while they squat in the corner. Biting ratty's head off while his paws kick and scratch at their chinny-chins! Rat blood and rat fur; gobble it, gobble it! Tee hee hee hee!

Sorry. Been watching too much of Ray and the MacDonald Brothers. It gets in your head and it changes you, badly.

Not Buck Rogers   [11 November 2006]

The future is a foreign country. They do things differently there. They wear tinfoil and fly around in hovercars, for starters. You wouldn't get that in the Dark Ages. Their most advanced piece of technology was the pointy stick, used for jabbing peasants in the eye or throwing at jabberwockies. Compared to the future, the past is rubbish, which is why TV science fiction is always a billion times better than costume drama. I don't want to watch people dressed in doilies curtseying to each other until everyone dies of consumption. I prefer lasers and dry ice. Give me the camp nonsense of Buck Rogers over the painful earnestness of Jane Eyre every time.

Actually, no. Not Buck Rogers. It's far too gee-whizz. Give me something British. Something depressing and dystopian. Something angry and idealistic and imaginative and scary and . . . well, give me half the things discussed at length in *The Martians and Us* (BBC4), an unmissable, timely documentary series examining the history of UK sci-fi.

I say 'timely' because it arrives a few weeks after the death of Nigel Kneale, who, in creating the BBC serial *Quatermass* back in the 1950s, single-handedly set the tone for all British TV sci-fi to follow. Kneale's work, which pops up repeatedly throughout this series, is well worth seeking out (and there's no excuse for not doing so, since it's largely available on DVD) – as a TV writer, he's up there with yer Dennis Potters and yer Jack Rosenthals, and with any luck the BBC will see his passing as a great excuse to screen everything he wrote all over again. In order. And ideally in 3D, even though that's not possible.

Anyway, back to *The Martians and Us*, which rather than being a dry chronological trawl through the past, tackles a different theme with each edition and sees how it evolved. Fittingly, episode one is about 'evolution'; specifically, the way Darwin's theories influenced H. G. Wells, who in turn influenced just about everyone else. Future episodes examine dystopian societies (*1984* et al) and Armageddon; they're all superbly researched and clearly sewn together with an almost unhealthy love for the subject matter (with an obvious bias in favour of television, but in this case that's no bad thing).

TV sci-fi is subjected to more than its fair share of derisive snorts, but as this series (misleading title aside) makes clear, it's always been about more than starships and rayguns. The best sci-fi explores ideas –– often deeply uncomfortable, challenging ideas about human society – in the most imaginative way possible. You may think 'dark' crime serials like *Cracker* or *Prime Suspect* tell you a lot about the sinister side of the human psyche, but they're nothing compared to the likes of *Quatermass* or *Threads*.

As a bonus, and in an apparent bid to make my last point sound like babbling nonsense, BBC4 is also repeating *The Day of the Triffids*, their early 80s adaptation of John Wyndham's biopocalypse pot-boiler. Yes, the one where a bunch of giant walking daffodils rise up and take over the Earth.

It's undeniably silly, with inadvertently funny FX, some dialogue so clumsily expositional it might as well be replaced with a diagram explaining who's who and what's what, and some alarmingly stiff performances (which serve as a jarring reminder that just a few decades ago, most TV actors sounded twice as posh as the royal family and spoke VERY CRISPLY AND LOUDLY as though appearing on stage before an audience of bewildered half-deaf paupers).

But get beyond all that, and you'll discover that at its core lurks a tale of startling bleakness, the likes of which rarely make it on screen in this mollycoddled day and age, when broadcasters think we prefer our entertainment with all the sharp edges sanded down, all the unpleasantness reduced to black and white shades or cuddled away completely. Stupid wobbling plant monsters aside, our TV used to have some bite – and our sci-fi often provided it. Laugh if you like, but cherish it too.

Might as well be dead   [18 November 2006]

As winter rolls in and the days shrink to the length of a depressive sigh, so a man's thoughts gradually acquire a melancholic timbre. Especially when said man is staring at *I'm a Celebrity . . . Get Me Out Of Here!* (ITV1) and sadly contemplating his symbiotic relationship with the people onscreen.

They bicker and preen; I write about it. They scrabble on their knees eating maggots; I mock them for it. They blow off in a hammock; I describe the smell. I am pathetic. My life is pathetic.

I truly, genuinely, might as well be dead.

Still, as I sit here, typing these words with one hand and clutching a kitchen knife to my neck with the other, I suppose I might as well run through the traditional abusive *Who's Who* list, to which the usual caveats apply, since the insane nature of newspaper-supplement lead times means I'm typing this on Tuesday morning – so if Toby Anstis hangs himself with a makeshift vine noose on Wednesday afternoon, not only will you find no mention of it here, but any abuse I pour on his head will seem particularly callous.

Then again, fuck him: this is Anstis we're talking about, not Hawking or a Beatle. Human civilisation might just survive his passing.

The chief freakshow draw this year is David Gest, the peculiar human-like organism which married Liza Minnelli a few years ago and divorced her a short time later. It looks as though plastic surgery has left Gest closely resembling the halfway point in a horror-movie transformation sequence; at a glance it's hard to tell which bits of his head it hears, sees, or talks through. If he didn't wear sunglasses all the time it'd be hard to know whether his face was on the right way up. Weirder still is his hair, which doesn't seem to be hair at all, but rather some kind of fine black smoke, loosely enveloping his scalp like a faint atmospheric haze. Whenever the sun hits it, it turns semi-translucent and looks like a force field effect from a computer game. This alone makes him the most interesting person in the camp.

Jason Donovan is also there, wearing the precise expression of a Teddy Ruxpin toy that's been through some tough times and currently finds itself timidly edging down an alleyway, toward an untended restaurant dustbin, hoping to steal some scraps without being spotted by the thickset whistling chef in the kitchen. At least that's what he looks like to me.

Others include erstwhile Thatcher substitute Faith Brown, owner of a bosom so outrageously huge it must render sitting at a table eating from a plate impossible, and former newsreader Jan Leeming, this year's posh-'n'-feisty mature matronly offering; you can just about picture her sponging down a retired colonel in a tin bath. And enjoying it. With any luck that'll be one of the bush-tucker trials.

There's also some frightened pop-eyed scamp from Busted, a who-the-hell fashion designer, Phina Thingypants with the broken accent from *Footballer's Wives*, Cherie Blair's sister, and Myleene Klass, professional eye candy.

It's a terrifying sign of age, and the most pathetic thing it's possible to admit, but the other day, while leafing through a tabloid paper, I stumbled across a picture of Klass in a bikini and 10 minutes later realised I was still staring at it, like a dog in a Perspex box dumbly contemplating a lump of meat dangling cruelly outside. Christ, I hate me.

All-out war with Scotland [25 November 2006]

OK. That's it. I've never been a patriot, because nationalist pride is clearly the pastime of choice for furious thimble-minded morons so thoroughly inadequate they need to leech off the history and status of an entire nation to bolster their own self-worth.

But all that's changed in the face of a sustained, maddening dose of the MacDonald Brothers, courtesy of *The X Factor* (ITV1). Suddenly, I'm declaring myself 100 per cent English and demanding all out war with Scotland.

Yes, Scottish readers, I'm sorry to tar you all with the same brush, and even sorrier to call for your heads on a silver platter – which, make no mistake, is precisely what I *am* doing – but I'm confused and I'm angry and you're the only easily identifiable group I can blame. This weekly atrocity cannot be allowed to continue. It's time for the Scottish community to stop making excuses and start policing itself; time to root out the extremists hell-bent on voting MacDonald and confront their twisted ideology head-on.

The extremists claim that by voting MacDonald they're simply doing their bit for Scotland. Yet their actions have caused misery and suffering for millions.

Imagine a world in which the MacDonald Brothers have won *The X Factor*. Gigantic billboards carrying their image dominate the skyline as a terrified populace scurries past. An anodyne MacDonald cover version of 'Unchained Melody' blares from a million speakers, drowning out the screams of men and dying children. Insane and unthinkable as it sounds, the extremists want to make this nightmare vision of the future a reality. We must stop them at all costs.

In return for the Scots co-operation, the rest of us can set about tackling anyone who votes for Ray, preferably by cutting their voting fingers off with pliers. Ray, a pirouetting kiddy vampire with a demented penchant for the big band sound, is even worse than the MacDonalds.

When Ray sings, music itself throws up. Not just a bit, like when you unexpectedly bring up half a gobful of baby sick and have to swallow it back down, but a lot. When Ray sings, music buckles in two, swings its jaws open and unleashes an unprecedented jet of acrid vomit. And it doesn't stop vomiting until strips of stomach lining are hanging off its teeth and it's spat its own ringpiece out like a hot rubber coin.

That's what Ray does to music. This is the worst *X Factor* line-up ever.

Meanwhile, *I'm a Celebrity* (ITV1) trundles on. Having spent a large portion of last week's column picking on David Gest, I've now warmed to him, just like the rest of the viewing public. Facially, he still resembles a cross between Paul Simon and the outermost fringe of madness, but inside lurks an endearingly dry sense of humour. Clearly he should win.

In other news, according to both the tabloids and the programme itself, Dean Gaffney's inaugural bushtucker trial was the single funniest event in recorded history. But it could've been far funnier. After all, he was on live television. He missed a golden opportunity.

If I was doing it instead of Gaffney, I'd have waited until the bit where they put me in the big wooden box thing, then deliberately stamped on a rat's head at the earliest opportunity. I'd crunch my heel around in its skull, pick its twitching carcass up by the tail and swing it in Ant and Dec's faces, shrieking 'LOOK WHAT YOU MADE ME DO! THIS PRODUCTION HAS BLOOD ON ITS HANDS! MURDERERS! MURDERERS!' at the top of my lungs.

And before they could respond I'd start sobbing and fighting the pair of them, mussing up their hair and getting rat blood all over their shirts. And then I'd whip down my trousers and unleash a curler, right there on the jungle floor.

And I'd sit there poking it with sticks and rubbing leaves on it and giggling. Although I guess they'd probably cut to a commercial by then.

A great leap forward   [16 December 2006]

This being a special 'award ceremony' edition of *The Guide*, it would be remiss of me not to devote this week's column to some awards of my own. So, let the ceremony commence with an awkward crunch of gears, as the award for the **Year's Most Jarring Show** goes to the *Doctor Who* spin-off *Torchwood*, which somehow managed to feel like both a multicoloured children's show and a heaving sex-and-gore bodice-ripper at the same time. The constant clash of mutually-incongruous tones meant watching it felt like stumbling across a hitherto secret episode of *Postman Pat* in which Pat runs down fifteen villagers while masturbating at the wheel of his van. Interesting, but possibly aimed at madmen.

The **Most Relentlessly Harrowing Drama** was *Prime Suspect 7*, in which Jane Tennison attempted to solve the murder of a pregnant fourteen-year-old while simultaneously battling alcoholism, nursing her dying father, facing retirement, and dealing with a world full of absurdly exaggerated ASBO youths who cared about ringtones and stabbings and very little else. There wasn't a chink of light in the whole thing. It was like being trapped in a coffin watching a depressed mouse slowly build a tiny gallows for itself out of lolly sticks, and being unable to stop it because you couldn't lift your arms. Well, vaguely.

An awkward silence now as the award for **Career Suicide** goes to nobody whatsoever. By rights it should have gone to George Galloway for his cat-impersonating antics on January's *Celebrity Big Brother* – except in retrospect, it didn't dent his career at all. He even introduces himself using the 'Top Cat' theme on his *TalkSport* radio show, just so no one forgets about it. Meanwhile, Busted's Matt Willis chewed his way through a kangaroo's anus on *I'm a Celebrity* and almost immediately won the public vote. In short, the public are now so desensitised to all manner of extreme or absurd behaviour, it's almost impossible to genuinely disgrace yourself on television. I can't imagine what you'd have to do to permanently wreck your career. Eat your own shit on Monday and you'd be cracking jokes about it on *The Paul O'Grady Show* by

Friday. I'm all for tolerance and forgiveness but somehow I doubt this represents a great leap forward.

Speaking of advances and the lack of them, the **Year's Most Outmoded Thing** was the television set itself – yes, even the fancy HD ones. What with torrent sites, YouTube, DVDs, PSPs and iPods with video playback, you don't need a telly to watch 'telly' any more. I probably spent a third of my telly-watching time in 2006 watching 'TV' on a laptop. And aside from the news, I saw hardly anything go out at its appointed time; thanks to PVR devices the entire notion of channels and schedules is rapidly becoming meaningless. The only problem is working out what we're going to call 'television' (as in the programming) now it's drifted free of 'the television' (as in the box itself). Tossers call it 'content', but that's (a) hideous and (b) so vague it might as well be French. Anyway, we'd best hurry up coming up with a name, or before long water-cooler conversations won't make sense any more ('Did you see that thing on the thing last night?', 'Nah, I was thinging the thing on the other thing – maybe I'll thing it tomorrow.').

Finally, the award for **Hugest Breakthrough** goes to Channel 5, which made history by actually showing it going in, then out, then back in again — right there on the telly. Yes, *The Girl's Guide to 21st-Century Sex* got away with showing hard-ons and fannies and full penetrative sex by claiming it was educational to do so (I certainly learnt a lot about how shocking it was to unexpectedly stumble across actual fucking on television).

By boldly introducing sweaty hardcore action to the TV schedule, they did more to blur the line separating TV from the internet than anyone else this year. See that spurting all over your screen? That, my friends, is progress.

Thus I win   [13 January 2007]

Celebrity Big Brother (C4) is one of those totemic shows people define themselves by. No, really.

Haughty types who consider it a glaring affront to humanity argue over which of them watches it the least ('I'm proud to say I haven't witnessed one second of that garbage' / 'Really? Well I tune in, then turn the sound down and deliberately sit with my back to the screen in protest – THUS I WIN').

At the other end of the scale, self-confessed trash addicts fight about how gloriously tacky they find it ('I sit for hours transcribing the live stream so I can read it back and chuckle about it later!' / 'Oh yeah? Well I watch it while literally reclining in a tin bath full of warm milky scum, farting and giggling and imagining I'm participating in one big steadily unfolding live-action cartoon version of the apocalypse – THUS I WIN').

Frustratingly, I'm somewhere in the middle. I think it's neither a work of lowbrow genius, nor a genuine harbinger of cultural death. I think it's a TV show. THUS I WIN.

Anyway, at the time of writing, this year's helping is a grinding, boring mess. It began with an uninspiring cast, then rapidly worsened as the most potentially interesting characters were prematurely driven out by the injection of Clan Goody.

Donny Tourette (Rick Parfitt from Status Quo impersonating Nathan Barley) was the first to bolt. Then surprise choice Ken Russell (a cross between *Withnail*'s Uncle Monty and a 500-year-old Pauline Quirke) decided he'd had enough, which was a personal relief since my attention span's so hopelessly depleted it can't cope with elderly contestants who move in slow motion. When he finally staggered for the exit, he took so long crossing the room I had to hit the fast-forward button twice, muttering 'hurry up' under my breath (I swear, if it were possible to grab the screen and tip the house sideways till he fell out the side, I'd have done it).

Now then. Jackiey. Picture a sandpapered orang-utan on the verge of grabbing a pool cue in anger and you've constructed a mental image more accurate than ten photographs superimposed on top of each other. It seems safe to assume the public will have ousted her by the time you read this, assuming the voters misspelled her name correctly when the texts were sent. (Jackiey. Jackiey. Jackiey. All that's missing is a wayward apostrophe and a few capital letters in the wrong place: jAcKie'y.)

This leaves us with a houseful of relative dullards. Jade we already know. Her silent Cylon boyfriend, Jack, is ultimately unknowable. Apparently too dense to speak or even perform basic facial expressions, he spends his time mutely propped up in the corner, like a broom leaning against the wall, or a tattooed sapling. At least Ken fidgeted from time to time.

Then there's Leo Sayer, who simply burbles the contents of his forebrain round the clock, like a radio station ceaselessly relaying the dislocated thoughts of a ball of pocket fluff as it drifts out of sight on a warm air current. Carole Malone, so repugnant in print you want to climb inside the page and vomit ink down her eye sockets, is merely tedious onscreen.

Cleo Roccos, Shilpa Shetty, Dirk Benedict and Danielle Thingy-bobs are equally dull. Likeable, attractive, but still dull. And the same goes for H from Steps and Jo O'Meara (the latter, incidentally, is played by Starbuck from the re-imagined *Battlestar Galactica*, which is well worth watching instead).

In other words, it's a long slow shrug so far. It's telling that the most interesting thing that's happened is something that *hasn't* happened: to date, no one's laughed uncontrollably in Jermaine Jackson's face when he mentions his son, Jermajesty.

Yes, Jermajesty: a name so bad, it never loses its magic. Jermajesty. Jermajesty. Still funny: Jermajesty. With any luck, inspired by his *Big Brother* experience, he'll hold a text vote to let the public decide the name of his next kid. In which case, I'd like to make an early bid for Jermwarfare.

The world's thickest coven   [20 January 2007]

As per tradition, whatever I write about *Celebrity Big Brother* (C4) on a Tuesday turns out not to be true come the time it's printed on a Saturday. Further proof that traditional print journalism is doomed. By the year 2015 all newspaper articles will be delivered to your cerebral cortex via wireless connection the moment they're written. Apart from Richard Littlejohn's columns, because he won't be writing them any more. Instead he'll scrape a living mastur-bating for pennies in abandoned shop doorways. I hope.

Anyway, last week I described the current *Celebrity Big Brother* as 'a grinding, boring mess', just before Leo Sayer livened things up immensely by turning into an enraged fusion of Alan Partridge and Derek-and-Clive-era Dudley Moore, then throwing a series of increasingly spectacular tantrums which culminated in the first proper 'break-out' the series has seen. In another weird first, we were shown plenty of footage of him outside the house, bickering with producers and tussling with security guards like a protester at the Downing Street gates. This is an alarming development – events outside the *Big Brother* walls aren't usually included in the highlights show, and lifting the 'fog of war' in this way raises the spectre of an endless, access-all-areas edition that follows escaping housemates wherever they run, like a fox hunt, shooting them in the thigh with a dart gun each time they get too far from the lens.

Following Leo's disgruntled exit, the remaining housemates decided to put on a brave face in the traditional fashion; i.e. forming two distinct groups and learning to loathe one another. At the time of writing, Jade, Jo and Danielle – collectively, the world's thickest coven – are relentlessly haranguing blameless Bollywood star Shilpa Shetty over an endless series of imaginary crimes, thereby prompting over 200 viewers to complain to Ofcom about alleged racism in the show.

I don't think they're racist, just unbelievably dumb. They're motivated by an intense, aching jealousy they're simply too stupid to process. After all, Shilpa is twenty times more successful than any of them, not to mention 400 times more beautiful. When you're a go-nowhere tit-flasher, a washed-up singer or a famous dunce, that's bound to rankle, especially since Shetty's also more intelligent, dignified, patient and likeable than you could ever, ever be.

There's a certain grim amusement to be had, watching the angry trio stropping about with faces like thunder, steadily dismantling their own careers, but equally, there's something profoundly embarrassing about having this lot representing Britain to a disarmingly gracious group of overseas visitors – the aforementioned Shilpa, plus sweetly gentle Jermaine and dry, debonair Dirk. This is humiliation on a national scale.

Mind you, dense as Jade, Jo and Danielle clearly are, even they're eclipsed by the staggeringly dim-witted Jack, a man so thick he'd have to study hard for six months just to make it to the level of 'vegetable'. A potato could beat him at noughts and crosses – assuming he could work out how to hold a pencil and make marks on the paper in the first place, which is doubtful. He doesn't contribute to the house, but slowly subtracts from it: moping, blinking, frowning at words of more than one letter, even frowning at noises that sound like they might be words (if the door to the diary room creaks when it opens, he gets a bit angry, thinking he's just heard yet another word he doesn't understand and vat ain't fair innit). And on the rare occasions when he opens his mouth to speak, he sounds like a leaden ten-year-old reading lines off a card.

Exactly what is Jack's purpose on Earth? There's a grisly YouTube clip of him apparently masturbating to orgasm beneath his duvet and firing his mess up Jade's leg. So maybe that's it. Maybe he was put here just to spunk on people's legs. Fucked if I can think of any other reason.

24 loses its mind [27 January 2007]

Sigh. So I started last week's column by pointing out how much things change between my Tuesday morning deadline and the printed copy appearing on Saturday morning, and wouldn't you know it, 'things' changed so much, it's probably safe to assume that by the time you read this, *Celebrity Big Brother* will have been ripped off air for inciting a full-blown race war with Jupiter.

In the unlikely event it hasn't, I'd still recommend tuning into this week's double-helping of *24* (Sky One) instead, since it'll doubtless provide happier viewing, even though it's one of the most relentlessly unpleasant things I've ever seen.

Let's be frank here: *24* has lost its mind. The hinges were always loose, but this sixth series is something else. It opened last week with Jack mute, scarred and bearded following months of torture in a secret Chinese prison. The man could scarcely walk. Two hours later he was cheerfully high-kicking a suicide bomber out the back of a train.

Nuts. But somehow it all seemed, to use a bit of internet parlance, a bit 'meh'. Jack's dealt with worse threats, right? Wrong. By the end of this week's two-hour televisual brain rape, you'll have trouble sleeping.

Aghast at the sheer swivel-eyed horror of the new episodes, several US commentators have condemned the show as a work of Neo-Con propaganda that promotes torture as a viable tool in the war against terrorism. It's hard to disagree. When 24 first began, Jack used torture as a shocking last resort, dabbling only occasionally, like an ex-smoker treating himself to a cigar on his birthday. These days, if Jack needs a piss, he'll torture anyone who might be able to tell him where the nearest bog is. Every other scene seems to run like this:

Jack (twisting screwdriver into waiter's tear duct): 'First on the left, or first on the right? TELL ME WHERE THE JOHN IS!'

Waiter: 'AUUGHHH left! It's on the left!'

Jack: 'About time' (nonchalantly shears waiter's face off with glass shard and nips off for a piss).

So far, so brutal. But the show has developed another, almost more disturbing signature move: the desperate 'against-my-will-kill' performed by an average Joe.

In season five, a grisly plot twist saw a young, quivering naval engineer being forced by circumstance to slit a terrorist's throat while Jack whispered gruff encouragement over the phone. This time round, a blameless civilian dad is coerced into battering a man to death with his bare hands. At this rate, by season seven, there'll be a convoluted storyline in which a weeping professor of ethics MUST bite the heads off ten babies IN THE NEXT TWO MINUTES or MILLIONS UPON MILLIONS WILL DIE.

Speaking of death, gleefully right-wing co-creator Joel Surnow calls the season-six terrorist threat 'smaller and more real' than before. He's wrong on both counts. Instead, it seems to consist of endless Space Invader waves of sharp-suited suicide bombers, overseen by a furious Middle East maniac who closely resembles a bald Dean Gaffney (which goes some way to explaining his fury).

Jack, meanwhile, has teamed up with a preposterous buddy-movie version of Osama Bin Laden, a ruthless jihadist leader who's suddenly decided to broker a peace deal – largely, it seems, so he and Jack can enjoy absurd getting-to-know-you banter as they drive from one bloodbath to the next.

Final absurdity: David Palmer's younger brother Wayne is now president of the US. He's about twenty-eight years old, sports a shaved head and a goatee, and looks like he's just stepped off the set of an upmarket R&B video. His inauguration must've been awesome.

In short, *24* has become a spiralling, undisciplined caricature of itself: *The Naked Gun* with blood-curdling paranoia in place of jokes. This is no longer a knockabout drama serial. It's mad crypto fascist horror. You can still laugh at it, of course. But only just.

Wanking for coins   [3 February 2007]

Four thousand years ago I used to write a website called TV Go Home, which consisted of capsule descriptions of imaginary television programmes – most of them ghastly creations teetering on the brink of plausibility. One of the earliest entries was *Wanking for Coins*, which was described as 'apocalyptic fun as Rowland Rivron tours the seedy backstreets of London's West End persuading the homeless to commit acts of self-degradation in exchange for pennies'.

I liked the phrase 'wanking for coins' so much I went on to use it again and again. The more I thought about it, the more it seemed to sum up an entire world of low-level employment. Stuck in a dead-end job? Wanking for coins. Obliged to smile at customers? Wanking for coins. Working extra shifts to pay the rent? Wanking for coins.

Imagine my surprise, then, all these years later, when I flipped on the box to discover the original *Wanking for Coins* is now broadcast in prime time on ITV1. A few things have changed, but the basic premise is essentially the same. The title's different, though. They're calling it *Fortune: Million Pound Giveaway* (ITV1).

The format is simple. Five slick entrepreneurs have a pot containing one million pounds of their own money (£200,000 each, although it's not clear whether they're paid more or less than that to do the show in the first place). They sit in a row, à la *Dragons' Den*, while members of the public come in and request some of the money. It's televised begging.

On the panel are Duncan Bannatyne (who I quite like), Jeffrey Archer (who I don't), two women who look the same, and Simon Jordan – who performs a mind-boggling miracle each week by coming across as a bigger, smugger arsehole than Archer. He looks like a cross between Gérard Depardieu and a thick waiter, and is one of those people you instinctively dislike the moment you clap eyes on them, presumably thanks to some weird, primordial twat-detector lurking in the evolutionary backwaters of the brain. Consequently, everything he says and does fills you with revulsion. Everything. Last week he raised an eyebrow and I vomited blood for an hour.

Archer, meanwhile, is clearly hell-bent on public rehabilitation, and exploits every opportunity to come across as 'the nice one' on the panel. He does this by pulling an expression so earnest it borders on insane, repeatedly straining forward and furrowing his brow so hard he looks like he's trying to screw his face into a tiny, pea-sized ball, then balance it on the end of his nose. Each contortion is accompanied by a hilariously melodramatic proclamation, delivered in the style of the 'once more unto the breach' speech from *Henry V*.

Speaking of the contestants: oh dear. They fall into four categories: elderlies ('lovable' pensioners wheeled on just so the panel can coo over them like they're four years old), do-gooders (people who need money for community centres and the like), tragics ('I lost all my limbs in a car crash and need £10,000 to have brightly coloured plastic windmills installed on the stumps – it's the only thing that'll cheer me up.'), and jokers ('Zoinks! I want £900,000 to get my bum tattooed! I'm mad, me!').

Basically, it's an hour of people desperately pleading for cash, with a cheering audience lobbed in for good measure. Presumably, it's supposed to be 'feelgood TV', but in reality, seeing people in wheelchairs beg Jeffrey Archer for money just doesn't warm the cockles. He pays out, the audience applauds, and the contestants sob for joy. But somehow they're all just wanking for coins in one sense or another, and Archer's wanking faster and more furiously than anyone.

I'd like to go on the show myself. My pitch would be simple – I'd whip out a rusting penknife and threaten to slit my throat right there and then unless they gave me the money. And if they didn't cough up, I'd do it – just to see Archer trying to work out what sort of face he should pull as my body hit the deck. What a way to go.

CHAPTER TEN

In which a wife is sought and not sought, Macs are slated, and
David Cameron is criticised in the most childish manner possible

Opinions R Us   [22 January 2007]

If there's one thing I can't stand, it's opinions. Opinionated people are everywhere. There's probably one standing beside you right now.

Look at them. There they stand, the great I-Am, eyes glinting with indignation, swinging their pompous little gobhole open and shut, spouting out one self-important proclamation after another. Have you actually heard what they're saying? Probably not. You doubtless switched off. And little wonder: it all blurs into one great big river of blah: it's all 'If you ask me . . .' and 'Well, what I think is . . .' and 'I think you'll find . . .'

They should all either shut up or be forced to shut up by stormtroopers. Or maybe we could seal them inside a Perspex chamber filled with angry bees swarming around with razor blades glued to their bellies. We could televise this. And encourage viewers to text in their opinions about what they're seeing. And trace those viewers from their mobile numbers, round them up, and slap them in the chamber too. And so on and so on, until we've whittled the population down to one person. Me. Watching everyone perish in a chamber of bees. That's my stock answer to everything.

Never in history have there been so many opportunities to put your opinion across. You can print it in papers, shout it on the radio, text it to the news channels or whack it on the internet. And it all happens so quickly, you don't even have to think your opinions through; if you can't be bothered doing the brainwork, you can simply repeat what someone else has said using slightly different words. And poorer spelling.

Most opinions, however, don't really need to be written down at all. They can be replaced by a sound effect – the audible equivalent of an internet frowny face. Imagine a sort of world-weary harrumph accompanied by the faintest glimmer of a self-satisfied sneer. That's 90 per cent of all human opinion on everything, right there. Internet debates would be far more efficient if everyone just sat at their keyboards hitting the 'harrumph' key over and over again. A herd of people mooing their heads off. Welcome to 2007.

Mind you, even the most bone-headed online debate is infinitely more sophisticated than any kind of 'public discourse' you'll see on TV, particularly if you're watching the news and they've just invited their viewers to call in for some kind of faux-democratic 'Have Your Say' segment, which inevitably functions in the same way as someone turning on a gigantic idiot magnet, given the sort of dribbling thicksicle it attracts.

In fact, that's what they should call it. The Idiot Magnet. At the end of each item on Sky News, they should say 'We're switching on the idiot magnet now. Let's see what we dredge up. Ah, Dick from Colchester, you're on the air . . .'

Cue five minutes of Dick repeatedly tapping the 'harrumph' key on his phone.

What is it with all this patronising 'Have Your Say' bullshit anyway? They don't call the rest of the programme 'Have *Our* Say'. I can have my say now, can I? What, right here, in this two-minute slice of airtime which no one's listening to anyway since they're too busy trying to get through themselves, or texting their disapproval or going online to moo at a rival? Why, thank you, Lord Media, and harrumph to you, sir.

Anyway, that's my two cents. Your turn.

It is a truth universally acknowledged that I must be in want of a wife [29 January 2007]

I need a wife. Strangers keep advising me to get one. Three times in the past fortnight, women unfamiliar to me have broached the subject with a blend of amusement and pity.

Two weeks ago I was on the phone to the bank, absent-mindedly bemoaning my own uselessness at opening bills until it's too late. 'You need a wife,' chuckled the woman at the other end.

A few days later I took a jacket to the dry-cleaners and asked the woman behind the counter if she could sew one of the buttons back on. She laughed and said she would, before explaining that what I really needed was a wife.

Today I was at a supermarket checkout, and when it was time to pay I delved in my pocket and pulled out a crumpled wedge of notes, receipts, distressed flecks of tissue, and a pen top. As I picked through the bird's nest in my hand, hunting for change, the cashier sighed that a wife would sort me out. Another woman, in the queue behind me, agreed. Quite loudly.

It's all quite warm and fuzzy really, this unsolicited maternal attention, but what's troubling is that they instinctively knew that I'm not married. Clearly I've been shuffling around emanating tragic waves of wife-needing energy. It shows up on their internal radar as a flashing alert: clueless bachelor at ten o'clock. Launch sardonic advice. Target patronised. Mission accomplished.

Well stop it, all of you. I don't want a wife. I can't imagine proposing marriage. Never. Not to a human. We're too unreliable.

Besides, marriage inevitably leads to kids, and that's just weird. I don't want to stand in a delivery room watching someone I'm supposed to love blasting a baby through her hips in an orgy of mucus, gore and screaming. My mind couldn't stand the horror. I would probably grab a rake and start thrashing at it like a farmhand startled by a rat.

Speaking of farmhands, don't assume that by ruling humans out of the marriage stakes I'm ruling animals in. Cows may have beautiful eyes, but no one wants to accompany their wife to a dinner party only to leave beneath a cloud of embarrassment because she spent the entire evening chewing with her mouth open and emptying her bum on the floor. On the drive home, the atmosphere would be poisonous. Silent opprobrium at your end, oblivious drooling at hers. What's more, a cow belches out almost eight pounds of methane a day, so good luck on your honeymoon.

But we're getting off the point here. If I must have a wife – and womankind has evidently decided I must – can't I just be assigned one by the government? It would take all the guesswork out of things – the root cause of the chronic commitment-phobia I've suffered for the past few years. The moment I so much as shake someone's hand I start assuming I will be sharing a cell with them for the rest of my life, and my subconscious ruthlessly scans them for character flaws that might grow annoying when experienced at close quarters for several decades. What's that? A faint lisp? Oh, sure, it's endearing now. But come the year 2029 you will want to smash yourself in the mind with a housebrick each time she opens her relentless, lisping gob. Better get out while you can. Run! Run for the horizon! And when you get there, keep running!

A government-arranged marriage would relieve all the pressure. Whenever my cellmate pissed me off, I would blame the powers that be instead of her. And it would work both ways: after six months of my shambolic company, she would want to punch the House of Commons into gravel-sized chunks. Our mutual loathing of the system that brought us together would keep us together. We would lie awake for hours, plotting our revenge against the bureaucrats who introduced us, sharing bitter jokes about how much we despised them. Just me and her against the world.

What could be more romantic? Mail me the forms. Show me where to sign. Finally, I'm up for it.

I hate Macs   [5 February 2007]

Unless you have been walking around with your eyes closed, and your head encased in a block of concrete with a blindfold tied round it, in the dark – unless you have been doing that, you surely can't have failed to notice the current Apple Macintosh campaign starring David Mitchell and Robert Webb which has taken over magazines, newspapers and the internet in a series of brutal co-ordinated attacks aimed at causing massive loss of resistance. While I don't have anything against shameless promotion per se (after all, within these very brackets I'm promoting my own BBC4 show, which starts tonight at 10 p.m.), there is something infuriating about this particular blitz. In the ads, Webb plays a Mac while Mitchell adopts the mantle of a PC. We know this because they say so right at the start of the ad.

'Hello, I'm a Mac,' says Webb.

'And I'm a PC,' adds Mitchell.

They then perform a small comic vignette aimed at highlighting the differences between the two computers. So in one, the PC has a 'nasty virus' that makes him sneeze like a plague victim; in another, he keeps freezing up and having to reboot. This is a subtle way of saying PCs are unreliable. Mitchell, incidentally, is wearing a nerdy, conservative suit throughout, while Webb is dressed in laid-back contemporary casual wear. This is a subtle way of saying Macs are cool.

The ads are adapted from a near-identical American campaign – the only difference is the use of Mitchell and Webb. They are a logical choice in one sense (everyone likes them), but a curious choice in another, since they are best known for the television series *Peep Show* – probably the best sitcom of the past five years – in which Mitchell plays a repressed, neurotic underdog, and Webb plays a selfish, self-regarding poseur. So when you see the ads, you think, 'PCs are a bit rubbish yet ultimately lovable, whereas Macs are just smug, preening tossers.' In other words, it is a devastatingly accurate campaign.

I hate Macs. I have always hated Macs. I hate people who use Macs. I even hate people who don't use Macs but sometimes wish they did. Macs are glorified Fisher-Price activity centres for adults; computers for scaredy cats too nervous to learn how proper computers work; computers for people who earnestly believe in feng shui.

PCs are the ramshackle computers of the people. You can build your own from scratch, then customise it into oblivion. Sometimes you have to slap it to make it work properly, just like the Tardis (Doctor Who, incidentally, would definitely use a PC). PCs have charm; Macs ooze pretension. When I sit down to use a Mac, the first thing I think is, 'I hate Macs', and then I think, 'Why has this rubbish aspirational ornament only got one mouse button?' Losing that second mouse button feels like losing a limb. If the ads were really honest, Webb would be standing there with one arm, struggling to open a packet of peanuts while Mitchell effortlessly tore his apart with both hands. But then, if the ads were really honest, Webb would be dressed in unbelievably po-faced avant-garde clothing with a gigantic glowing apple on his back. And instead of conducting a proper conversation, he would be repeatedly congratulating himself for looking so cool, and banging on about how he was going to use his new laptop to write a novel, without ever getting round to doing it, like a mediocre idiot.

Cue ten years of nasal bleating from Mac-likers who profess to like Macs not because they are fashionable, but because 'they are just better'. Mac owners often sneer that kind of defence back at you when you mock their silly, posturing contraptions, because in doing so you have inadvertently put your finger on the dark fear haunting their feeble, quivering soul – that in some sense, they are a superficial semi-person assembled from packaging; an infinitely sad, second-rate replicant who doesn't really know what they are doing here, but feels vaguely significant and creative each time they gaze at their sleek designer machine. And the more deftly constructed and wittily argued their defence, the more terrified and wounded they secretly are.

Aside from crowing about sartorial differences, the adverts also make a big deal about PCs being associated with 'work stuff' (Boo! Offices! Boo!), as opposed to Macs, which are apparently better at 'fun stuff'. How insecure is that? And how inaccurate? Better at 'fun stuff', my arse. The only way to have fun with a Mac is to poke its insufferable owner in the eye. For proof, stroll into any decent games shop and cast your eye over the exhaustive range of cutting-edge computer games available exclusively for the PC, then compare that with the sort of rubbish you get on the Mac. *Myst*, the most pompous and boring video game of all time, a plodding, dismal 'adventure' in which you wandered around solving tedious puzzles in a rubbish magic kingdom apparently modelled on pretentious album covers, originated on the Mac in 1993. That same year, *Doom* was released on the PC. This tells you all you will ever need to know about the Mac's relationship with 'fun'.

Ultimately the campaign's biggest flaw is that it perpetuates the notion that consumers somehow 'define themselves' with the technology they choose. If you truly believe you need to pick a mobile phone that 'says something' about your personality, don't bother. You don't have a personality. A mental illness, maybe – but not a personality. Of course, that hasn't stopped me slagging off Mac owners, with a series of sweeping generalisations, for the past 900 words, but that is what the ads do to PCs. Besides, that's what we PC owners are like – unreliable, idiosyncratic and gleefully unfair. And if you'll excuse me now, I feel an unexpected crash comin##f;@

Read it and weep [26 February 2007]

You know how sometimes you develop an obsession with a writer's work, and decide to seek out their entire oeuvre and inhale their every word, even if you don't really know what an 'oeuvre' is or what it looks like? Well, I do that for masochistic reasons. I actively enjoy reading people I can't stand. When they write something particularly horrid, a wave of nausea surges through me and my pulse quickens. I'm hooked on it, like a BASE jumper compelled to leap off chimney stacks for the adrenaline rush. Consider it a sickness.

Previous obsessions have included Liz Jones of the *Evening Standard* (specialist subjects: new age spa treatments and marital despair) and the Barefoot Doctor, who used to write for the *Observer*.

The latter took over my life for several months. Everything he said incensed me. He gushed a wild river of bullshit, which I swam through open-mouthed, savouring the taste. I even bought one of his books – a 'guide to urban survival', an incredible how-to manual apparently designed to help shallow, cosseted airheads become even more self-obsessed, justifying their unhinged narcissism as spiritual development.

It outlined concepts such as 'people-surfing' – which seemed to involve deliberately developing superficial relationships for personal gain – and 'visualisation'. If you wanted a new laptop, he said, you should picture yourself throwing a magic lasso around it, and before long it would be yours in *real life* (assuming you walked into a shop and bought it at some point).

I read the book from cover to cover, pausing occasionally to hurl it across the room in disgust. Even the typeface annoyed me. It was brilliant.

And now I've got a new obsession, this time with a blogger. Not just any old blogger, mind – this one's a showbiz journalist with a celebrity girlfriend. He's called Joe Mott and he writes for the *Daily Star*. His blog, archived at dailystar.co.uk/blog, is the single most dazzling body of work I've encountered in years. I urge you to read it yourself. It heaves with demented beauty.

At the top of the page squats a photo of our hero, grinning like a man who's just found £10,000 up his arse, beside the legend 'Joe Mott's HOT'. The word 'HOT' appears to be made of gold. Over this, a little textual strap informs us that Joe Mott's HOT is 'AWARD-WINNING'. Sadly it's not clear what sort of award it was. Perhaps he entered a competition to see who could devise the most infuriating byline imaginable. If so, he deserved his prize.

The byline on its own is enough to trigger my coveted puke-surge, but beneath it, thrillingly, Mott has actually written several hundred words about his incredible life. Within seconds he's describing a rowdy night out with some 'fellow journos' and bragging about getting a Lotus Europa ('it's small, fast and arousing'). Slightly annoying, but this is Mott Lite. Scroll further down and you strike gold.

Mott recounts his night at the BAFTAs. He starts by ticking off 'charmless man' Daniel Craig, who 'had less charisma than the spotty youth who took my ticket on the way in . . . come on son, you're James Bond . . . you could have larged it at the parties after-wards . . . sort it out.'

Yeah, Craig. Pull your finger out.

He attended the evening with his current beau, Sarah Harding from Girls Aloud. 'Fittest one there was my girlfriend. And you know that is an actual fact, which statisticians could validate using their craft.'

He clearly loves Sarah a lot – almost as much as himself, in fact, because he's recently bought her a 'well flash gift . . . it's a Swarovski crystal-covered bottle in pink and it's blinger than everything in the world . . . the only other person who's got one at the moment is Jay Z.'

But his life isn't all chuckles and flashbulbs and 'larging it at the parties afterwards'. There's also beauty. 'I woke up this morning in

264

the converted church I live in, to find snow settled beautifully on the slate rooftops', he muses. 'It's funny how I've started noticing that sort of thing as I've got older . . . my younger self would still have been thinking about garters, g-strings and possibly women's volleyball.'

Magical. But sadly his joy doesn't last long.

'I turned up at Cirque for the launch of a new mobile phone fronted by David Blaine,' he writes. 'I just wanted a free phone – simple. But look after me and you'll get plugs and a decent party write up.' Instead, outrageously, an 'Aussie-sounding bloke from God knows what PR company' holds him up at the door because 'we thought you were bringing Sarah'.

'You do not invite national press to cover an event, make them wait at the door, tick them off for not publicising you properly last time . . . then express disappointment that you haven't brought your celebrity girlfriend', Mott fumes. 'That's first room stuff . . . the idiot should . . . admit defeat and go to his natural home in telesales'.

'And did I even get a phone? Nope.'

Fighting back sympathetic tears, I read on. Mott visits Spearmint Rhino for a magazine launch, where his problems get worse still.

'My mate fancied a girl who was there for the event, so I started talking to her ugly friend to try and get him in there . . . [she] didn't even want to pass the time of day . . . being snubbed by a rough bird is not a good experience. "Look woman. You'd be lucky if I did fancy you and I'm only trying to help my friend out plus I've got a fit girlfriend already, so don't flatter yourself you riverpig," was what I didn't say to her. But I thought it, a lot.'

Marvellous stuff. But not my words. The award-winning words of Joe Mott. Right now he's my favourite writer in the world. That a prick this immense could actually exist in our universe is utterly inconceivable – yet Mott, clearly the most brilliant parodist of our age, almost has you believing it's true. If I bump into him some day, while I'm 'larging it' at a swanky press-awards ceremony, I swear I'll kiss him full on the lips, whether Sarah Harding's there or not. I urge you to read him. The man is HOT.

On a mobile twit machine [5 March 2007]

It is astounding how quickly you get used to technological change. For instance, within the space of 18 months, I have gone from regarding wireless broadband as an outlandish novelty to considering it my God-given right. Cables appal me – they belong to the stone age – alongside electric typewriters, fax machines, video recorders, pagers and the plough.

But there is one device I just can't get comfortable with – my mobile phone. I'm not some medieval yeoman, infuriated by mobiles full stop. Just this particular model.

The trouble started the afternoon someone from Orange rang me up to say, 'Hey, valued customer – do you want a free phone?' At first I wasn't interested, but he went on and on about how popular and great the Samsung E900 was, then promised me free texts at weekends for life if I said yes. So I gave in.

The phone arrived the next day and immediately began elbowing me in the ribs. It seems to have been designed specifically to irritate anyone with a mind. It starts gently – a pinch of annoyance here, an inconvenience there – but before long the steady drip, drip, drip of minor frustrations begins to affect your quality of life, like a mouth ulcer, or a stone in your boot, or the lingering memory of love gone sour.

The menu system is a confusing mangle of branching dead ends. It has touch-sensitive buttons that either refuse to work or leap into action if you breathe on them. One such button also terminates calls, so it is easy to cut people off merely by holding the phone against your ear to hear them. It has no apparent 'silent' mode, and when you set it to vibrate, it buzzes like a hornet in a matchbox.

It is lumbered with a bewildering array of unnecessary 'features' aimed at idiots, including a mode that scans each text message and turns some of the words into tiny animations, so if someone texts to say they have just run over your child in their car, the word 'car' is replaced by a wacky cartoon vehicle putt-putting onto the screen. There is also a crap built-in game in which you play a rabbit

('Step into the role of Bobby Carrot – the new star of cute, mind-cracking carrot action!').

When you dial a number, you have a choice of seeing said number in a gigantic, ghastly typeface, or watching it moronically scribbled on parchment by an animated quill. I can't find an option to see it in small, uniform numbers. The whole thing is the visual equivalent of a moronic clip-art jumble-sale poster designed in the dark by a myopic divorcee experiencing a freak biorhythmic high. Worst of all, it seems to have an unmarked omnipresent shortcut to Orange's internet service, which means that whether you are confused by the menu, or the typeface, or the user-confounding buttons, you are never more than one click away from accidentally plunging into an overpriced galaxy of idiocy, which, rather than politely restricting itself to news headlines and train timetables, thunders 'BUFF OR ROUGH? GET VOTING!' and starts hurling cameraphone snaps of 'babes and hunks' in their underwear at you, presumably because some pin-brained coven of marketing gonks discovered the average Orange internet user was teenage and incredibly stupid, so they set about mercilessly tailoring all their 'content' toward priapic halfwits, thereby assuring no one outside this slim demographic will ever use their gaudy, insulting service ever again. And then they probably reached across the table and high-fived each other for skilfully delivering 'targeted content' or something, even though what they should really have done, if there was any justice in the world, is smash the desk to pieces, select the longest wooden splinters they could find, then drive them firmly into their imbecilic, atrophied, world-wrecking rodent brains.

Anyway, over the past week, I've bumped into other people scowling at the same poxy phone as me. And in each case, the story is the same: Orange rang up and offered them one for nothing. It's spreading like a sinister virus, putting me in mind of the meteor storm at the start of *Day of the Triffids* – a seemingly innocent event that rapidly cripples humankind. My theory: the government is offloading these twittering handheld crapstones on to as many people as possible in a bid to whip us all into a state of perpetual, simmering anger in readiness for some kind of bare-knuckle street war. Don't say I didn't warn you.

There's only one way for Bush to dig himself out of this unpopular hole: with an ironic shovel

[12 March 2007]

You've got to feel sorry for George W. Bush. No, really. Bear with me. At the time of writing, he's just arrived in Brazil as part of a 'good-will tour', only to be greeted by 10,000 protesters banging drums and carrying banners with 'Bush Go Home' printed on them. And Hugo Chavez is due to address thousands of people in an Argentinean stadium – an event at which, according to BBC News, 'he is expected to hurl insults at Mr. Bush', an act likely to garner 'an enthusiastic reception'.

Most of the time, when people take a holiday abroad, they return home gushing about how friendly the locals were, how helpful, how accommodating. They whip out their digital cameras and bore you with pictures of them grinning alongside that nice bloke who ran that lovely little restaurant, the one who gave them that recipe for that thing. Bush doesn't have any photos like that. His holiday snaps, assuming he takes any, must consist of brief glimpses of landmarks as seen through a ten-inch layer of bulletproof glass and a billowing cloud of tear gas.

It can't be good for the psyche, being reviled around the world. And I can't see it getting better any time soon. When Bush retires, where's he meant to go for a nice relaxing getaway? Let's face it, even in the year 2025, if he pops out for some curried goat during a Caribbean break, chances are the kitchen staff will be queuing up to dribble all manner of bodily fluids in his food. He'll wind up thinking all global cuisine tastes vaguely similar and possibly a bit too runny for his liking. On the plus side, his hotel minibar will be perpetually overstocked with complimentary packets of pretzels.

All is not lost. He's got just under two years left in office: plenty of time to recover. The solution is simple: he needs to become an ironic 're-imagined' version of himself. And here's how:

1) Grow a big floppy schoolboy fringe. Like Bush, Boris Johnson is a blustering, incompetent right-wing buffoon. Every time he opens his mouth, a herd of stupid horses gallops. He's offensive, clumsy, childish, frequently lost for words and hopelessly prone to scandal. But he's also got a big floppy schoolboy fringe, so everybody loves him. Start growing one now, George. Within six months you'll be greeted with a warm, lairy cheer at student unions worldwide.

2) Leak a sex tape on the Internet. Never did anyone any harm, and besides, according to estimates, by 2015 everyone on the planet, Pope included, will have starred in some form of 'stolen honeymoon video'. Politicians will be forced to out-do one another in order to gain our respect – so if Blair's sex tape features a rather polite threesome at Chequers, Cameron will top it with a noisy twelve-way orgy on a solar-powered yacht. To make a mark, Dubya must create the most shocking and explicit video yet, something so grotesque the computer itself starts vomiting. Look up 'necrophilia' and 'zoophilia' in the dictionary, Mr Bush. Then marry the two. That's your starting point. It'll be the worst evening of your life, but you'll be an Internet hero.

3) Disappear for a bit, then return with a game show. This is the Noel Edmonds manoeuvre. No matter how much everyone dislikes you, if you hang on in there long enough, your very unpopularity will eventually make you a prime candidate for ironic reinvention. All you need is the right format, and *Deal or No Deal* is it. In the US, it's currently hosted by a weird, bald goatee-sporting guy called Howie Mandel. Action a little regime change and it's all yours, George. And instead of conversing with 'the banker', you can receive special instructions from God, which under the circumstances will seem like a fun gimmick, rather than a terrifying indication that the world's most powerful man has completely lost his mind.

4) Be more cringeworthy.
Richard Madeley has become wildly popular for saying whatever's in his head, no matter how embarrassing it may be. Bush is already pretty good at this, but needs to try harder. Next time you're at a global summit, turn to the Japanese Prime Minister live

on air and ask him if it's true about those vending machines full of schoolgirls' knickers – that kind of thing.

5) Stop invading nations and killing people. While not quite as simple as suggestions 1–4, this is nevertheless vital to anyone's ironic appeal. You can be as big an arsehole as you like – bigger even than Piers Morgan – but you've got to appear ultimately harmless. Witness the way Jade Goody's ironic charm vanished the moment she became a bully. Unfortunately, whereas she could at least try to claw back a few atoms of goodwill by publicly apologising to Shilpa Shetty, you'll have to visit the afterlife and grovel before the 650,000 Iraqis and 3,188 US soldiers estimated to have died since the whole clumsy war thing started. And that's going to take some time.

Actually, it's probably best to hope there isn't any kind of afterlife at all, because if there is, chances are they're already working on those 'Bush Go Home' placards with their magic indelible ghost pens. And God knows what kind of bodily fluids you'll find in your food. Whatever you do, don't order the milk and honey.

A fool and his money are soon parted. A bastard and his money are best friends [19 March 2007]

Only a few things separate us from the apes: (1) there's no direct ape equivalent of *The Apprentice*; (2) apes are hopeless at changing duvet covers (they pull them over their heads and panic because the sun's disappeared); and (3) apes don't use money. This third fact alone makes them vastly superior to humankind.

Money is the most terrible thing in the universe. It causes more stress, disputes and wars than religion, which ought to be impossible. Everything about it drives me up the pole, which is why I'm useless with it. I pay bills at the last minute, rarely check my bank balance, and get ripped off left, right and centre because I just can't bring myself to care about it. Friends gasp at my ineptitude. A few think me insane.

Immediate convenience. That's important. Not money. It's a wonder I bend down to pick up coins I've dropped. And it's nothing to do with how much money I have at any given moment. It's always been this way. In my early twenties, when I worked in a second-hand music store for peanuts, I'd regularly take cabs to work because I'd overslept and couldn't wait for the bus. And at the end of the day, I'd often take another cab home because I was tired, thereby blowing my entire daily wage ferrying myself to and from a job I despised. This was, admittedly, astronomically stupid, but so what? I'm still alive, thanks to dumb luck.

As you might imagine, I'm incapable of haggling. I avoid it like beasts avoid fire, because any discussion about money depresses me into a mental coma. So my current situation is my worst nightmare – my day-to-day comfort is under direct threat, and the only way out is to plunge headlong into a protracted financial negotiation. I live in a rented flat which has just been put up for sale. The thought of moving genuinely makes me pray for death. Looking round flats, signing contracts, packing things up, lugging them around, sorting out the phones and the bills and the countless petty irritants – just crack me over the head with a paving stone and have done with it. Please. Anything but that.

So I'm going to have to buy the place. Trouble is, I live in London, where houses are (a) satirically expensive and (b) people crawl over themselves like rats, scraping each other's eyes out with their selfish, grasping claws at the sight of a halfway desirable property.

And as luck wouldn't have it, my place is slap bang in the middle of the catchment area for about ten thousand flouncey schools full of horrible, bawling little Hitlers called Josh and Jake and Jessica, every single one of whom will doubtless grow up to be as effortlessly brilliant with money as Mummy and Daddy, while I rot to mulch in the old folks' home equivalent of a pound shop, beaten and abused by underpaid care workers who'll film my misery on their cameraphones and upload it to the internet for chuckles because I was too financially apathetic to sort a pension out.

I mentioned rats earlier – pertinently, since that's how I feel. The estate agents are trying to send potential buyers round to view the place every three minutes, but I keep thwarting their plans by, like, living here and stuff. I'm not a tenant any more: I'm an infestation.

I keep expecting them to kick the door in and chase me out with a broom.

And I will do literally anything to make it stop, including sorting out a mortgage, but everyone I know is urging me to negotiate over prices and haggle and fuss over this and that and God knows what and make an offer, then another, then another . . . Dance the financial tango. Get your money's worth. Play the game.

But I hate the game. Hate it. It's a boring game, of interest only to the soulless. A fool and his money are soon parted. A bastard and his money are best friends. Financial negotiation is the opposite of music, of laughter, of sunshine, of ideas, of absolutely everything that makes life worth living. It's a blank-eyed shit in a coalhouse. It's hell.

Which is why I'll probably end up paying more than the asking price, gleefully bankrupting myself just to make it all go away – especially if, as seems likely given my run of luck, the estate agents read this and the words on the page start rearranging themselves into dancing pound signs but I JUST DON'T CARE ANY MORE. Do your worst, you awful, boring, terrible world of finance, you. Then leave me alone. Forever.

Is there no end to my ignorance? [26 March 2007]

One of the most terrifying lessons I've learned is that, by and large, grown-ups don't really know what they are doing. As a schoolkid, I mistook my teachers for all-knowing, infallible beings protected by an invisible forcefield of adulthood. Even as I grew older, left school, became a student, left polytechnic and became a fledgling adult myself, I laboured under the delusion that people in positions of authority were inherently more 'adult' than I was – that they possessed some kind of on-board mental computer that guided them towards making the right decision, even if I didn't always agree with it.

My overdue epiphany finally arrived in my mid-twenties, at a barbecue, when I found myself talking to a girl the same age as me who was a schoolteacher, and she described how, much of the time, she was teaching the kids things she had only read the week before in the textbook. As long as she stayed one chapter ahead, she was fine. At first I was genuinely surprised; I'd thought all that knowledge was stored in their heads. Then it got worse. I met a doctor, not much older than myself, who was (a) drunk and (b) pretty stupid. I realised that in terms of age, I had caught up with the 'adults', and was horrified to learn they were all just as ham-fisted as me. At least the young ones were. The older generation surely had a better handle on things, I reasoned. They had to, or the world would slide into chaos. Then I passed thirty and realised I still didn't have a clue what was going on. Now I'm thirty-six, and if there is one thing I do know, it's that I still don't know that much. No one does. Everybody's winging it. Everything is improvised.

And the world never 'slides into chaos' – it's perpetually chaotic because all of us, from beggars to emperors, are crashing around trying to make the best of an unpredictable universe. We are little more than walking mistake generators. Dumb animals, essentially. Things would be just as messy if hens ruled the world. This is true, and it's scary. But also sort of glorious.

Consider that an extended caveat for the following humiliating confession: I don't understand the news. Not entirely. Let me explain: I watch and read the news, not obsessively, but probably often enough to be doing my bit as a concerned citizen. But I can't keep up with it. I follow it, but I don't always truly follow it, if you see what I mean.

Entertainment news aside, every story comes with a complex back story consisting of a million tiny events, of countless shades of right and wrong, of mistake piled upon mistake, successes and fail-ures, injustices and struggles. It's like trying to follow the plot of the most complicated and detailed soap opera ever made, one that was running for centuries before you started tuning in. To truly under-stand a major news story often requires real effort – more than many people are willing to give – which is why most of us know more about celebrities than, say, the Israel–Palestine situation.

I think people who work in hard news often forget this. They are submerged in it. They know the cast, they have followed the storylines and they can't help assuming their readers or viewers have similar knowledge. In reality, most people probably missed the crucial, earlier episodes, and subsequently can't quite relate to the story. We can see it's important – it's the news! – but we don't always *feel* its importance. If more of us did, there would probably be open revolt – or at least more revolt, more often.

In my mid-twenties I wrote for video-games magazines. I was proud of my work. It was just an excuse to write jokes really, and it was great fun. But while video-game fans seemed to like what I did, it was baffling to the average Joe: peppered with terminology about polygon counts and frame rates, and gags that referenced other, older games. To the casual observer, it was a minefield of unfamiliar acronyms.

This is fine for specialist writing but it alienates the outsider. A lot of news coverage is specialist writing. It's news written for news fans. And the stuff that isn't seems to consist of stories about Sienna Miller's arse, which is easy to follow because, well, there's not much to it. Because she is so thin.

I can't help thinking that what we need now, perhaps more than ever, is a populist and accessible *Dummies' Guide to Now*. The BBC News website does this brilliantly, with regular bite-sized primers attached to major stories which attempt to explain the back story to newcomers clearly and concisely, without being patronising or stupid. It has simple titles such as 'Who is Scooter Libby?', and is a rare oasis of clarity. I would like to see it launch some kind of 24-hour 'news companion' channel, or red-button service, that does the same thing on TV: a rolling fill-in-the-blanks service that helps you get up to speed. A catch-up service for reality, if you like. Not dumbed-down news, but clear information – something that often gets lost in the 24-hour scramble of breaking developments and updated headlines.

Maybe it's just me who craves that. Maybe I'm thick. Maybe the rest of you understand everything and I'm alone in my ignorance. But I doubt it. I think the vast majority of us are winging it, at least eighteen chapters behind in the textbook and secretly praying no one else will notice. If we all knew more, we would do more to lend a hand, instead of shrugging and hoping the news might some day go away or submerging ourselves in comforting trivia. Don't just tell us what is important. We might not have paid attention earlier. Toss us a bone. Tell us why.

On David Cameron [2 April 2007]

David Cameron is an idiot. A simpering, say-anything, dough-faced, preposterous waddling idiot with a feeble, insincere voice and an irritating tendency to squat near the top of opinion polls. I don't like him. And I've got a terrible feeling he'll be prime minister one day. Brrr.

These are unthinking snap judgements, based on little more than his media profile – but since he appears to consist of little more than a media profile designed to appeal to unthinking snap judgements, that seems fair enough. On that basis, let's stick to gut instincts, shall we?

There is nothing to him. He is like a hollow Easter egg with no bag of sweets inside. Cameron will say absolutely anything if he thinks it might get him elected. If a shock poll was published saying 99 per cent of the British public were enthusiastic paedophiles, he would drive through the streets in an open-top bus surrounded by the Mini Pops. He's nothing. He's no one.

It's notoriously tricky to find out much about his past, in the same way that Morgan Freeman and Brad Pitt found it tricky to find out much about the serial killer John Doe in the movie Se7en. He'd managed to erase his entire existence, even slicing the skin off his fingers to avoid leaving prints. Ever seen a close-up of Cameron's fingertips? Of course not. Think about it.

The apparently self-penned bio on Cameron's website begins, 'I was born in October 1966,' and then leaps straight forward to 2001, missing out the decades he spent as a guffawing, top-hatted toff in between. The infamous photo of Dave posing alongside his posho chums from the Bullingdon Club in an expensive royal blue tail-coat is one of the few clues we have. It looks like precisely the sort of photo a detective might end up studying in a murder mystery, one where a group of friends accidentally killed a prostitute during a drunken, stormy night, and collaborated on a cover-up. I'm not saying the Bullingdon boys kill prostitutes. I'm just saying I wouldn't be surprised. And that's his fault, not mine. He's gone out of his way not to mention his blue-blooded carousing, because he knows it would make the average citizen puke themselves into a coma, and one side effect of this is that he seems shifty and suspicious.

Every time I look at Cameron, I'm reminded of video-game characters: not the lovable, spiky ones like Sonic or Mario, but the bland, generic dead-eyed avatars you can 'create' for use in a tennis game or a tedious Tolkienesque adventure. You start with a bald clone, then add features drawn from a limited palette – eye colour, one of three noses, an optional goatee beard and so on – and invariably end up with an eerily characterless zombie straight out of the boardgame Guess Who? Simulated choice, as opposed to genuine variety. It is easy to build a Cameron lookalike. Just simulate the smuggest estate agent you can think of. Or some interchangeable braying twit in a rugby shirt, ruining a local pub just by being there. Easy.

Naturally, I'm biased. I've instinctively hated the Tories since birth. If there was an election tomorrow, and the only two choices were the Nazis or the Tories, I'd vote Tory with an extremely heavy heart. In descending order of vehemence, my objections to the Tory species stem from (a) everything they do, (b) everything they say, (c) everything they stand for, (d) how they look, (e) their stupid names and (f) the noises I imagine they make in bed. I once overheard two posh people – almost certainly Tories – having sex in a hotel room. It was grim. The woman kept saying, 'Fuck me, Gerald,' in a cut-glass accent, which was funny, but Gerald himself soon wiped the grin off my face with his grunting, which wasn't really grunting at all, but instead consisted of the words 'oh' and 'ah' crisply orated aloud, like Sir Laurence Olivier reading dialogue off a card at an early rehearsal. I didn't stick around long enough to hear the climax, but I imagine the words 'gosh', 'crumbs' and 'crikey' probably put in an appearance.

And here is why that's relevant: Cameron almost certainly says 'crikey' at the vital moment. Go on, picture it. Right now, in your mind's eye. You know it's true. If nothing else in this puerile one-sided hatchet job has convinced you, that's reason enough not to elect him, right there.

In summary, then: he's an idiot. But you knew that anyway. In fact the only reason I've written this is because it is going to be printed in a newspaper, which means his advisers will have to photocopy it and include it in some official internal press file, where it will sit alongside all the unnecessarily positive coverage he has generated for himself. It gives me a pathetic, childish, self-indulgent thrill, and in today's world of cookie-cutter choiceless-ness, that's as good as it gets. So nyahh nyahh, Dave, you fair-weather, upper-crust guff-cloud. Nyahh nyahh.

Safe beneath the watchful eyes   [9 April 2007]

In case you missed it, last week police in Middlesbrough unveiled a startling new weapon in the ongoing war against crime: CCTV cameras that shout at you whenever you do something wrong. Currently, they are chiefly used to warn drunken revellers hell-bent on stealing traffic cones, or to dish out virtual bollockings to litter-bugs. 'Respect tsar' Louise Casey says it 'nips problems in the bud', while home secretary John Reid praised the scheme on the grounds that rather than being 'secret surveillance' it was 'very public' and, most importantly, 'interactive'.

Of course, the word 'interactive' is regularly wheeled out to make any old bullshit sound exciting and modern. Hey, it's not a humiliating infringement of civil liberties – it's interactive! You know – a bit of democratic fun, just like *The X Factor* or *MySpace*! Woo hoo! Now put that in the bin or I'll blow your head off.

There are two major problems with justifying the bellowing CCTV cameras on the grounds that they're 'interactive'. Firstly, just because something's 'interactive', that doesn't automatically make it right. Coprophilia is interactive, and that doesn't belong in the street either.

Secondly, they're not interactive at all. They're faceless electronic scrutinisers that scream when you break the rules. What John Reid has done here is confuse the word 'interactive' with the word 'nightmarish'.

And wait, it gets worse. As if the scheme wasn't already unsettling enough, according to news reports 'children's voices are to be used initially to make the encounter less confrontational'.

This would be a brilliantly disturbing twist in a dystopian sci-fi movie in which the traditional adult-child relationship has been thrown into reverse, and misbehaving grown-ups are publicly scolded by eerie, disembodied infant voices, but unfortunately it's not happening in a dystopian sci-fi movie at all, but in Middlesborough. And, later this year, in Southwark, Barking and Dagenham, Reading, Harlow, Norwich, Ipswich, Plymouth, Gloucester, Derby, Northampton, Mansfield, Nottingham, Coventry, Sandwell, Wirral, Blackpool, Salford, South Tyneside and Darlington.

Incidentally, it's not yet clear whether the children's voices will address miscreants using formal language ('Attention, citizen: you are committing a felony; you have 20 seconds to desist') or in 'kid-speak' ('You're a bad man and I'm telling on you and my dad's going to tear your head off'). Perhaps they could also allow kids to control the cameras and decide what constitutes a crime. And rather than mounting the cameras on poles, why not make them mobile and more kid-friendly by placing them inside full-size, remote-controlled Daleks, which can patrol the streets dishing out near-fatal electric shocks to those who disobey?

Actually, using the Daleks would be a masterstroke. Everyone loves *Doctor Who* – who wouldn't be thrilled by the sight of a real-life Dalek squadron rolling down the high street, glinting in the sun? The sheer excitement would genuinely make the accompanying loss of liberty seem worthwhile.

To liven things up even more, our rasping pepperpot overlords could be colour-coded. Blue Daleks would deal with minor infractions, and would spend most of their time issuing warnings and administering minor shocks – but they'd also be chummy and approachable, and willing to pose for photographs with your

278

nephew. Red Daleks, on the other hand, would be emotionless killing machines.

Imagine the atmosphere outside a pub on a hot summer's day: a Red Dalek trundles past, and the convivial hubbub suddenly fades to a whisper. Everyone stiffens. And then he turns the corner and a communal sigh of relief goes up, and the drinking continues and the jukebox plays louder and louder . . . community spirit lives again. Admit it: it'd be fantastic.

Of course, to maximise the psychological impact of the Red Daleks, they'd have to be fewer in number than the Blues. Ten per citizen, tops.

If anyone from the Home Office is reading this, incidentally, it's absolutely imperative that you license the actual, 100 per cent official, BBC Daleks, as seen on TV. Don't just try to create some sort of rip-off close-as-dammit lookalike and hope we'll start calling them 'Daleks'. We're not idiots. And if you draw a blank with Terry Nation's estate, don't bother negotiating for the rights to the Cyber-men instead. It won't be the same. Daleks or nothing. Pull that off and I guarantee we'll willingly accept it. Even Shami Chakrabarti, denouncing the plan on *Question Time*, would have to start her complaint by saying, 'Obviously I love the idea of Daleks as much as anyone, but . . .'

So come on, Reid. Stop pissing about with twittering cameras on sticks. The technology for an army of wirelessly controlled mobile CCTV spybots already exists – and it's interactive. There's nothing stopping you. Show some balls for once in your poxy life. Give us the Daleks.

CHAPTER ELEVEN

In which 9/11 is not a conspiracy, Fearne Cotton and Pac-Man are pitied, and Mussolini makes everyone laugh

A terrible crime   [17 February 2007]

Mark Twain once said that a lie can travel halfway round the world before the truth can put its socks on. Now, thanks to the internet, a lie can travel round the world, head home, take a dump, watch the entire *Lord of the Rings* trilogy on DVD, make supper and die of old age before the truth has opened an eyelid. It's not Twain's fault. In his day the internet was made of string.

Chinese whispers spread online faster than any computer virus. I know this better than most because I was at the centre of one a few years ago, when I ended a *Screen Burn* column by recycling a very old tasteless joke (a variant of a graffiti I first saw during the Thatcher years), and within minutes half the internet seemed convinced the *Guardian* was officially calling for assassination.

My inbox overflowed with blood-curdling death threats, and it was all very unfunny indeed – a bit like recounting a rude joke at a dinner party, only to be told you hadn't recounted a joke at all, but molested the host's children, and suddenly everyone was punching you and you weren't going to get any pudding. I've had better weekends.

Incidentally, in case the entire internet is reading, it seems prudent at this point to unequivocally state that I've never wanted to see *anyone* murdered, injured, or even lightly bruised. Not even Mac owners, and frankly they're pushing it.

As anyone who read the original column will know, I'm not a huge fan of Bush. He's a dangerous idiot who's dragged America's name into the mud, and crapped all over it, grinning as he does so. As for Americans themselves, I can honestly say I've never met one I didn't like. Maybe I'm shallow, maybe it's the accents. But really – every single one of them: lovely.

So, having established that (a) I don't like Bush but (b) I love Americans, it's time for a third revelation – namely, (c) I don't believe 9/11 was an inside job orchestrated by the Bush administration. Which is a pity, because I love a good conspiracy theory, and that's a humdinger.

Thing is, people like me will eventually be in the minority if the

Chinese whisperers have their way. I'd like to think tomorrow's excellent documentary *9/11: The Conspiracy Files* (BBC2) will redress the balance – but I doubt it, since the story it tells (i.e. the real one) isn't half as exciting as the other story doing the rounds (i.e. the bullshit cuckooland version).

In cool, measured tones it steadily dismantles the Loose Change conspiracy theory until there's nothing left to see besides a slightly snotty young director and a few unhinged talking heads. No rational person could watch this and come away thinking otherwise.

But whoops: people aren't rational. They believe what they want to believe, and when evidence mounts to the contrary, dig their heels in and refuse to change their minds, like dogs that won't be dragged through a doorway. Sometimes the sheer pressure of all that stubbornness causes them to lose their senses completely and become creationists, at which point they're beyond help.

But there's still hope for the 9/11 conspiracy theorists. Their hearts are still in the right place, even if their brains have fluttered off to spaceland. One day they'll return, like butterflies, and all will be well.

Here's what really happened on 9/11. A terrible crime was committed by a group of determined terrorists. Appalling mistakes were made both before and after the terrible crime. The terrible crime was capitalised upon. The world was shit before the terrible crime, and got steadily shittier afterwards. That's it! So please, please, stop pissing your pants about controlled demolitions and the like – you're wrong. You're wrong! And it's OK to be wrong. You can still distrust or even hate the government. But on this one? You're wrong. And continuing to bang on about it isn't heroic, it's embarrassing. The rest of the world isn't asleep. You're just dreaming out loud.

Right-wing funnies [24 February 2007]

Political humour is rarely a boxful of chuckles. It largely consists of clever-clever point-scoring, weary cynicism and lolly-stick gags about the size of Prescott's arse. There's surprisingly little anger, considering the piss-poor state of the world – and when rage or passion does appear, it's often elbowed all the jokes out of the way. Mostly though, political satire seems to be stuck in a strange, woozy rut: half-heartedly sniping at the powers that be with an underpowered peashooter, breaking off every 10 minutes for a fag break and a shrug.

Three cheers then, for *24* co-creator Joel Surnow, who's recently given birth to *The Half Hour News Hour* (Fox News), a topical comedy show which manages to be angry, opinionated and genuinely political all at once. In fact, there are only two things wrong with it: (1) it's dementedly right-wing, and (2) radiation sickness is funnier.

A lot of people think right-wingers aren't capable of being amusing at all. Not true. Mussolini looked hilarious swinging from that lamppost. And besides, hardcore lefties aren't a barrel of laughs either. They're a crushing, life-depleting bore. People who stand firmly to one side of the political spectrum tend by their very nature to be stiff, crotchety sorts with a persecution complex and an axe to grind. These are not prime credentials for clown school.

For my money, the best satire floats somewhere in the centre – not in a non-committal sense, but a tactical one: positioned between the two sides, you're capable of lashing out in either direction. The first one to say something ridiculous gets a slap. It's the rational option. Genuine satire ultimately consists of the outraged application of cold rationality to whoever deserves it the most.

The Half Hour News Hour isn't rational. It's intended as a riposte to Comedy Central's *The Daily Show* (More4), the show that made stars of Jon Stewart and Stephen Colbert.

The Daily Show isn't perfect. Understandably, for a programme airing four times per week, it's often hit and miss. When it misses, it's cringeworthy; but when it hits, it's laugh out loud funny. It attacks both Republicans and Democrats, but leans more heavily on Republicans because, hey, they're the ones in power. This makes sense comedically: there are more jokes to be had in lampooning the governing party since their actions carry more weight. And besides, it's hard to generate giggles by attacking the underdog. If Hilary Clinton were in charge, she'd be pilloried nightly. But she isn't. Bush is.

Rational viewers understand this. Eye-swivelling nutrags don't. They believe *The Daily Show* is a far-left propaganda tool. Hence the advent of *The Half Hour News Hour*, which Fox claims offers 'balance' by adopting an enraged conservative stance. The end result, if the first episode is anything to go by, is a bizarre, unnatural beast: a topical comedy show that ignores the present government completely and concentrates its fury on environmentalists, civil rights campaigners, Barack Obama and Cindy Sheehan. The set piece was a shockingly dismal skit starring right-wing talk-radio hog Rush Limbaugh and joyless crypto-fascist commentator Ann Coulter, who wandered on screen looking so haunted and drawn I briefly mistook her for a ghost and kicked my television from its stand in a blind panic. Spewing all that negative hate speech must've hollowed out her spirit, poor thing; her eyes are now a portal to a world of infinite nihilistic oblivion – gaze into them too long and you can feel the air growing cold around you.

To be fair, there were one or two decent gags, but they felt like aberrations thrown up by the law of averages. There is one thing to be said in the show's favour: at least it *has* an agenda, which is unusual in modern comedy. But an agenda is all it has. It's government-approved satire – as oxymoronic, pointless and wretched as church-sanctioned porn. But probably easier to masturbate to, assuming you get off on abject desperation.

Carpet of the stars   [3 March 2007]

Celebrity worship has reached such a demented peak, it won't be long before they're legally allowed to mount the pavement and run us over for chuckles. In fact, it'll be considered an honour. We'll voluntarily hurl ourselves beneath the wheels, jizzing for joy as the tyres churn our bodies to ribbons, screaming that it's the most amazing thing that's ever happened to us.

We'll watch celebrities do anything. We'd watch Brad Pitt sit on his front lawn throwing acorns into a can. Christ, we'd watch Eamonn Holmes buying a cabbage. If there's someone famous involved, we're there.

Last Sunday, I watched *Oscars Red Carpet Live* (Sky Movies 9 HD). Ninety pin-sharp minutes of people walking along a carpet. That's all it was. Plod plod plod. Carpet carpet carpet. Every few minutes my brain protested. It screamed at my fingers to grab the remote . . . but then a voice would assure me that what I was seeing was desperately exciting and a privilege and the remote stayed put and the plodding carried on.

It wasn't my own voice, incidentally, but the voice of Fearne Cotton, who was presenting the show. I think she's nine years old, and there's something slightly odd about her. She's got a cute-but-sad expression, like a pleading mouse in a vivisectionist's cage, or that mass-produced painting of a crying boy.

Recently, in an interview with *GQ* magazine, she claimed to be 'good in bed', adding that she wears 'sexy lingerie' and had her fanny waxed – revelations which doubtless set their entire readership wanking like an angry orchestra, but only made me picture that boy from the painting – shaved, knickered, crying in a bedroom. This kind of horror has no place in anyone's head. Don't say it again, Fearne. Please.

Anyway, back on the red carpet, the crying boy was interviewing the stars as they passed by like celebrity livestock. When Michael Sheen appeared, she asked him if playing Tony Blair in *The Queen* had been 'fun', then called him 'Martin' to his face.

She asked Al Gore 'What message have you got for the Brits about keeping the environment safe?', and seemed surprised when he didn't trot out a three-word answer. She told the women they looked gorgeous, amazing and, in one case, 'top-notch'.

She was the ideal presenter. They needed someone to cover a bunch of people walking down a fucking carpet. Who do you expect? Noam Chomsky? At least Fearne got something out of it – she kept telling us how crazy and brilliant it all was. She had a night she'll remember for the rest of her life. Who are we to gripe?

Between interviews, the camera cut to shots of other stars as they arrived: grinning, posing for photos, and in Will Smith's case, proudly displaying his wife and child as though they were papier-mâché sculptures he'd made in remedial art class.

Whenever even this got too boring to sustain, we were treated to pre-recorded VTs in which a selection of who-the-hell talking heads blathered about Hollywood and glamour and fashion and God knows what else – teaspoons perhaps – and then it cut back to Fearne and she was talking to Penélope Cruz, one of the most beautiful women in the world, but instead of looking at her, I was staring at all the publicists jostling in the background, because thanks to the wonder of HD broadcasting I could make them out clearly, and each one looked like a furious gum-chewing monster who'd slit your throat if you coughed inappropriately in their client's presence, and suddenly I felt infinitely sorry for Fearne, and violently protective.

And then poor Fearne said goodbye and it was time for the ceremony itself, which turned out to be an unbearably odious five-hour tantric masturbation session in which the carpet people told the world how magical they were.

Still, it's probably worth enjoying this glittering bullshit while it lasts. In ten years' time, when we're battling 20-foot radioactive scorpions for the last six molecules of water, we'll look back on it all and emit a wistful sigh.

Same clothes. Same cars. Same sky [17 March 2007]

I used to pity Pac-Man. Not because he was relentlessly pursued by ghosts (what had he done – fucked their sisters?) but because he was a prisoner in that maze. There were exits either side, but they didn't lead anywhere. They spat him back into the haunted labyrinth. No wonder he ate so many of those suspicious looking pills. Getting off his face was his only escape.

You don't have to turn yellow and consist of pixels to experience a similar sense of déjà vu. Just trot round contemporary Britain. Chain store after chain store. Ten billion supermarket doppel-gangers. Identikit architecture. Same clothes. Same cars. Same sky.

Same sameness. It's like walking the wrong way on a travelator: hours of plodding, and you've gone nowhere.

It's the same on TV. Not so long ago, not only were our towns and cities markedly different, the ITV regions were too. A small thrill, to switch on the box in your B&B and see unfamiliar announcers, exotic logos. Different programmes too. It was like being abroad.

As a youngster, I scanned the 'regional variations' in the listings and felt faintly jealous if I spotted something interesting which I couldn't see on Central TV (my local). Gus Honeybun. Who or what was Gus Honeybun? He was always in the Westward listings, taunting me from afar.

I've just Googled him: he was a puppet rabbit. At last I know.

Anyway, since 2002 it's generic ITV, all over (apart from the hold-outs – STV in Scotland, UTV in Northern Ireland). Local identity hardly gets a look-in.

But hmmm. Glancing at the cascade of unnecessary nationwide channels available through my Sky box – UKTV *Canoe History* +2, anybody? – I can't help thinking local broadcasting is due to make a comeback.

In fact, it already is. There, nestling in the EPG: local stations for Manchester, Milton Keynes and, most exciting of all, Solent TV (Sky Channel 219) – an entire network devoted to the Isle of Wight.

Solent TV is strikingly confident. Brash, even. It's just like an ITV region circa 1989. Its flagship show is a daily newscast called *Solent Tonight*, which looks and feels just like a 'proper' news programme, except the headlines consist of minor traffic incidents and council squabbling. To a Londoner, this isn't boring, just comforting. Our news has a bodycount: it's all stab this and arson that and guns and bombs and phonecam footage of babies hurled under tube trains. It's nice to know that somewhere a hay bale blowing across a B-road is still big news. I watch it to relax.

The hosts are far younger than the national norm, yet work with absolute conviction (apart from one cub reporter, who the other day was conducting vox-pop interviews in a baseball cap). They've clearly got a minuscule budget, but they wear it well. The studio's so small, when they interview a guest they have to sit so close their knees are almost touching. But I'd rather watch that than the absurd virtual aircraft hangar you see on ITV news.

Aside from the news, there are other homegrown programmes like the brilliantly titled *See It, Like It, Cook It*, which seems to star a fifteen-year-old chef, and a chat show called *Hannam's Half Hour*, in which a kindly bloke called John Hannam converses with leading Isle of Wight figures. Thrillingly, last week the listings promised an interview with 'local character Derek Sprake', which I genuinely couldn't wait to see – but this seemed to change at the last minute. Nevertheless, the edition I *did* watch was twice as cosy and reassuring as the local news – 30 minutes of jovial chat between two likeable men in that familiar cramped studio.

Between shows, you can enjoy commercials for local shops, and occasional televised 'notice boards' promoting jumble sales or talks at Ventnor town hall ('Entry fee £1: coffee and sandwiches included'). It's a trip back in time to a more reassuring age – but also, it seems to me, a glimpse of a cosier future. It's truly heartening. Tune in. See for yourself.

Lie upon lie upon lie upon lie   [31 March 2007]

Did you see that Catherine Tate sketch on *Comic Relief* the other week? The one where Tony Blair played himself? He gave a fantastic performance. Genuinely – a fantastic performance. He actually made me laugh out loud. Admittedly, not as loud as I'll laugh the day he and Bush are found guilty of war crimes following a six-month show trial at the Hague, but close.

When he unexpectedly delivered the 'Am I bovvered?' catchphrase, his timing was immaculate – for a second, I guffawed so loudly I almost forgot about the teetering stacks of skulls, the foaming geysers of blood, the phosphor burns, the pictures of young children with their arms blown off, and the constant metronomic background tick-tock of lie upon lie upon lie upon lie.

Obviously future generations will use Blair's name as a swearword so offensive it currently has no equivalent in the English language (the closest possible translation at present being 'idiot turd stuffed in dead horse vagina' – that's your name, that is, Blair), and obviously he's doomed to spend eternity shrieking in unimaginable agony as he's boiled alive in a gigantic cauldron by a cackling, masturbating demon in the fieriest corner of Hell – but boy, he was funny in that sketch. Perhaps the custodians of Hades will cut him some slack for that. Give him a four-minute break from gargling molten lava once a millennium, something like that. Fingers crossed, eh, Tone?

I'm in a bad mood, in case you hadn't noticed, but for the best of reasons. I've just watched *The Mark of Cain*, an intensely powerful drama about the abuse of Iraqi prisoners at the hands of British soldiers, and it's made me very angry indeed. That's its job: it's a protest film. A work of fiction, based heavily on fact, written by Tony Marchant, featuring taut direction and some superb central performances.

So far, so worthy. Because it's on Channel 4, and because, on the face of it, it looks like a 'difficult' work, I suspect it'll draw a respectable-but-not-astounding audience, as opposed to the five to six million it might find if it were on ITV or BBC1 – a pity, because in addition to being angry and moving and extremely well made, it's also hugely accessible. Place this slap-bang in the mainstream and it'd go down a storm. And then cause one. It opens feeling almost like a thriller – and an effective one at that – before sliding into gut-wrenching tragedy, including some truly shocking final scenes that should redefine the phrase 'harrowing TV drama' for some time to come. And despite the subject matter, it's perhaps the most genuinely sympathetic examination of the pressures facing our troops I've seen in years.

It's not perfect (it sags slightly in the middle, and one character feels like a stock TV nasty), and it's not always subtle, but it's the best thing on the box this week by a long chalk. People need to see this. And by people, I mean you.

A roomful of squealing Josephs [14 April 2007]

Musicals are not to be trusted. They're not right. They're creepy.
If the performing arts are a family, musicals are the suspect uncle
inviting the kids to sit on his knee and play horsey. Serial killers
hear show tunes in their heads while slicing up their victims.
Musicals aren't right.

And right now, there's no escaping them. Saturday night TV has
become one big amateur chorus line, what with *Any Dream Will Do*
on BBC1 and *Grease Is the Word* on ITV. You can't move for grinning,
twirling bastards bursting ineptly into song. It's like being trapped
in a Halifax commercial.

The BBC's effort is a follow-up to last year's *Sound of Music*
search-a-thon, which posed the question 'How Do You Solve a
Problem Like Maria?' and successfully answered it with the words
'Connie Fisher'. This time, they're trying to fill the lead role in
Joseph and His Amazing Technicolor Dreamcoat – a musical so
uniquely irritating, even its title makes you grind your teeth.

The programme itself is the campest example of mainstream
BBC entertainment since Larry Grayson took over the *Generation
Game* in 1978: Graham Norton, John Barrowman and a roomful of
squealing Josephs. Yes, Josephs. They call the aspiring stars
'Josephs', which somehow sounds like an insult, especially if you
were a schoolkid circa 1981, when the word 'Joey' was regularly
employed as a term of abuse on the hilarious basis that it was the
name of a man with cerebral palsy who'd featured heavily on *Blue
Peter*. It was a cruel and infantile way for kids to get an easy laugh.

Anyway, this bunch of Joeys are set to annoy the nation for weeks
to come. Two stand out: Lewis, a blond-haired Gillette-advert-in-
waiting who looks like he's auditioning for a role in *Wilmott-Brown:
The Early Years*; and sweet-natured Johndeep, pronounced 'John
Deep' – perhaps the greatest pornstar name in history.

The live studio shows start tonight, which is just as well,
because last week's 'boot camp' episode was so choppy and packaged it felt like an extended trailer, packed with obviously manu-
factured moments of drama, yet oddly devoid of substance even

though emotions amongst the Joeys were clearly running high.
I've never seen so many grown men crying. Either someone kept
letting off spectacularly eggy guffs in the rehearsal room (I'm looking at *you*, Denise Van Outen) or they're taking the whole thing far
too seriously.

Or maybe they were simply scared of Andrew Lloyd-Webber,
whose repeated arrivals were accompanied by a burst of *Phantom
of the Opera* organ music on the soundtrack, which had the unfortunate effect of making him seem like a monster in a silent
movie, which isn't hard, given that he looks like the sort of thing
that normally breathes through gills on its neck.

Actually, that's unfair. He's not scary-faced at all. He looks like
Droopy. He does! Google it. See for yourself.

While the BBC's Joey Hunt restricts itself to sifting through irritating men, ITV's *Grease Quest* is also open to irksome women.
They're seeking a Danny and a Sandy to play the lead roles in a new
production of the popular high school musical. ITV have two main
advantages here: (1) thanks to the movie, *Grease* is more familiar
to viewers than *Joseph*; (2) they've got David Gest on the panel,
who's always entertaining (even if he doesn't speak, you can simply
marvel at his face, which coincidentally looks like Lloyd-Webber
impersonating Paul Simon).

As a programme, it's all packaged together in precisely the same
way as *The X Factor*, and I mean precisely: the main difference
being that in addition to singing, the wannabes are also required
to dance and act, thereby affording the producers three separate
opportunities to humiliate them. It's telling that so far, we've only
been shown 'acting' from the terrible auditionees, where it's used
as an extra bucket of shit to throw over them. Just how brilliant at
acting were your shiny happy chosen ones, then, eh? Eh? *Eh*?

Further proof that edit suites, like musicals, are not to be trusted.

Steamy hand-on-Bible close-ups   [21 April 2007]

One hundred per cent uncensored judicial procedure! Steamy
hand-on-Bible close-ups! Hardcore gavel-banging action! Girls

who love oaths and want to swallow YOUR testimony! Yes! It's *Sex in Court* (E4) – the show in which sexual intercourse and the British legal system are combined at last, to create the creepiest bit of broadcasting in quite some time.

It works like this. Find a couple with some kind of sexual dysfunction (she can't climax without using a vibrator; he insists on shrieking 'You can't *handle* the truth!' just before ejaculating, etc. etc). Invite them into a convincing replica courtroom. Find a real-life judge who doesn't mind presiding over this sort of 'case', and twelve members of the public prepared to form a 'jury'. Switch the cameras on. Done.

Prospective masturbators lured by the title are likely to be disappointed. The programme largely consists of close-ups of old women on the jury listening attentively to sexual problems being discussed using explicit terminology. The judge, who also features a lot, resembles a cross between the dead one out of *Two Fat Ladies* and the Queen of Hearts from Disney's *Alice in Wonderland*. In a recent edition she discussed cunnilingus at length with an eighteen-year-old who wanted his girlfriend to let him perform oral sex because 'Every woman would like to get her pussy licked – even you, your honour – you'd like to get your pussy licked, innit?' Occasionally, they call an 'expert witness' – often an old doctor who holds up medical diagrams of genitals and spends rather too long pointing out the sensitive bits.

In other words, it's less erotic than choosing a door handle from a Dutch home-fittings catalogue. The only way they could make it less arousing would be to intermittently cut to footage of a squatting farmhand crapping into a pail – shot from the pail's point of view, so it looks like a fat brown snake squeezing through a quoit. In fact it's so powerfully unsexy, I suspect it's part of some government initiative aimed at curbing procreation. Remember that scene in *A Clockwork Orange* where they feed Alex some kind of nausea drug and force him to watch footage of rapes and beatings until he can't contemplate either without feeling ill? This is more effective, and doesn't require drugs. After half an hour of *Sex in Court*, you won't be able to have sex for weeks without haunting close-ups of jurors' faces drifting through your mind's eye. That must be what it's designed to do, because it doesn't seem to serve any other purpose. Weird.

Speaking of weird, a quick update on *24* (Sky One) seems in order, simply because the current season surely constitutes the most awesome example of wholesale shark-jumping in TV history. First they detonate a nuclear bomb in the Los Angeles outskirts in episode four, which initially caused a bit of panic and general running-around, but now, a few hours later, doesn't seem to have affected the infrastructure or population one iota (in fact, round episode seven, there was a hilarious shot of the mushroom cloud on the horizon, which then panned down to a motel where a maid was blithely going about her minimum-wage job as usual).

The terrorist plot, which is so incomprehensible as to be meaningless, has already involved Islamic terrorists, Russian generals, an Australian, an autistic hacker, and Jack's own brother and father. People have been tortured with injections, carrier bags, cigar clippers and drills. Last week a terrorist chopped his own arm off with an axe. The vice president is nuts, and the president, who's been in and out of a coma, is about to launch a nuclear strike against an innocent country just because someone called him a pussy.

To cap it all, the blond boy from cloying 1980s sitcom *Silver Spoons* has turned up, playing an ultra-tough CTU agent. All they need now is a robot, and the transformation from must-see thriller to flailing joke is complete.

Then again, I've said that before, and I'm still hooked on the poxy thing. It's worse than bloody smoking.

In no way similar to *The Apprentice* [28 April 2007]

Everyone likes to think they do a difficult job. After all, if anyone could do what you do, what's the point in turning up? You might as well be replaced by an empty cereal box with a face drawn on it. Makes sense from your boss's point of view: he doesn't have to pay a box anything, and he can kick it or shag it as often as he wants, without fear of a tribunal. In many ways it's the perfect employee.

All of which explains why people feel the need to exaggerate how tough their day's been, even though listening to someone bang on about what a nightmare they've had at work is twenty times as boring as hearing them describe their dreams, i.e. so boring it almost qualifies as physical assault.

'Oh God right first I spend all morning on this report and then the email goes down so I can't send it and then this cow from HR turns up and . . .' FOR CHRIST'S SAKE SHUT YOUR THICKHOLE.

Yes, most jobs are tedious beyond measure. Which is why it's far more entertaining to see an ostensibly reasonable occupation rendered impossible for the sake of entertainment, as *Deadline* (ITV2) proves. The setup: a bunch of glittering stars try their hand at producing a weekly celebrity magazine under the aegis of Janet Street-Porter, the Fleet Street legend famous for sounding like she's rolling five broken dice in her mouth whenever she speaks.

Each week, there's a tense showdown in the boardroom (sorry, 'meeting room') during which she fires someone (although she doesn't actually say 'you're fired', she says 'clear your desk', thereby convincing the viewer what they're watching is in no way similar to *The Apprentice*).

Janet's assisted by two deputies: Darryn Lyons and Joe Mott. Mott (played by a young Kenny Everett) spends most of his time quietly moping at the edge of frame in a stupid flat cap, a bit like Jack Tweedy in this year's *Celebrity Big Brother*. He seems almost depressed, which is possibly something to do with having to share an office with paparazzi supremo Darryn Lyons, a monumental bell-end who looks precisely (and I mean precisely) like Mel Smith playing a King's Road comedy punk, circa 1981.

This being a fabricated telly job, the bosses will have been instructed to behave like rude, uncompromising, dick-swinging bastards throughout – an opportunity Lyons gleefully seizes with both hands. He struts, he barks, he bollocks, and he bangs on and on about how important it all is, in the dullest and most macho manner possible, as though he's single-handedly leading an SAS task force into Syria. It can't be much fun being bellowed at by a man who looks like a forty-six-year-old Woody Woodpecker impersonator undergoing a messy divorce, especially when he's shouting at you just because you failed to get a decent photograph of Pete Doherty – something the world needs like increased carbon emissions.

Yes, because unlike a real editorial team, the celebrity trainees are expected to take their own photos as well as writing copy, which makes it about as accurate a depiction of the magazine production process as an episode of *Ugly Betty*. Of the trainees, only Dom Joly, who seems to have turned the whole thing into some surreal personal adventure, shows any promise whatsoever. The rest just mill around bumping into each other like blind chickens. Considering this, and the fact that 50 per cent of the job (i.e. typing) isn't very televisual, the end result is far more entertaining than it has any right to be.

Still, there can't be many more careers left for TV to 're-imagine'. We've had farming, hairdressing, teaching, catering, and now journalism. A different job each week. It's like Mr Benn. What next? *Celebrity Balloon Factory*?

Actually, how about an all-star branch of Ryman's? Yeah! It'd have to be needlessly tough for telly purposes, obviously. The boss kicks you in the nuts each time a stapler goes missing. Instead of customers, it's drunken giraffes. And every Friday, the shop bursts into flames for no reason. And one of you WILL get fired.

A terribly serious drama   [5 May 2007]

In life, certain things are designated 'funny' and others are designated 'not funny'. You're supposed to laugh at the former and nod sagely at the latter. And while what officially constitutes 'funny' has altered throughout the years – at one point it was custard pies and fart noises; now it's awkward pauses and catchphrases so simple a dog could recite them – the contents of the box marked 'not funny' have remained largely unchanged throughout history. War crimes, terminal disease, children's funerals . . . they're the polar opposite of a laugh riot, and to react with anything other than pained reverence would be inhuman.

Unless you can't help it. Even funerals can be funny in the right circumstances. Say one of the pallbearers blows off, and they drop the coffin, and a dead kiddy spills out and everyone flails about trying to pop it back in his box, but they keep trapping its head in the lid, and its arms are all poking out, and it's all so inappropriate that before long you're doubled over, slapping your thighs and hooting your lungs dry in front of his horrified parents. Any reasonable person would forgive you for that.

Likewise, I expect to be forgiven for guffawing my way through *Saddam's Tribe* (C4), a terribly serious drama about Saddam Hussein's family based on interviews with his daughter Raghad, which inadvertently straddles the funny/not funny divide. On the one hand, it's the inside story of an insane, brutal, real-world regime in which torture and murder were commonplace. On the other, it's a bit like *Dynasty*. And once you've decided it's a bit like *Dynasty*, it's impossible not to laugh, even when Saddam walks around shooting dogs in the head and things like that.

Speaking of Saddam, he comes across as a less subtle version of Ian McShane's Al Swearengen character from *Deadwood* (minus the swearing). Plus he's got an oaky, baritone voice which makes him sound like Joss Ackland doing the voice-over for a gravy commercial. And for some reason I can't put my finger on, he reminded me visually of Captain Pugwash. I doubt this is the effect they were aiming for.

Stealing the show, however, is his son Uday – an outright psychopath highly reminiscent of Al Pacino in *Scarface*. In reality, Uday was apparently an unspeakable bastard who raped and tortured people for breakfast. The fictional Uday, however, lights up the screen like you wouldn't believe. He's played with absolute conviction by the naturally charismatic Daniel Mays, who had me in fits, not because he gives a bad performance (he doesn't – quite the reverse, in fact), but because by the time he's shown gleefully machine-gunning a crowded cocktail bar, my brain had already decided none of this was real and was actively willing him to commit even greater atrocities.

At one point I actually shouted 'Go on Uday, have him!' at the screen, which is pretty weird behaviour however you look at it.

On this evidence, they should turn the whole thing into a sitcom (the theme tune's already been written: 'They're creepy and they're kooky/ Mysterious and spooky/ They're altogether 'ooky/ They're Saddam's family'). I'd Sky Plus the lot.

The problem is that the current trend for fictionalised accounts of real events is inherently camp. *The Queen*, for instance, was bloody ridiculous. And there can't be many stories left to cover. Saddam this week, Robert Maxwell last week, Blunkett, Blair and co. already in the bag . . . Who's next?

My money's on Sir Clive Sinclair. A ninety-minute TV drama spanning the period from the introduction of the ZX81, taking in the triumph of the ZX Spectrum and the failure of the Sinclair QL, culminating in the ill-fated launch of the Sinclair C5. Starring David Thewlis as Sir Clive, and John Thomson as a young Alan Sugar waiting in the wings. And with Uday Hussein thrown in for no good reason. You'd have him torture Rod Hull with a hammer or something, just to sex things up. Ratings dynamite – and audience chuckles – guaranteed.

Obsessed with Katie Hopkins [19 May 2007]

According to the popular imaginary superhero Jesus Christ, it's easier for a camel to pass through the eye of a needle than for a rich man to enter heaven. In either case, it's not impossible. To solve the camel/eye-of-needle puzzler you need a liquidiser, an extremely tiny spout, a steady hand, and a shit-load of patience. To get a rich man into heaven, get him to take part in a televised public atonement exercise, such as Channel 4's *Secret Millionaire*, or *Filthy Rich and Homeless* (BBC3)

The set-up: five loaded members of the public give up their cosseted existence to live like homeless people for ten days – sleeping on the streets, begging for scraps of food, arguing with drunks – accompanied only by a cameraman who leans in for a good hard watch each time they snap and start beating the pavement with their fists, shrieking and wailing and begging to be taken home.

Among the volunteers is Clementine Stewart, twenty-one-year-old-daughter of pint-sized ITV news-bellower Alistair Stewart. In 'normal life' she spends most of her time riding horses and chortling. Here, she's dumped, late at night and in sub-zero temperatures, in the 'crack triangle' of Soho, and commanded to find somewhere to kip. It's hard not to feel sorry for her as she tearfully wanders the streets with her mangy sleeping bag, desperately seeking a dry shop doorway to lie down in. Hard, but not impossible. Bastards will laugh themselves blue. (Clem spoils things the next day, spectacularly breaking the rules by hanging around outside the *This Morning* studios until spotted by family friend Fern Britton – who immediately whisks her into a dressing room for a wash, a drink, a bite to eat and an illicit £20 note.)

No one finds it easy. The toughest-looking contender – an imposing, skin-headed booze magnate named Darren, who looks like he could punch a battleship unconscious – breaks down after one night on the streets and resorts to phoning his mum in tears. Multi-millionaire Ravi, meanwhile, mistakes the whole thing for an *Apprentice*-style task, and sets about trying to make money by flogging things on the street. (This being a BBC show, he has to settle for selling flowers – Channel 4 would have let him sell bootleg fags and crack, thereby giving him a sporting chance).

Anyway, the show ultimately *is* reminiscent of *The Apprentice*, but only as a startling contrast. It's even edited in similar fashion, although instead of sweeping aerial shots of the London skyline, you get footage of dustbins and pigeons being sick.

The whole thing is clearly a life-changing eye-opener for the contestants; whether viewers will feel fresh sympathy for the homeless, or simply enjoy a cheap holiday in other people's misery before flipping channels is open to question. Two final thoughts: (1) cute title, but they should've called it *Moneybags Masochists* instead; and (2) the weird over-zealous duo overseeing the whole thing scared me silly – especially former US probation officer Rebecca Pettit, who's all finger-pointing, wake-up-call attitude and mad googly eyes. I wouldn't want to bump into her in a dark alley.

Speaking of mad googly eyes, I'm now obsessed with Katie Hopkins from *The Apprentice* (BBC1) – the bitchiest, most venomous contestant in the show's history. Apparently played by the old *Spitting Image* puppet of the Queen, wearing a blond wig and glowing pale-blue contact lenses, Katie enjoys sticking the knife into her fellow contestants so much, she can't help smiling as she slags them off to camera. I can't help imagining if one of the others accidentally fell down the stairs, and lay at the bottom in a broken-necked comatose heap, she'd stand at the top grinning like a carnival mask and frantically rubbing her mimsy till the ambulance arrived. There's something unholy about her, like a possessed Ermintrude. Lord help Sir Alan if he finally decides to fire her. Her head'll start revolving and spewing green vomit. Here's hoping Nick Hewer carries a crucifix in his pocket.

Sir Alan, Margaret Mountford, and Gandalf

[26 May 2007]

This series of *The Apprentice* (BBC1) is cursed. As far as I'm concerned, I mean. In week one, I had trouble getting preview DVDs. Since then, the PR company couldn't be more helpful. Today they bent over backwards to secure me a last-minute, hot-off-the-press, edit-suite-fresh copy of the next episode. They said it would be ready this evening, and sure enough, it was – just in time for my deadline. Excited, I arranged for a courier to pick it up. Being a twat, he decided to post it through the letterbox of the interior design showroom next door, then ride away without telling me. I discovered the error around 10.30 p.m., and subsequently spent fifteen minutes on my knees in the street, trying to retrieve the Jiffy bag from their welcome mat by reaching through their letterbox with a pair of kitchen tongs, like some kind of *Crystal Maze* cunt.

A jogger glared at me. Then two smartarse teenagers asked if I was a burglar. And then I gave up. It'd make a better anecdote if a neighbour's dog had unexpectedly turned up and screwed my arse inside out with its hot red doggy little dick, but nothing that exciting happened, which in itself makes the whole thing more annoying. Here's hoping that courier prick hits a speed bump at the wrong angle and accidentally drives his entire bike up his own arse some time soon.

So, rather than deliver an appetite-whetting critique of this week's episode, I'll simply have to pour needless abuse on the heads of each remaining contestant instead, in the guise of a tipster's form sheet. It's what I was going to do anyway.

If *The Apprentice* were a personality contest, as opposed to a wacky 'business simulation' in which a trio of white-haired 800-year-olds (played by Sir Alan, Margaret Mountford and Gandalf) tut and fuss and disapprove of the young, the obvious winner would be Tre – even though his 'personality' apparently consists of fury and cockiness, with not much in between. As ambitious as a harpoon gun, Tre clearly has no intention of becoming Sir Alan's apprentice, and every intention of becoming his conqueror. Unlikely to be chosen on that basis, he'll probably be PM by 2009 and World Emperor by 2013. Odds: 10/1.

Next, Naomi – lopsided, booby Naomi. If Katie resembles *The Magic Roundabout*'s Ermintrude, Naomi is Brian the snail. With twin stomach bumpers. Seems to have spent most of the past fortnight nodding at anything Kristina says. Can't see her winning. Odds: 9/1.

Then there's Lohit, the eerie space butler. Lohit is one of those people whose age is tricky to gauge (I figured he was in his mid-thirties; actually he's twenty-five). The winner of *The Apprentice* always seems to come from nowhere; on that basis Lohit, who spent the first six weeks hanging around like a barely perceptible gas, is almost certainly bound for the final, but he's possibly too much of an android to actually win. Odds: 3/1.

What about Simon? The nice-but-dim estate-agency one who looks a bit like a Disney boy turned adult. Too bland to win, like Naomi he's presumably still in the show simply to provide a bit of non-threatening human filler. Not a winner. Odds: 11/1.

Next, freak candidate Katie – like a female Blue Meanie, but pink; boiled-baby pink; an evil, peeled dormouse that can't wait to watch you die. I'd previously noted her tendency to smile while sticking the knife in. More worryingly, she also smiles whenever Sir Alan slags her off in the boardroom, which is just plain sick. Tellingly, Katie is the only contestant you could picture constructing a gallows and hanging a baby koala in front of a schoolyard full of horrified children. Not human. Odds: 100/1.

Finally, my tip: Kristina. Trustworthy, glamorous and a little bit leathery, like a seasoned air hostess keeping her head during a hijack; Kristina is the most promising all-rounder by far. For some reason, I keep picturing her playing Ian McShane's love interest in a contemporary 're-imagining' of *Lovejoy*. If she doesn't win, perhaps the BBC drama department would like to take that idea and run with it. Odds: 1/1, Favourite.

Twelve sure-fire ways to save *24* [2 June 2007]

So it's the finale of *24* (Sky One) tomorrow night, and – wait! Come back! I know, I know, it bores you senseless now. I agree. This season has been so dreadful, I'm not going to watch the climax. I don't have to. I've saved myself the time by reading the episode synopsis on Wikipedia. That's how bad this once-unmissable show has become: I'm willingly seeking out spoilers just to get it over with. And I'm not alone. *24*'s ratings have plunged in the US. The producers are promising to make changes in time for season seven – possibly a complete reboot. With this in mind, and in an attempt to revive a show I used to love, I humbly present twelve sure-fire ways to save *24*. Free of charge. I'm good like that.

1) Introduce plausible enemies. At present, *24*'s bad guys are such humourless, hard-arsed drones, they might as well be replaced by shop window dummies with 'BAD GUY' scribbled on the forehead. If they must be one-dimensional cartoon villains, go the whole hog. Make them Terminators. This would be far more exciting, and probably only about 3 per cent less realistic than the show is anyway.

2) Think small. You don't need mushroom clouds to hold our attention. Give Jack a compact-yet-urgent threat to handle – a lone serial killer perhaps – and we'll be just as entertained.

3) Enough of CTU's teenage office politics. Things reached a new

nadir this season, where the moronic Chloe/Morris, Milo/Nadia storylines resembled a soap opera aimed at people recovering from head injuries. Either make them bang each other over the desks, or don't let their love lives intrude at all.

4) Make the next season a blatant *Fantastic Voyage* rip-off, in which Jack is miniaturised and injected into Lindsay Lohan's body. He has 24 hours to save her liver from permanent damage by fighting off invading 'alcohol cells' with his bare hands. Not only is this a superb cautionary tale for younger viewers, it means the finale will culminate in an eye-popping sequence in which Jack, midway through transforming back to his original dimensions, squeezes out of Lohan's bottom and flops triumphantly into an aluminium medical tray, where he thrashes around, covered in mucus, the same size as a rat. Don't tell me you wouldn't remember *that* for the rest of your life.

5) *Rest Home 24*: recast the show with eighty-five-year-olds who take an entire episode to stagger from one side of a room to the other, and half a season to make a cup of tea with their brittle, quaking fingers. It'd have true morbid appeal. Will Jack make it to the front door before the postman stops ringing the bell? Can Chloe climb into the bath unassisted before the water goes cold? The clock is ticking! (Literally – you'd replace the iconic digital timer with an Edwardian grandfather clock.)

6) The Chinese have created 240 identical clones of Dick Cheney! One has an essential microchip hidden in its balls, and the only way for Jack to retrieve it is to suck it out through the end of its winky. That's 240 clones – in order to save the world, Jack must perform ten blowjobs an hour, for twenty-four hours. On Dick Cheney. Brilliant.

7) Jack travels back to 1963 and must race against time to stop Lee Harvey Oswald shooting John F Kennedy.

8) Jack travels back to 1990 and must race against time to stop himself making *Young Guns II*.

9) Jack wants to buy a hen, but all the hen shops are closed (hey, it *could* work).

10) Make each episode cover a year instead of an hour; instead of

playing a government agent fighting terrorists, Kiefer plays a glacier fighting the effects of climate change. You'll need to play loads of dramatic up-tempo music to keep the pace jaunty.

11) Do a *Memento* season, in which each episode takes place an hour before the previous one (Note: instead of 'Previously on *24* . . .' the pre-credits summary would have to say 'Consequently on *24* . . .')

12) Don't do any of the above. Apart from the first three.

A collector's edition of Barely Legal   [9 June 2007]

People on TV aren't people; they're distorted electronic drawings of people, and only an idiot would judge someone based on how they come across on a reality show. Reader, I am that idiot. *Big Brother 8* (C4) began with a gimmick presumably designed to quell sour memories of the race war. The house was pumped full of girls. Since a woman can't walk from one side of the room to the other without provoking a catty feud with at least three other females, even if you offered to pay them £100 per minute of camaraderie, these are ideal breeding conditions for a summer of life-enhancing squabbling.

At the time of writing, the house contains the following: Sam and Amanda – chirping, identical borderline foetuses resembling the cover of a collector's edition of *Barely Legal*, their entrance was terrifying; toting lollipops and squealing about the colour pink, they seemed to have stepped out of a sinister, perverted remake of *Charlie and the Chocolate Factory*. Lately, they've calmed down a bit; just as well, since thanks to all those mirrors, there often appear to be eight of them.

We'll skip Nicky and Chanelle for now, since both seem far too nice to succeed, and instead ponder Charley, an instant villain (played by Neneh Cherry) who made the classic error of assuming international celebrity status in her own mind the moment she entered the house. Not so much a person as a damning indictment of everything, I assume she'll have been evicted and booed to the moon and back by the time these words reach you. Almost a pity.

Next, Shabnam. An over-excited *Meg and Mog* blabbermouth

cursed with demented eyes (the self-adhesive, googly ones you'd stick on a sock puppet), Shabnam has tucked her personality behind a wall of breathless prattle and is therefore hard to read. As is Tracey. Worzel Gummidge. Jimmy Savile. The Face of Boe. That witch from *Chorlton and the Wheelies*. Cackling rave Womble Tracey provides an inexhaustible supply of cruel lookalikes to choose from. For this reason alone, she's one of the more entertaining inhabitants, better than, say, Emily, because Emily doesn't really look like anyone or anything, in the way that the cast of Hollyoaks don't look like anyone or anything either. A classic example of anonymous prettiness; the second your brain registers that she's attractive, it simultaneously deletes her face from memory.

Then there's Carole, Laura and Lesley. The most likable housemates since Pete or Aisleyne, Carole and Laura haven't put a foot wrong; Lesley however, is becoming increasingly peculiar, and appears to have wandered into the house by mistake during a distracted 'turn', like a menopausal shoplifter.

At the time of writing, there's only one man about the house – and he's a girl too. The human equivalent of Leslie Phillips saying 'well, helllll-oh', oily, lipless Ziggy seems to have based his entire persona on Anthony Head's portrayal of a smug yuppie twat attempting to bag Sharon Maughan in the old Gold Blend commercials. For some reason I have a recurring fantasy in which Ziggy eats something that disagrees with him, and spends an afternoon staggering around with liquid dribbling down his thighs, in full view of the girls and cameras. Anything to knock that self-satisfied look off his fizzog.

And that's it so far. Chances are by the time you read this, they'll have put some more men in. And, with any luck, Clyde the orangutan and a wisecracking robot. We can dream.

Finally, *The Apprentice* (BBC1) roars to a close, following last week's chilling boardroom finale, in which Katie Hopkins cemented her position as the most terrifying, unpredictable screen villain since Sadako from the movie *Ring*. What – WHAT – was going on in her head? We shall never know, just as we'll never know what motivated the Zodiac killer. The final is now a showdown between the sole credible contestant (Kristina) and a shivering puppy (Simon). Surely a foregone conclusion. Surely.

No it wasn't. Simon won.

The Amazing Mister No Lips   [16 June 2007]

If the past is a foreign country, the future is a foreign country in space. It's an absolute pig, the future. Intriguing yet ultimately unknowable – a bit like Moira Stuart. There's a whole industry devoted to working out what's going to happen in the future: jittery governments paying big bucks to learned men and women who call themselves 'futurologists' (or 'guessers') and make informed predictions (or 'guesses') about the shape of things to come. Of course, the problem with all this crystal-ball-gazing is the wild card, the spanner in the works, the unpredictable random occurrence that irrevocably alters the course of everything that follows. Like if the Ice King from Planet Shiver suddenly beams down and reverses global warming with his magic snowman army. That kind of thing.

Judging by last week's column on *Big Brother* (C4), I'd make a useless futurologist, having predicted that (a) Charley would be out in week one, and (b) the 'women only' gimmick had distracted attention from the CBB race war. I hadn't foreseen Emily's Nathan Barley impression – the dumbest passing utterance by any house-mate ever – and its consequences.

Now it seems rash to blithely assume the house itself is even standing. Maybe someone daubed a cartoon of Muhammad on the walls five minutes after I wrote this. Or maybe Ziggy ate a load of honey and blew off and the guff-cloud attracted a swarm of bees which flew up his arse and repeatedly stung him on the brain till he started speaking a new language. Hope so. I hate Ziggy, the Amazing Mr No Lips: him and that open-handed 'hey, I'm a reasonable guy' shtick he pulls at every opportunity. He's like a surfer impersonating Tony Blair. Or maybe he's nice and I'm nasty. The truth will out.

Speaking of which, I think – I *think* – it's safe to assume Charley will be out by the time this gets printed. Surely to God. Sharing a house with her must be like sharing a cramped train carriage with a sleeping bear, afraid the next tiny bump will wake her up and set her off. She's a hovering attack droid: the moment her sensors detect the faintest whiff of disapproval, she corners her subject and mercilessly machine-guns them with words. I've never heard anyone talk so fast. It's like someone fast-forwarding through an audiobook version of *The Oxford Dictionary of Accusatory Dialogue*.

Another thing I didn't see coming was the introduction of two fresh housemates, Gerry and Seany; both gay, both likable, although it took a while to warm to Seany simply because he's so strange. The moment he entered, Laura mistook him for a clown. He looks like a cross between Gene Wilder and Simon Weston, and dresses like Flavor Flav at a Klaxons gig. At the time of writing, he and Gerry (played by a very young Oliver Hardy, voiced by Borat) appear to be warming to each other and have started holding hands, which should launch a thousand 'hilarious' *Brokeback Mountain* poster mock-ups in the tabloids. If they start snogging in earnest, I hope Big Brother issues them T-shirts with Richard Littlejohn's face printed on the front, so they can sit in front of the cameras, necking like teenagers, just to confuse him.

Actually, what with Laura, Gerry, Seany, Carole and Nicky, there's a higher concentration of likable housemates than at any point in the show's history – although of course, since I, the master futurologist, am saying that, you can bet they're about to cause a disgraceful international incident from which the nation will never recover.

A few words, now, on *Doctor Who* (BBC1), which I've neglected to mention for weeks. This third series had a big wobble with the 'human Dalek' and spaceship-into-the-sun episodes, before hitting a stellar home run with 'The Family of Blood' and last week's brilliant 'Blink'. Tonight's episode is also unmissable, albeit for slightly different reasons. Oh, and I need to say this, because it's true: David Tennant is the best Doctor Who ever.

Monsters Got Talent   [23 June 2007]

Last week, the final of *Britain's Got Talent* got almost 13 million viewers, which in this multi-channel age is the equivalent of a *Morecambe and Wise Christmas Special* watched twice by everyone in the country through a kaleidoscope. Hits don't come any bigger. Former *Sun* TV critic and Bluto-lookalike Garry Bushell used to repeatedly bang on about how the viewing public was yearning for old-fashioned variety shows, and on this wonky evidence, he was right.

Ultimately, it was proof you *can* polish a turd. The finale consisted of a breakdance troupe, a faintly creepy Julie Andrews MiniPop (played by the girl from the 'if you hit me at thirty, I'll live' ad), some juggling barmen, a man whose act consisted of a monkey waggling its arse, a foetus singing 'Somewhere over the Rainbow', and an opera singer with a face like the Stay Puft Marshmallow Man from *Ghost Busters* reading a disappointing bank statement. Under normal circumstances, a line-up that wouldn't fill a village hall; in the grip of collective madness, a nation-uniting clash of the titans.

The astronomically smug and watery Piers Morgan (who – and this is a reference only three of you will 'get', but it's true – looks precisely like a Chris Ware cartoon character) went on *This Morning* to pipe a load of guff through his blowhole about how the Great British Public had rallied around the show like the World Cup or Wimbledon. Infuriatingly, he was right. They've already started trawling for next year's contestants; expect ITV to expand the 2008 run to 2008 daily episodes. Plus a two-hour special showcasing all the contestants they had to eliminate for being on the sex offenders' register: *Monsters Got Talent*.

In official ratings parlance, ITV's barnstorming end-of-the-pier show kicked the shit out of *Big Brother* (C4), which has now had so many housemates passing through it, it's starting to resemble an over-designed airport lounge. I keep expecting to spot a duty-free Sunglass Hut in the background.

Anyway, a fresh meat injection arrived in the form of four new dick-owners: Brian, an earnestly thick nineteen-year-old played by Grace Jones; Liam, a pudgy, ruddy-cheeked tree surgeon; Jonathan, a forty-nine-year-old millionaire media magnate who looks like he should be reading the news in a wizard's hat for some mad reason, and Billi, a haircut from Middlesex. The latter has less personality than a cardboard ghost, but has at least put the wind up my least favourite housemate, the sanctimonious aftershave splash-post Ziggy, by having designs on Chanelle, Ziggy's in-house squeeze, who appears to be having designs back.

At the time of writing, one of my predictions from last week has just done the unlikely thing and come over all true, as Seany and Gerry 'made *Big Brother* history' by sharing an enthusiastic man-on-man snog. Something about Gerry has been bugging me for the last few weeks, and I think I've finally cracked it: if you ignore his hair and wispy goatee-beard-type-growth, he's got exactly the same face as Gordon Ramsay.

Speaking of look-alikes, casual channel-surfers could be forgiven for mistaking the first episode of season six of *The Shield* (Five) for an especially frantic episode of *Ross Kemp on Gangs*, since he and lead actor Michael Chiklis look eerily similar, although the arrival of Forest Whitaker should put paid to that delusion. Next to the solemn pace and meticulous attention to detail of greatest-show-on-television *The Wire*, The Shield feels like a hard-boiled Frank Miller cartoon, all banging doors and wise-ass dialogue, a hundred miles from reality, but it's fearsomely addictive once you're in. Like *The Wire*, despite arriving in big season-shaped chunks, it's telling one long, winding tale. If you haven't been on board from the start, you're missing out – and annoyingly, the release of previous seasons on DVD here in the UK has fallen way behind the US pace. But sod it: order them from abroad. Or download them. Hours of thrilling goodness await, and it's well worth catching up.

CHAPTER TWELVE

In which penises are measured, fashion and Facebook cause bewilderment, and the author is blackmailed into attending the Glastonbury Festival.

On knife-in-the-eye shop signage [23 April 2007]

I live in a town you may have heard of. It's called London. In many ways, it's a great place – excellent local amenities, a giant Ferris wheel, and more than a few famous faces (Toby Anstis lives here, as does that woman off Holby City – you know, the nursey one). But there is a downside, too. London – like many other places – has a cancer; an unwelcome phenomenon that has been gradually spreading over the past decade, and is now reaching saturation point. I am talking, of course, about modern laser-printed uPVC retail signage.

Shop fronts have never been uglier. I'm not talking about the big chains here – they've spent millions designing their logos. Theirs look crisp and clean and occasionally even demure. I've got nothing against, say, Nando's. Nando's is awesome.

No, I'm annoyed by the little guy – the pound shops, the cheapo grocers, the off-licences and the takeaways with their horrid, shrieking signs. Frankly, I couldn't give a toss if Tesco bulldozed the lot of them and turned the entire nation into one huge super-market. At least there'd be some typographic consistency.

A few years ago, shopkeepers had three basic options: (1) paint the store front yourself; (2) hire a professional to paint it for you; (3) buy some metal or plastic lettering and screw it over the door. Now, there's a fourth option: get a bunch of clueless, cut-price fuck-wipes to design a banner on a computer in six minutes flat, stretch it to fit and print it out using some hideous modern laser-jet device filled with fifteen thousand waterproof inks, each a virulent shade of sick.

As a result, we live in a cluttered optical hell of carelessly stretched-and-squashed typefaces and colour schemes that clash so violently they give you vertigo. Stroll down the average high street and it's like being assailed by gaudy pop-ups on the internet. It makes your eyes want to spin inward and puke down their own sockets.

As if thoughtless font abuse isn't enough, some signs even incor-porate scanned photographs: a garish snap of sweating meat sur-

313

rounded by a yellow Photoshop 'haze' effect, hovering over an electric blue background, flanked by the words KEBAB DUNGEON in bright red, foot-high Comic Sans crushed to 75 per cent its usual width. Jesus. Why not punch me in the face and have done with it?

The overall effect is depressing and disorientating. One computer-assisted eyesore after another, jostling for position, kicking good taste in the nuts. Surely this is more than the human mind can process? I wouldn't be at all surprised if the local crime rate rises each time one of these poxy signs go up. It's enough to put almost anyone in a knife-wielding frame of mind.

And that's not just idle speculation. Well, all right, it is. But there's little doubt that environment affects mood. That's why we tend to paint our bedroom walls soothing, neutral, off-white shades as opposed to frantic lime green with Day-Glo orange swastikas. When I walk the streets of the tiny Oxfordshire village in which I grew up, my mind feels clearer. I can concentrate in a way that simply isn't possible in London, where my subconscious is too busy trying to filter out the billboards and the lettering and the POUNDLAND ANY ITEM £1 OR LESS.

Laser-printed uPVC shop signs are an atrocity. A sanctioned act of vandalism. They should be outlawed or, at the very least, be put through some kind of approval process in which a panel of graphic designers inspects each proposed sign, rejecting those with squashed typography or obnoxious colour schemes.

Something has got to be done because it's only going to get worse. You know what's coming: animated shop signs with moving 'wallpaper' backgrounds. Storefronts resembling god-awful homepages from 1998. Row upon row of them. Visual bedlam wherever you turn. Two months of that and our cities are going to be overrun with screaming maniac gangs, hitherto law-abiding citizens driven insane without knowing why, like the jittering zombies from *28 Days Later*.

It's your fault, shopkeepers. It's your ugly font-abusing fault.

Who are these people and what are they wearing?

[30 April 2007]

Who says Britons are apathetic? It's all a question of priorities. We can hardly muster so much as a shrug as our leaders drag us toward Armageddon, but dangle something fashionable in front of us and we'll gladly queue round the block and beat our own neighbours to death for a chance to momentarily brush against its hem. Last week, hardcore idiots across the nation stood in rows at dawn, desperate to get their hands on a cotton bag with 'I'm not a plastic bag' printed on it. Right now, a group of determined oafs is camping out in preparation for tomorrow's launch of the new Kate Moss clothing range at Topshop. If *Grazia* magazine printed an article declaring it fashionable to smack yourself in the forehead with a limited-edition ball-pein hammer designed exclusively by Coleen McLoughlin, a mob would form outside your local B&Q before the ink had dried on the page.

It's a mystery to me. If the whole point of fashion is to distinguish yourself from the herd, why queue up to be part of it? Am I missing something here? I suspect not. But then I don't 'get' fashion. I once went out with a girl who was obsessed with dressing up; a real clothes nerd. While we were together, she developed a serious jeans habit. Each week, a new pair. She'd bring them home and show them to me, bubbling with excitement. I honestly couldn't tell the difference between one pair and the next, and I was staring pretty hard, in case there was a quiz at the end of the relationship. Doubtless a fellow jeans spod would've been thrilled by her purchases. To me, it was like trying to spot minute discrepancies between two marked playing cards. She virtually bankrupted herself buying items of clothing that looked identical to anyone other than an similarly obsessed expert. They were only jeans! Blue bloody trousers!

As far as I can tell, fashion is nothing more than a handy visual system that gives people with no personality some palpable criteria to judge each other by. Anyone who regularly contemplates clothing for more than five minutes a week is wasting their life as surely as the most lethargic, do-nothing heroin addict imaginable. Yet despite this, interest in fashion seems to be spreading.

Take men. Youngish men. Men in their late twenties and early thirties. What's happened to them? They've had a collective makeover. Not so long ago they were content to slob around in vaguely ironic T-shirts. Suddenly they've lost nine stone. They wear trousers so thin you could mistake them for shoelaces. Cardigans and flat caps. Flat caps! Talk about trying far too hard to please. Every time I see some flat-capped little tit bobbing down the pavement towards me I have to fight the urge to rip that cloth disc off their head and toss it, Frisbee-style, way up onto the nearest roof. Just to see what their face does. They'd probably just stand there, blinking dumbly, like a robot awaiting instructions. These people are hopelessly lost.

What exactly is the thought process that leads someone to buy a bloody cap anyway? Or any à-la-mode accoutrement, come to that? Is it motivated by fear? Do you see someone influential wearing something preposterous and find yourself irresistibly compelled to follow suit, like a cry-baby sheep? Or is there a secret fact-sheet being handed round – one that lists all the elements of the unofficial tosser's uniform and commands you to buy them? Who's issuing the orders here? And why does everyone seem so eager to obey?

Youngish men have gone all wrong. But the younger ones are worse. They've got haircuts now. Quirky, angular, idiosyncratic haircuts; haircuts like elaborate designer lampshades; haircuts they've downloaded off the internet. Some of them wear eyeliner. Presumably they're aiming somewhere between Russell Brand and Marc Bolan, but somehow end up resembling Muppet Baby incarnations of Danny the dealer from *Withnail and I*.

Jesus Christ. That's another popular look: Jesus Christ. I went to a gig the other day and saw at least eighteen Christs, none of them a day over twenty-five. At one point, three of them stood in a corner chatting to each other. I thought I'd stumbled across a religious triptych. God knows what they were talking about. Eyeliner tips, probably. Or parables.

Don't get me wrong. I'm all for freedom of expression. I just don't understand why people choose to flaunt their individuality by dressing alike. Maybe I'm just jealous. I've got less fashion sense than the average PC World sales assistant. I shop in the high street, and only then under duress. (Incidentally, is it just me, or would it be handy if clothes had 'recommended age group' labels, alongside the waist, chest, and leg measurements? It'd stop literally thousands of people from making fools of themselves each year.)

I hate shopping for clothes so much, I wear things until they fall apart. Right now, the soles of my shoes have worn so thin I can stand on a penny and tell if it's heads or tails. And I've only got the one pair, which means when they finally disintegrate I'm going to have to shamble into the nearest shoe shop looking like a tramp. I may not have dignity, but I've got my priorities right. And those caps wouldn't suit me anyway. I've got a head like a loaf of wet bread.

On a face on a book [7 May 2007]

Modern life is hectic. So hectic you don't have time to think, and instead have to rely on snap judgments to do your thinking for you. Malcolm Gladwell wrote a book about this in 2005. It was called *Blink: The Power of Thinking Without Thinking*, and became a bestseller when thousands bought it without thinking. I was one of them.

It began as an entertaining treatise on why you should always trust your gut instincts. Mine told me this incredible book would change my life, so I read on. In the event, my gut was wrong. It was bullshit. The second half of the book argued that, hey, actually, you shouldn't always trust your gut instincts. By the end I'd learned precisely nothing about 'thinking without thinking' except that in future I'd avoid making any impulse book-buying decisions. Particularly ones that benefit Malcolm Gladwell. Proof, if any were needed, that you shouldn't judge a book by its cover.

It's easier said than done. Book covers – like TV programme titles, magazine covers and newspaper headlines – are increasingly designed to draw in passers-by via any means necessary. Subtlety doesn't get a look-in. Nor does common sense. I had first-hand experience of this several years ago when a book I'd written, a spoof version of the Innovations catalogue, was published. It was full of outrageous mock inventions, most of them electronic gadgets of some kind, apart from one: a 'guilt-free' Christmas turkey which lived its last days in the lap of luxury before being slaughtered (look, it seemed funny at the time). Anyway, the marketing department insisted said turkey should appear as the main image on the book's front cover. Why? Because the book was coming out in the run-up to Christmas, and they figured that might help it sell. Never mind that it was the single most atypical item in the book, never mind that it made the front cover a confusing mess, and never mind that it instantly rendered the book redundant the moment Boxing Day arrived – some arrogant dunce had decreed the turkey might help sales, and that was that. At the time of writing, it's ranked 239,952nd on the Amazon bestseller chart. Way to go, faceless marketing guy! You rock!

Substantially higher up the sales list, currently at number 32, is a book that absolutely can be judged by its cover, largely because its cover features the words 'Richard Littlejohn'. In fact, just for fun, let's review it by its cover. That seems fair. So, the full title is *Littlejohn's Britain*, which is spelled out in hideous red lettering with a thin white border, across two lines, spaced slightly too far apart, as though the designer were consciously emulating a cheap pizza delivery menu. It's so ugly, it seems almost deliberate – as though they made this section of the cover as offensive and nasty as possible in a desperate last-minute bid to distract attention from the large photograph of Richard Littlejohn that hovers below it.

A noble effort. But it doesn't work. I can't help noticing Littlejohn's picture, even when my eyes are looking elsewhere, because his face smells – or at any rate, I think it does. I can smell it in my brain. Even when it's just a photo. It smells like someone breaking wind in a pair of cheap nylon trousers while eating a Scotch egg in a hot car passing the Tilsworth Golf and Conference Centre on the A5 outside Dunstable. But worse.

Fortunately, it's not a facial close-up. Unfortunately, his whole body's on there. Littlejohn is pictured standing astride the United Kingdom, like a colossus (or, more accurately, like Fred Talbot, the weatherman who used to do the forecasts on *This Morning*). Surrounding him are three things presumably intended to sum up the very worst of 'modern Britain': a speed camera, a recycling bin, and the London Eye – a triumvirate so utterly despicable, Littlejohn can't even muster the will to shake a fist in their direction. Instead he merely shrugs with exasperation: his arms are outstretched, palms up, and he stares down the lens, bemused, as though saying, 'Cuh! Speed cameras, eh? It's basic concern for human safety gone mad! Recycling bins? Typical! And if that bloody Ferris wheel doesn't sum up Blair's Britain, I don't know what does. You couldn't make it up!'

Weirdly, they've chosen not to include any of Littlejohn's other bugbears on the cover: there are no gays or asylum seekers here. Unless, perhaps, they're crushed beneath Littlejohn's feet. It's hard to tell from the preview image on Amazon. I mean, I'd go into a bookshop and examine it in closer detail, but then I'd get Littlejohn on my hands, and my fingers would have that Scotch-egg-car-fart stink on them for the rest of the day.

Speaking of Amazon, the site recommends *Don't You Know Who I Am?: Insider Diaries of Fame, Power and Naked Ambition*, by Piers Morgan, as a 'perfect partner' to *Littlejohn's Britain* – presumably on the basis that once you've desensitised yourself with Littlejohn, Piers Morgan's going to be a doddle. On the cover, Morgan is standing on the wrong side of a velvet VIP rope, pulling a strikingly similar pose to Littlejohn – arms outstretched, palms up, like he's measuring an imaginary fish or grossly overestimating the size of his penis. Clearly, this is a trend. It's the stance du jour, the latest dance craze sweeping the nation.

Anyway: covers. You can't judge a book by them. But you can point at them and laugh.

On Facebook [21 May 2007]

Two's company. Three's a crowd. And whoever they are, I don't trust them. Yes, in the ever expanding list of things I don't 'get' – fashion, Apple Macs, David Cameron, etc – the most crippling entry has to be people. I don't get people. What's their appeal, precisely? They waddle around with their haircuts on, cluttering the pavement like gormless, farting skittles. They're awful.

As you might imagine, given my inability to relate to the rest of the human race on even the most cursory level, I'm somewhat socially inept. Slide me between two strangers at any light-hearted jamboree and I'll either rock awkwardly and silently on my heels, or come out with a stone-cold conversation-killer like, 'This room's quite rectangular, isn't it?' I glide through the social whirl with all the elegance of a dog in high heels.

A friend once tried help by coaching me in small talk. Step one: take note of what day it is. On a Monday or Tuesday, ask what they got up to at the weekend. Thursday or Friday, ask if they've got any plans for the coming weekend.

'What about Wednesdays?' I asked, wide-eyed. 'Or what if I meet them at the weekend? What the hell happens then?' 'Oh, for Christ's sake. Just ask what they do for a living.'

That Friday, I attended a reasonably sized get-together and boldly stood in the corner, trying to avoid everyone and everything. When this plan failed, I tried out my newfound small-talk skills. But having dealt my opening gambit, I drifted off, gazing at eternity as their stupid wobbling faces outlined their weekend plans in punishing detail. I didn't care what they were doing at the weekend – nor, indeed, whether they lived or died. Afterwards my friend asked how the party had gone. I complained that the key to small talk had merely opened a door into a world of tedium.

'Well, duh,' they said. 'No one really cares what anyone else is getting up to. Why do you think it's called small talk? It's just shit you say to make things less awkward.' What, just a pointless noise you make with your mouth? 'Precisely,' they said. 'Cows moo.

People small-talk.' And I thought: I hate this world. This stinking, unbearable world.

Fast-forward several years until you hit now. Then rewind a few weeks. Some of my friends tell me they've signed up to Facebook. It's a bit of silly fun, they say. So I sign up too. Even misanthropes hate feeling left out. Facebook, for the uninitiated, is 'a social utility that connects you with the people around you'. It's like a stream-lined, refined take on MySpace. No gaudy backgrounds and hideous customised cursors, just crisp whites and pale blues. You create a profile for yourself, locate other people you know, and add them as 'friends'. You can then swap messages, share photos, invite one another for drinks, and so on. There's also a status window you can easily update, so if your friend Dave is feeling pensive, he types 'feeling pensive' in and you see a little bulletin saying, 'Dave is feeling pensive.' For some reason, this is endlessly amusing. My friends were right: it was a bit of silly fun.

There was one drawback. Being on Facebook involves submitting yourself to cheerful, yet merciless surveillance. Your friends can automatically see more or less everything you're doing – who else you're making friends with, which groups you've joined, and so on – and vice versa. So when a girl I'd once been semi-involved with but oh-dear-that-ended-badly added me as a friend, I found myself confronted with an unrelenting, unfolding, up-to-the-minute news feed of her fantastic new life and her fantastic new man, replete with photos. It doesn't yet treat me to an automatic update each time they have sex, although that feature can't be far off.

Anyway, last week I mentioned my burgeoning Facebook obses-sion in print. This was my first mistake. By the end of the day I had received several hundred 'friend requests', mainly from students so desperate to escape the tedium of revision they'd idly befriend literally anyone, including me. Probably out of pity.

When someone sends you a friend request, you're confronted with three options: 'confirm', 'reject', or 'send message'. Confirming all of them would make it hard for me to find my real friends among the influx of strangers. Coldly hitting 'reject', however, seemed far too mean. Most of them were smiling.

Instead, I chose 'send message', and invited them to join a group I'd set up for people I didn't really know, but who had been kind or bored enough to send a request. This was my second mistake. After sending about thirty such cut-and-pasted invites in quick succession, my account was blocked for twenty-four hours: Facebook thought I was a spammer. Worse, people who signed up wondered what my plan was (I didn't have one), while others refused, and instead sent me messages pointing out how pathetic it is to smugly fish for new Facebook friends, then arrogantly shove anyone who applies into a custom-made holding pen. Besides, in Facebook terms, several hundred people isn't that many. Ian Huntley could generate more friends in an hour. 'You're not exactly Joan Bakewell or John O'Farrell,' rasped one irritated ex-admirer.

So, for the sake of a bit of silly fun, I've generated a roster of wannabe friends I can't reply to, organised a small group of people baffled by my motives, and convinced several perfect strangers that I'm a conceited, desperate prick. In other words, it's comforting to know my crashing social ineptitude adapts in line with technology. I can be awkward and useless anytime, anywhere. Even when pixellated, there's no bloody stopping me.

Because we're worth it [28 May 2007]

So it's come to this. Traffic wardens waddling around with cameras on their heads, like a 70s sitcom approximation of *RoboCop*. Miniature, pilotless spycopters hovering overhead, simultaneously fighting crime and peering down girls' dresses. And – as mentioned a few weeks ago – CCTV cameras audibly shrieking at yobs, litter-bugs and anyone with a slouchy walk. The future's not only arrived, it's entered our lives with all the breezy assurance of a character from *Neighbours* popping into Harold Bishop's kitchen and casually helping himself to an orange juice. The air is thick with magic wi-fi atoms. We're literally breathing technology.

All of which should make us the most depersonalised generation in history, right? After all, we're analysed and observed, prodded and scrutinised, catalogued and chronicled, twenty-four hours a day. As far as the software's concerned, a human being is nothing more than a 3D barcode made of animated pork; a blob on the radar.

Yet thrillingly, we refuse to be beaten. We may have willingly submitted to this unfolding mass experiment in passive-aggressive suppression, but we're not going to feel like meaningless pixels, goddammit. No siree. Instead, we've gone the other way and become hugely self-important. Every single one of us is the centre of the universe. Our mantra: have it your way. Because you're worth it. Because you're special. More special than, say, the person standing beside you – can you believe that idiot actually thinks you're talking to them? Ha ha ha! As if! You're the special one. Right? Don't let anyone tell you different. Keep repeating: You are special. And if you detect a whiff of desperation in your own voice, don't worry. That's just part of your specialness.

Remember the time that bad thing happened to you? You know. The bad thing? Knocked you for six, didn't it? Perhaps you were left wondering whether the universe is a godless, random sort of place which doesn't understand the concept of favouritism. Well, you were wrong, silly! The bad thing happened for a reason. Everything happens for a reason. No, really: there's a gigantic Department of Reason deciding these things, located somewhere between the spirit realm and the superstition junction; a shimmering celestial office where invisible civil servants plot out Your Fate and Your Destiny on an almighty chart. The paperwork involved is mind-boggling, but it's worth it. You're worth it. You're special. Keep repeating: You are special

So yes, you have a destiny all of your own, and in the meantime, while it's slowly being fulfilled – while all these things are happening to you for a reason – you should demand nothing but the best. The greatest comfort, the tastiest meals, the widest possible choice of entertainment. It's all about you. Look! Movies on demand! Widescreen movies, movies you can play and pause and repeat as you see fit. Hey, fast-forward the damn thing if you like! Go crazy! It's your movie!

And we'll adapt to your mood. You're in control. Want chuckles?

You got 'em! More than 200 Adam Sandler movies at the touch of a button. Want romance? It's yours! More than 200 Adam Sandler movies at the touch of a button. Want Adam Sandler? Yes sir! More than 200 Adam Sandler movies at the touch of a button.

You've never had so much choice. It's part of your destiny. Because you're worth it. Everything in those movies happens for a reason. And it happens in front of your eyes because you're special. Keep repeating: You are special

Now, if you'd just like to pop that special fingertip of yours on this scanning device for a moment . . . that's the way . . . and just keep your special eyelids open while the iris recognition software does its thing . . . that's lovely . . . now, you might get a bit bored during this next bit – we're going to analyse your prior credit trans- actions and generate a purchasing destiny chart – so while we're doing that, slip some headphones into your special little ears (white headphones, pink headphones, red, blue, olive – pick a colour that you feel expresses your personality best) and listen to your very own choice of music while our computer chugs away in the background. Are you comfortable? Would you like to lie down? We've got 1,000 pillows for you to choose from. Pick the one you feel expresses your personality best. Plump it up (or don't! You decide!). Lie back. Close your eyes (quickly or slowly! You decide!).

Tell you what. We can pump some dreams into your brain if you like. Want dreams? More than 2,000 Adam Sandler dreams at the touch of a button. Have it your way. And we'll do what we like while you enjoy your little snooze. That's right. That's good. That's special. You're special. Keep repeating: You are special.

Dicks, lies and measuring tape [4 June 2007]

It's what you do with it that counts. And, according to the *Sun* newspaper, what almost half of men 'do' is fret about it. 'MEN FEAR TOO SMALL PENIS SIZE' bleats the headline, which, like all *Sun* headlines, sounds a bit like 'red injun' dialogue from an old cowboy film (quite a racy one, in this case).

Apparently, Dr Kevan Wylie of the Royal Hallamshire hospital has recently overseen the completion of a sixty-year study into penis size, during which 12,000 penises were 'analysed' – an average of 200 penises a year. Assuming they took weekends off, that's 0.76 penises a day. At some point you'd drift off and start doodling on them.

The survey ultimately concluded that 'the average erect penis was 5.5 ins to 6.2 ins long and 4.7 ins to 5.1 ins in girth'. And looked hilarious resting on a Petri dish.

If we generously take the average to be six inches, and multiply that by the total number of appendages, it means they examined a total of 72,000 inches of penis, which sounds impressive until you input that figure into a conversion calculator and realise it's a mere 1.136 miles. A frail old lady could cycle that distance in less than five minutes, assuming she could keep her eyes on the road.

Anyway, it wasn't all warm hands and tape measures. The researchers also asked the owners of the penises some probing questions – presumably in a misguided attempt to break the ice, or make the whole scenario feel faintly less awkward. They found that 'those with a "normal-sized" penis often mistakenly thought theirs was too small'. Perhaps the researcher had huge hands.

No. It seems pornography is to blame, as 'almost 40 per cent blamed their insecurity on watching porn as teens'. Presumably they also felt insecure that they weren't a smooth-chested, oily West German pulling a face like a man undergoing an ingrown toe-nail operation under insufficient local anaesthetic. On the plus side, they'll have learned to pronounce the phrase 'Ich komme', witnessed countless body-fluid tributes to Jackson Pollock, and perfected the art of slamming a laptop shut at the sound of approaching footsteps.

The tragedy here is that most of them are anxious for no reason. The *Sun* reports that 'there is no need to worry as 85 per cent of women ARE satisfied with their partner's penis proportions. The study found **GIRTH** matters more than length to 90 per cent of women.' That's how they printed it – **GIRTH**, in bold capital letters, no messing about. It's a raunchy paper, the *Sun*.

(Speaking of suns, or rather sons, if I ever have one – a son –

I've just decided that I'm going to call him Girth, to give him a subliminal advantage with any would-be suitors. Girth Hammer Lointhump Brooker. He'll thank me for it one day, if only because having a unique Googlewhack-of-a-name is a real boon in our thrilling online age. Finding him on Facebook will be easy, and who wouldn't want someone like that listed among their 'friends'?)

To assist worried readers, the *Sun* thoughtfully accompanied the article with a 'Pecker Checker' – a graphic of an actual-size ruler with the 'average zone' clearly labelled. In doing so, it is actively encouraging male readers to press their erect penises against the page, which is a cheery way to pass a few minutes on a quiet afternoon – or it would be, if the article weren't surrounded by adverts for MFI kitchens and BT broadband hubs, a column called 'The Whip' topped by an illustration of a gloved hand wielding a lash, a photograph of silver-haired sixty-year-old aristocrat Benjamin Slade and, most alarmingly of all, a headshot of Mr Bean hovering perilously close to the ruler's tip, gazing directly into your eyes. Anyone who can maintain even a below-average erection under those circumstances is precisely the kind of psychopath who shouldn't be allowed to own a penis in the first place.

So, then. Penises. Men fret about them too much. The answer, perhaps, is to remain erect at all times, as the moment a penis starts engorging, it drains blood from the brain, leaving the owner incapable of worrying about anything more complex than where he wants to put it. Long or short, fat or thin – they're good for depleting common sense, soiling sheets, terrifying bystanders, creating selfish offspring and precious little else. Plus they look ridiculous. If you've got one, or access to one, take a good look at it this evening and ask yourself: how can this possibly be the work of a sane God?

Washing machines live longer with Calgon

[11 June 2007]

My favourite advert at the moment is for Calgon. A kindly looking handyman is sitting behind a washing machine and a box of Calgon, addressing me directly. 'You've heard about Calgon, but why should you use it?' he asks. It's true. I have indeed heard of Calgon, but don't know why I should use it. It is as if he has looked into my soul. This guy understands me better than many of my closest friends, and I've only known him four seconds.

Better still, he follows his ice-breaking question with a straight-forward answer. Apparently Calgon stops your washing machine turning into a crumbling chalk sculpture. 'Calgon protection,' he says, patting the box. The advert ends with a good old-fashioned jingle – a small choir singing: 'Washing machines live longer with Calgon!' It couldn't be simpler.

Now obviously, I'm never going to buy Calgon; popping a Calgon tablet 'in every wash' might make the washer 'live' longer, but (a) it sounds like too much trouble to go to on behalf of a machine and (b) I could probably spend the money I'd saved on not buying Calgon on getting a new machine when the old one finally dies of limescale cancer – and I bet new washing machines are thrillingly advanced these days, with wi-fi iPod connections and sat nav and everything. But I appreciate the ad's straight-talking nature. It's refreshingly unsophisticated, and unlike almost every other advert on television, not glaringly over-pleased with itself.

Right now, there's a rash of commercials which combine 'twee' with 'patronising' – 'tweetronising' if you like, although that's quite tweetronising in itself. You can spot a tweetronising commercial a mile off – it'll have a modern folk music backing track, a cast of non-threatening urban hippy replicants, and a drowsy hello-birds-hello-sky overall attitude that makes you want to chase it down an alleyway and kick it until the police arrive.

Furthermore, tweetronising takes infantilism to a new level. They're like children's programmes in miniature – not so much talking down to the viewer as placing the viewer in a cot and tick-ling his chin. George Orwell once described advertising as 'the rattling of a stick inside a swill-bucket'. These days it's more like the rattling of a rattle.

Take the current Orange ad in which a woman stands in a forest unfolding a range of ain't-it-cute props while a self-consciously lo-fi recording of a female voice recites the following:

> *I like conversations that last for hours and hours*
> *Full of jokes about singing bees and talking flowers*
> *I like it when they take up whole mornings*
> *And fill up whole nights*
> *When they mention books and cocktails*
> *And trumpets and kites*
> *I like them when they talk about parties and talk about dreams*
> *And talk about cakes covered in cream*
> *And all that they need is me and a friend*
> *And the talking to go on and never to end.*

Never to end? I'm all for a bit of pointless digression, but this bitch wants to witter about 'singing bees' and 'trumpets and kites' for *eternity*? This is a description of hell. Orange does not think insipid babble is the sole preserve of womankind, incidentally – there is a companion ad backed with a man moronically singing about how he likes to talk about dinosaurs, cars and 'anything that pops in my brain/ and then falls out my mouth/ kind of like the rain'. He is either naturally stupid or recovering from a head injury. Or maybe years of intensive mobile phone use have caused a brain tumour so huge it's crushed his IQ to the back of his skull, leaving him with the conversational skills of a six-year-old.

The rule of thumb seems to be that the more grimly impersonal the product, the more ingratiatingly syrupy the ad. Cars, for example, were until recently portrayed as cold mechanical sharks; selfish metal cocoons that transported men in sunglasses across isolated desert roads at fearsome velocity. Now, apparently, they are cuddly scamps with an impish sense of humour. Or toys. Or skateboards.

But they're not. Cars are bastards. You know that advert where the smashed-up little girl whines about being run over at 40 miles an hour? A car did that. And the car was such a bastard, it probably thought it was all her own fault. (And to be fair, it's got a point: if she's OK with being hit at 30 mph, why didn't she start running away at 10 mph the moment she saw it heading toward her at 40?

No, she'd rather laze about on her back at the side of the road, moaning about it. I've got no sympathy. She's an idiot.)

In summary: phones are little plastic boxes, cars are large metal boxes, and no amount of goo-goo gurgling will change that. Please, advertisers: enough with the sugar and folk music. It's time to get puritan. Washing machines live longer with Calgon. Ronseal does what it says on the tin. That's all we need to know.

On Glastonbury [27 June 2007]

Here's an entirely random list of things I hate. Mud. Rain. Inconvenience. Any form of discomfort whatsoever. Loud noises. People. People's friends. People standing next to other people, with yet more people in between. Drunks bumping into you and being sick down your leg. Poorly maintained public toilets. Camping.

You'll find all these things and more at the Glastonbury festival, which is why it has always struck me as heck on earth. A long weekend in a wet field surrounded by students on cider, thirtysomething Faithless fans, and everyone I avoided at school. That's not a holiday. That's a penance.

On top of that, I'd heard my share of off-putting Glastonbury myths. Tents bobbing in a mud-slide. Widespread trench foot. A man on ketamine eating his own hand. One of my friends swore blind she knew a man who'd been sitting in a Portaloo when some passing japester decided to tip it over, door side down, leaving him trapped inside a coffin full of foaming crap for fifteen horrifying minutes; it went in his eyes and mouth. He got dysentery.

In summary: pretty far removed from my idea of fun. Consequently, I've never been. Until now. I got talked into it by the *Guardian*. From the start, I was adamant about one thing.

'I'm not camping,' I said. 'I hate camping more than I hate the Nazis. Plus I can't use sleeping bags because I get restrictive claustrophobia.'

'What's that?' they asked.

'It means I panic in any situation where I can't fan my arms and legs out to their fullest extent.'

'Are you making this up?'

'Almost, but no. Anyway, I'm not camping.'

'But we want you to experience it properly,' they said.

'Sod "properly". I don't want to experience it at all. I can't do it. I won't do it.'

Many complain that Glastonbury has become too corporate and sanitised. These days you're more likely to see Alan Yentob slipping in a puddle than a naked hippy up a tree; celebrities outnumber acid casualties. There are phone-charging tents and cashpoints. It's a theme-park ride. All of which should make it ideal for cosseted, mid-thirties media cry-babies like me. Instead, here I was falling at the first hurdle. To a wuss like me, a mere tent represented intolerable squalor.

In the end, we struck a deal: the paper would supply me with a magic pop-up tent, so simple a cat could assemble it. All I had to do was promise to camp for one night, and I could spend the rest of the festival sleeping off-site in a winsome, rustic cottage full of potpourri. During the day, if I got scared of the crowds, the press pass meant I could hide out in a backstage compound, gawping at Pete Doherty. The toilets were the clincher: apparently the ones backstage flush properly .

And so I agreed. But even the prospect of one night of camping terrified me. A seasoned outdoorsman I ain't. Within an hour of the phone conversation, I was standing in a branch of 'outdoor experts' Black's – true alien territory – panic-buying like a man who had foreseen Hurricane Katrina. Cagoules, wellies, rucksacks, pocket torches, a rain hat – even waterproof socks. Anything capable of repelling the elements. All that was missing was a sword and a shield.

But who should I go with? Everyone I knew either didn't want to go or already had a ticket. In fact, the only person who'd expressed any interest at all was Aisleyne Horgan-Wallace, the 'ghetto princess' from last year's *Big Brother*, who has, inexplicably, become a friend of mine in recent months. So I invited her.

Since Aisleyne knew even less about camping – or Glastonbury – than I did, it gave me the chance to play the expert. Over the phone, I sagely listed all the equipment she'd need, down to the waterproof socks, while she took notes. The day before the festival, she rang to double-check her inventory.

'I've got a tent from Argos,' she said. 'It was only £7.99.'

Unfortunately for Aisleyne, I didn't know enough about camping to realise that wasn't a good idea.

We bagged a lift with some friends of mine, both Glastonbury veterans who wouldn't raise an eyebrow all weekend. The arrival was a shock. Being an almighty and unashamed puss, I'd never been to a music festival before, let alone the biggest one in Europe.

Having parked somewhere behind the smallest of Saturn's moons, you have to trudge on foot across what feels like the width of a small county, lugging all your equipment on your back, staring grimly at smartarses who'd had the good sense to cart their stuff on to the site in a wheelbarrow. Laden with half the contents of the Clapham branch of Black's, I scarcely fitted through the gate. Straps dug into every square inch of my flesh. My shoulders grew extra muscles just so I could pull them. And the walking never stopped. This was like being in the army, except at least there you get to let off steam by machine-gunning people in their thousands.

Once you're in, the sheer scale of it is initially overwhelming. Imagine forcing the cast of Emmerdale to hurriedly construct Las Vegas at gunpoint in the rain. Then do it again. And once more for luck. That's Glastonbury: a cross between a medieval refugee camp and a recently detonated circus. Roads of sloppy mud and drunken civilians shivering in tents; this is what London would look like if I'd been in charge for a hundred years. Not because I'm some kind of laid-back dreamer, but because I couldn't organise a piss-up in a pissery. It'd take me six decades to assemble the most rudimentary infrastructure. There'd be no museums in my London. Maybe a bin or two, at a push.

Wherever I looked, there were options. Things to do. Food stalls, poetry huts, henna-tattoo dungeons . . . and music. It was only Thursday, and the headline acts weren't due till Friday, but already there were sound systems and bands and people banging musical pots together. Yet in the midst of so much choice, I had focus. I knew what I wanted to do. Leave.

Instead, I had to pitch my tent. The *Guardian* wanted me to camp out in the main fields, among the public. I chickened out and opted to set up home in the backstage compound (which turned out to be a mistake – more on this later).

The pop-up a tent was a joy. It comes flat, disc-shaped. You throw it in the air and it unfurls into a canvas shell. Within seconds I was the proud owner of a home fit for a tramp. Aisleyne's Argos special took longer to assemble, and turned out to be a striking visual definition of the word 'flimsy'. If Christmas crackers came with folded-up tents inside, they'd look like this. It seemed to be made out of soluble material – possibly the same stuff as those translucent breath-mint strips that dissolve on your tongue.

But it wasn't raining yet – in fact, the air was downright balmy – and I was optimistic. Perhaps camping would be fun. Hell, I might stay here for the whole thing. I went to the backstage bar, which seemed to be full of people hugging themselves with joy at being 'allowed' backstage. (The sole advantage to a backstage pass, incidentally, is that the area doubles as a short cut between the two main stages. That's it. That's all you're 'missing'.)

We left the backstage area and headed off into the 'proper bit'. Getting in touch with my festival-hardened friends soon proved impossible – text messages were taking two hours to arrive, making it impossible to sync up a meeting.

Outside the backstage compound, everyone was astonishingly friendly. And astonishingly everywhere. It was like the height of rush hour conducted by lazy people in love. When someone stepped on your foot, they apologised. There was laughter and music, genuinely funny T-shirt slogans and a palpable sense of relaxed excitement. We walked up to the Lost Vagueness area and saw people eating in dodgems and children dressed as spacemen. For an eight-year-old, Glastonbury probably makes more sense than, say, Basingstoke.

After hours of walking and gawping, we headed back to the hospitality section, stopping at a food stall along the way. (The food at

Glastonbury was far, far better than I'd expected, by the way.) Then, full and happy, I headed to my tent for an early night. Which is when things started to go wrong.

If there's one piece of Glastonbury advice I can give you, it's this: don't camp backstage. On the plus side, there was no flooding, no thieving, and the toilets did indeed flush properly. On the minus side, at 3 a.m. a group of post-pubescent upper-middle-class music-industry git-sacks pitched their tent beside mine, and no power on Earth could make them stop braying witless bullshit at the top of their idiot lungs.

For hours they tramped round my tent, tripping over the guy ropes and gurgling. One of them had a bassoon. All of them were howlingly impressed with themselves. It suddenly occurred to me that if you fashioned a thick block of concrete the precise shape of the backstage compound, and dropped it from a helicopter, crushing everyone below, you'd improve the quality of life on the planet by at least 3 per cent.

The most annoying one was an infuriating raspy-voiced nincompoop who kept waving a blue light-sabre around, subtly flirting with his female companions by pretending it was a glowing penis. And when he wasn't doing that, he was bragging about how much ketamine he'd taken.

'George, I'm fucked . . . I'm going to fall over any second,' he rasped. He was saying this while bouncing up and down next to my head. He's going to break my neck, I thought. I'm going to have my neck broken by a prick with a light-sabre.

All the goodwill for humankind I'd built up during the day drained away in seconds. I felt like ripping through the side of my tent and pushing his eyes into the back of his skull with my thumbs – which isn't really in keeping with any festival spirit I know of.

Instead, I sulked off for a charming moonlight piss. But by now, the bog was overflowing. Someone – maybe Pete Doherty – was defecating noisily in the cubicle beside me. I returned to my tent only to discover someone had taken my wellies and inexplicably left them outside. Then I unzipped the door and found a stranger sleeping on the floor. And then I realised it wasn't my tent. Of course, even in the dark, mine should have been easy to spot. It was the one with a bunch of light-sabre-swinging twats beside it.

The next morning I awoke feeling as if I'd been beaten up. But I'd had it easy compared to Aisleyne, whose joke tent had been kicked to death by an early-morning downpour. She was soaked through, and claimed to have cried herself awake – which is quite a skill.

And then it rained and rained and rained. The whole site resembled a war zone: I couldn't believe the mud, which seasoned visitors were already shrugging off as nothing compared to '97. All I wanted was a hot bath in the cottage, which by now sounded like the promised land. I couldn't face this merry hell without my creature comforts. Sod camping. Sod it to the moon and back. The thought of being kept awake another night by Captain Lightsabre was too much to bear. Macho be damned. I needed cosseting.

I didn't see any bands that afternoon. I had a bath, stretched out on a comfy sofa, drank tea and watched *Operation Petticoat* on Channel 4. Then I went back to the site, headed up to the Healing Fields, and got an excellent neck massage. Thus recharged, I returned to the breach and proceeded to drink heavily. This, I discovered, is key to enjoying the festival. Your mind needs to be dislodged from its normal position; your filter adjusted to the point where stomping through endless mud ponds seems gently amusing rather than, say, grindingly depressing. In fact, the mud eventually becomes nothing more than an ever-present slapstick punchline. The first time you fall over in it, you feel angry and stupid. Second time you shrug and laugh and scarcely care.

Mind you, I had a flouncy cottage with hot running water. The people in tents must be idiots.

The rest of Friday night became a bewildering, enjoyable blur – so much so, summing up individual moments feels pointless. I bumped into a friend with kids and carried her daughter on my shoulders through half the Arctic Monkeys set, like I was Phil bloody Hogan or something, before heading for the Jazz stage to catch the end of Damian Marley (who was fantastic). Then there was more drink and more things to see. At some point, I realised something was wrong with my face. It was smiling.

Saturday was equally strange and fun. I ended up backstage at the Roots tent watching Damian, Stephen and Ziggy Marley, after one of the 3 a.m. girls blagged us in. Hanging around with Aisleyne has unforeseen advantages. Aisleyne, incidentally, had recovered from her tent trauma and was now in her element. Although she failed to teach me to skank.

At Glastonbury, I've learned, for every high, a low will inevitably follow, generally a low involving a large amount of rain or mud or both. If you're lucky the highs cancel out or even outweigh the lows. So far, I've been lucky. Fate dictates that'll have changed by the time you read this – there'll be a tornado or a massacre in the interim to redress the balance. But for now, at the time of writing, here in the *Guardian* Portakabin, I'm enjoying the Glastonbury festival. Something, somewhere, has gone terribly wrong in my universe.

All men are created equal, just like airline seats aren't [9 July 2007]

Cease wailing, rain-lashed scumsacks, and gasp at my jet-set lifestyle. I've just returned from a bracing whistle-stop tour of Baltimore – or more specifically, the most impoverished, crime-blighted corners of Baltimore, where we were shooting a documentary about the drama serial *The Wire* (which is largely set on said corners).

To a wuss like me, it was an industrial-strength eye-opener: boarded-up windows, needles in the grass, crack vials littering the pavement and open-air drug markets aplenty. A staggering corpse of a neighbourhood, so ravaged and despairing that each time you spot a dead rat (roughly every ten minutes) you assume it committed suicide.

In short, an obscenity; standing in stark relief to the toothless tourist-oriented central waterfront, where our hotel, a faceless slab running on Windows, sat coolly humming its way through a minor heatwave. Two worlds, same city. Madness.

Just to make the rich/poor contrast even more apparent, I'd

flown there First Class for the first time in my life. Not by choice, you understand. The production paid for 'Premium Economy' tickets, and on top of these I was unexpectedly granted an upgrade. When I stepped on board the stewardess ushered me leftward, to the promised land.

In First Class, I had a seat that reclined far enough to become a flat bed. I drank champagne and ate smoked salmon from a china plate with weighty silverware while watching a flat-screen TV. When I got bored of that, there were a couple of framed pictures on the wall. That was the weirdest, most needless touch. They weren't interesting – just photographs of city skylines — but they weren't there to be looked at. They were there to make me feel special.

'If a terrorist shoe-bombs a hole in the fuselage right now,' I thought, 'and the plane corkscrews toward the ocean at 1,000 mph, I'm going to fix my gaze on that gilt-framed photograph and remind myself I'm dying in the lap of luxury.'

At the time, I didn't really appreciate these myriad notional blowjobs. But come the return flight, stripped of any upgrade, I missed them so hard I went through the five stages of grief: denial, anger, bargaining, depression and acceptance. Apart from the last one.

Just as Starbucks serves buckets of hot milk in 'Tall', 'Grande' and 'Venti' sizes instead of 'small', 'medium' and 'large', so airline seating distinctions, whatever they're called, actually break down into 'Misery', 'Misery Lite', and the highest achievable grade — 'Slightly Comfortable'. I was now seated in 'Misery Lite', which was twice – *twice* – the cost of mere 'Misery', despite the only difference being a slight spatial increase. Every aspect of Misery Lite was a just a tad crapper than First Class, for no reason other than it *had* to be, in order to keep First Class seeming First Class. The seat reclined (but not too far), the blanket crackled with static, the cutlery was plastic, and the meal smelt like a stomach wound. The in-flight TV had the same movie selection, but a smaller screen. Even the headphones were cheaper. If it were possible, they'd make the air thinner too.

Trouble is, the people in First Class never get to see any of this, because they're separated by a curtain. For all they know, the whole notion of seating classes could be a con: there might be an open fireplace and conveyor belt sushi bar at the back of the plane. Surely this is missing the point. Whip back the curtain. Treat the First Class fat cats to a guided tour of the poky sardine conditions. Only then can they appreciate their fortune.

Mind you, since comfort is relative, the airlines could, in turn, raise the spirits of the Economy section by introducing a new Sub-Economy class, in which society's most impoverished passengers travel for free, provided they stand atop rickety stools with a noose round their necks for the duration of the flight. Suddenly your cramped Economy seat will feel like a gilded throne in comparison. For about ten minutes. Until the veins in your leg explode.

If they must take the rich/poor divide to the skyways, they could at least be creative about it. Here's the ultimate in First Class entertainment: an interactive screen displaying a floorplan of the economy section. Tap any seat, and up pops a live shot of its luckless proletarian inhabitant. Now, using a videogame-style joypad, you control his environment. You can halt his in-flight movie forty minutes in, turn the sound so low his ears have to squint to hear it, or play it at half normal speed, so *Die Hard 4* seems to be taking place underwater.

You can slowly slide his seat forward, gradually reducing his legroom for chuckles. Blow cold air in his face. Shine lights in his eyes. Remorselessly goad him with a stick. Hidden beneath his seat is a turbulence simulator: activate this if he reaches for orange juice. Seated beside him is an animatronic baby which will scream, dribble or belch half-digested rusk down the side of his face whenever you see fit.

And if physical discomfort isn't enough, why not mess with his mind? Pipe in a faked announcement from the pilot claiming the plane's accidentally flown through a time-hole and will now remain airborne for eternity. Chortle through mouthfuls of roast goose as he tries to slash his own throat with his stupid plastic dinner knife. Revel in his desperation! That's what it's there for!

Of course the inequality of air travel is a caricature of what happens on the ground: space and resources for all, doled out disproportionately. Yet no matter what relative comforts we're gifted, we're all screwed if the wings fall off. And the bolts holding them in place have been loosening for some time.

Here endeth the tortured metaphor. Good night.

INDEX

342